TRANSFORMING HITLER'S GERMANY

TRANSFORMING HITLER'S GERMANY

DEVELOPING WESTERN CULTURES UNDER THE THREAT OF THE COLD WAR

TIM HEATH AND ANNAMARIE VICKERS

PEN & SWORD
HISTORY
AN IMPRINT OF PEN & SWORD BOOKS LTD.
YORKSHIRE – PHILADELPHIA

First published in Great Britain in 2022 by
PEN AND SWORD HISTORY
An imprint of
Pen & Sword Books Ltd
Yorkshire – Philadelphia

Copyright © Tim Heath and Annamarie Vickers, 2022

ISBN 978 1 52677 777 5

The right of Tim Heath and Annamarie Vickers to be identified as Authors of this work has been asserted by them in accordance with the Copyright, Designs and Patents Act 1988.

A CIP catalogue record for this book is available from the British Library.

All rights reserved. No part of this book may be reproduced or transmitted in any form or by any means, electronic or mechanical including photocopying, recording or by any information storage and retrieval system, without permission from the Publisher in writing.

Typeset in Times New Roman 11.5/14 by
SJmagic DESIGN SERVICES, India.
Printed and bound in the UK by TJ Books Ltd.

Pen & Sword Books Limited incorporates the imprints of Atlas, Archaeology, Aviation, Discovery, Family History, Fiction, History, Maritime, Military, Military Classics, Politics, Select, Transport, True Crime, Air World, Frontline Publishing, Leo Cooper, Remember When, Seaforth Publishing, The Praetorian Press, Wharncliffe Local History, Wharncliffe Transport, Wharncliffe True Crime and White Owl.

For a complete list of Pen & Sword titles please contact
PEN & SWORD BOOKS LIMITED
47 Church Street, Barnsley, South Yorkshire, S70 2AS, England
E-mail: enquiries@pen-and-sword.co.uk
Website: www.pen-and-sword.co.uk

Or
PEN AND SWORD BOOKS
1950 Lawrence Rd, Havertown, PA 19083, USA
E-mail: Uspen-and-sword@casematepublishers.com
Website: www.penandswordbooks.com

Contents

Introduction vi

Chapter 1   Tentative Steps 1

Chapter 2   On Jaundiced Pages 23

Chapter 3   When the Owls Sang at Schlactensee 39

Chapter 4   Alternate Fatalities 62

Chapter 5   Velvet Purses and the Bruised Violets 76

Chapter 6   Breaking the Black Mirror of our Past 97

Chapter 7   Allied in Love 125

Chapter 8   Adventures in Sorority 145

Chapter 9   Let Them Eat Cherry Pie 167

Chapter 10   Black Dogs and Near Misses 189

Chapter 11   The Perfume of Purgatory 205

Chapter 12   A Barbed-wire Bodice 219

Chapter 13   The Ever-changing Sculpture that is Fire 233

Afterword 248

Sources & Acknowledgements 253

About the Authors 254

Introduction

*In 1945 Germany's invaders were met with a hell-storm of gunfire;
in 2015 they were greeted by pacifists holding candles.*
Eulogy of a Nation

As the last flames of the Second World War flickered and died, Germany resembled a terminally ill patient on life support. She had entered into a pact with the devil, emerging from the nightmare of National Socialism twelve years later as the accused in perhaps the greatest murder trial of the twentieth century. She had witnessed hope, persecution, bombs, fire, death, rape and occupation, with the sense of abandonment which left her feeling as if she were yet another lost child, whose existence had been swallowed in the destruction, which just a few months previous had raged in virtually every street of German territory. Many emerged into a half-light of hell, a stunned silence of which echoed a defeat where Hitler's name was no longer mentioned in either jest or scorn. It was as if Adolf Hitler and the National Socialists had never existed. Only the tattered and torn remains of Swastika drapes which now lay discarded in the gutters and rubble where homes once stood, remained as some grim testimony to the madness which had consumed the German nation.

The Hitler Youth generation would be cursed with the exploded boil of National Socialism; in the view of the victors this was to be an obligatory curse, an indelible birthmark to be worn unto death in recompense for their own costly naivety.

As the *Wolfkinder* (wolf children) gathered around bonfires fuelled with the ever-increasing piles of Nazi flags and literature, they stood impassive, staring into the flames, as if mourning their own lost childhoods. They watched as the plumes of thick, black smoke rose up into the blue sky above. One of the girls clutched a small plastic doll, holding it close to her chest as she gently swayed from side to side as if attempting to nurse a real infant to sleep. These *Wolfkinder* appeared as

Introduction

daylight ghosts among those citizens going about their daily business; no one cared about them or whether they lived or died. It painted a scene of dejection, void of all hope and unworthy of human compassion.

Tia Schuster and Lisa Kraus were two young Berliners and, like many of West Germany's post-Second World War youth, they would have to be shoehorned into what would be the second 'new era' of their young lives. The first had brought about only death and destruction, yet this second possessed a cold unfamiliarity. They were made to sit and watch the Holocaust films in stuffy tents crammed with thirty or more other children at a time, films which would haunt the German conscience for decades to come. Yet hope had to begin somewhere, and Tia and Lisa, along with thousands of other young girls and boys, would have to sometimes fight to claim their rightful place within this new mechanism. Germany's females under the Nazis had been raised as bearers and carers of children, but the obligatory posts of nursing or childcare appealed little to Tia and Lisa, these being the requisite duties of a regime which had brought only death and misery to the masses. The girls' good looks almost assured their employment in the many brew houses, coffee shops and cinemas which began to open for business, places which would soon be frequented not only by the locals but the hordes of young foreign servicemen and -women who would be posted to western Germany throughout the years following the end of the Second World War.

The steadily escalating tensions between East and West provided some distraction from the funeral pyre of Third Reich Germany. With the uncaged bear of the Soviet Union flexing its muscles across a barrier consisting of little more than a roll of barbed wire, and the subsequent division of East from West, those living in western Germany soon understood that they were the geological bulkhead, a vital component in the prevention of communism spreading throughout the infant peace of post-war Europe.

Despite all the destruction and political tensions which surrounded them, the youth of West Germany were keen to experience the world beyond their own precarious borders. As the late 1940s gave way to the 1950s and 1960s, a series of new, decadent eras were on the horizon. Rock 'n' roll, fashion, music festivals, flower power with its flagship sexual revolution attractively packaged as 'free love' and fuelled by marijuana and LSD, were viewed as subversive elements which posed a threat to the traditional German way of life. Western decadence threatened to bury not only the home, church and children ethos so beloved of the Nazi regime and post-war West German governments, but it also threatened to reverse the image of German males as the traditional masculine upholders of German culture.

The young people of western Germany were anxious to experience the freedoms and excesses brought about as a result of western youth cultures. Soon teenage girls and boys all over West Germany were keen to rebel against their perceived traditional roles still expected of them by state and parents. Both state and parents soon had to understand that whether they approved or not, the new youth of post-war western Germany were Germany's future, who now demanded equality, respect and a freedom many had never thought possible within their society both past and present. It was a freedom that those unfortunate to find themselves living in communist East Germany would not have the pleasure of experiencing for many years.

Is it not then touching that within this heady mix of newfound freedom, makeup, beauty products, trendy fashion and vibrant music that the youth of West Germany would perhaps unwittingly become the symbol of everything that both fascism and communism despised?

This unique work tells the story of a group of friends and their tentative steps into the afterlife of Nazi Germany, encompassing the memoirs of other young men and women along the way. This work also embraces memories of young Allied services personnel stationed in West Germany in the aftermath of the war. It is a portrayal of charm, humour, mischief and accomplishment along with a vitally important slice of West Germany's social and Cold War history that has remained hidden for decades from the world.

As Tia Schuster remarked early on in the formulation of this book:

> The sky above Berlin appeared as if it too were writhing about the heavens in agony. It was a mixture of colours, yet none clearly definable – yellow, grey, white, blue, orange and black. It was as if the sky were permanently bruised by the once thousands of aircraft which had somehow torn it and the city's inhabitants apart. It looked like something that [Andy] Warhol himself would have been proud to have captured on canvas. Yet, the world suddenly became a very big piece of pie and we wouldn't be happy with just taking a slice of this pie; no, we wanted the whole damn thing and we didn't care if it made us sick or not!

Chapter 1

Tentative Steps

Even the heavens are bruised and torn,
seems like just yesterday to me.
Shattered dreams and broken hearts,
laid in the rubble for all to see.
Lasting fragments of Hitler's reign,
as the landscape gently weeps.
Time to rebuild,
stand tall again,
if just for now she sleeps.

She Sleeps AV I

It's the dead of night. The brown Bakelite radio suddenly begins to crackle, as if switched on by some invisible hand. A crackly static-filled robotic voice begins to issue the alarm, 'warning, warning, warning, enemy aircraft approaching, evacuate immediately, repeat evacuate immediately'. The radio falls silent, switching off as mysteriously as it had switched on. The room is pitch black. I jump out of my bed and try desperately to find the handle of my bedroom door. I feel around with my hands, stumbling over unseen objects in the darkness; I can't find the door handle. Next, I hear the rumble of thousands of aircraft overhead; there is the whistle of bombs, followed by a deafening explosion. The ceiling comes crashing down, huge pieces of plaster fall upon my head. I awake in a state of panic. I am fighting to get my breath, beads of sweat run down my face, as outside the window dawn is just breaking.

Yet another nightmare has jolted me awake. I sit up for a few minutes until my pounding heart returns to its normal rhythm. I lie down again; my pillow and the white cotton sheets are damp from my own perspiration. I lie staring at the ceiling for a few minutes before closing my eyes again. In what seems like just a few minutes my mother is waking me up, it is 8 am and I must attend school. The school is little more than a large tent with just twenty pupils including myself. The teacher is a volunteer, as all the former Nazi teachers are banned from their professions under the new denazification laws imposed by the Allied authority. The school we kids used to attend is a pile of rubble; it was bombed a few months ago before the war ended. By the time it's rebuilt we will have all probably left school. On the way I meet my close friend Lisa Kraus; we have known each other since early childhood, not only bound by the friendship of our families and the experiences of the past six years under Adolf Hitler, but bound only as the experiences of those who have lived through a total war could be. We are both 14 years of age now and we are inseparable. We walk the streets which are now strangely unfamiliar, even though we were born and raised here. The Allied bombing, in combination with the vicious street fighting that ensued between our army, the people and the Red Army, has disfigured this city beyond recognition. There are few remaining landmarks with which one can navigate one's way around, yet we seem to know where we are going; it hardly makes any sense, I know. In places dry blood is still evident on the ground, testimony to the fury of the battle that raged here just months before. If you go inside those ruined buildings which still stand, you will see enemy propaganda daubed on the walls with what looks like human blood and excrement. The stench inside tells you that bodies or at least parts of bodies are still lying trapped and decaying within the rubble. Soldiers have defecated and urinated in these ruins which compounds our revulsion ever further.

Walking the streets of my lost childhood,
still smell death on the summer breeze.
Miles of rubble stretch before me,
trapped in time, our eternal freeze.

Tentative Steps

Walking the streets of my lost childhood,
memories of buildings still remain.
Everything is so unfamiliar,
though the foundations are still the same.

Haunted AV II

We use some of these ruins with the newly cleared walkways as shortcuts to our destination. The rubble gangs of older girls and women – the *Trümmerfrauen* – are busy clearing the mess up. As we walk past them, they look at us as if to say, 'You should be here helping us with this' – it's just the feeling we get judging by their facial expressions. These women and older girls are the wives and girlfriends of our soldiers, many of whom are now dead or missing and these wretched women have no idea as to the fates of their loved ones. Their angst is perfectly understandable. We are separate entities, young and adult. They are the ones some say who should have known better, whereas we are the children – that brainwashed, lost generation that the occupying forces are now desperate to re-educate toward a better future for Germany, one where war is not the prerequisite to greatness. Lisa and I never quite understood Hitler or the Nazis. We understood there were sets of ideals we had to conform to along with every other child in the Reich. We were all the same in that respect. We were told that Jews were evil, and we accepted those teachings just as any child accepts the logic of a parent when lecturing it to not engage in conversation with or accept sweets from strangers. Now it's all over its like it never happened, like some bad dream, yet our surroundings are a daily reminder of the fact that it did happen along with our own personal experiences, some of which haunt our sleep on a nightly basis.

Delousing was our first rite of passage into what would be the Allied-brokered 'new era'. A revolting procedure where we were lined up and one by one covered in this chemical powder discharged from a cone-shaped metallic vessel. The Allied soldiers carried out this delousing procedure. It was meant to kill lice in our hair and clothing, yet I swore it almost killed us too. We came away choking with a foul taste in our mouths; we felt sick later. I felt shit for three days after this and swore I would never let them do this to me again.

As we walk through the skeletal remains of the city, we pass many soldiers. Most are American and British, as we are within the western sector or western Allied zone as it is sometimes called. We get stopped occasionally as the servicemen like to take photographs; they like to be able to pose with us. I guess these snapshots end up in letters home or even in newspapers, I don't know. We sometimes feel like minor celebrities in some budget horror picture. We laugh to ourselves after the photographs are taken; one of the soldiers puts his arm around me, as Hershey's chocolate bars are thrust into our hands without us even having to ask for them. Lisa tears open the wrapping like some excited toddler and takes a bite of the creamy-tasting chocolate. She mumbles with a full mouth, 'Hmmm, god this is very good,' her eyes closed in an ecstasy that only a sweet heaven might produce. We see the big tent as we called it up ahead, with other children going inside. Lisa has chocolate all around her mouth and I can't help but laugh at her.

She asks me, 'Where is it? Can you wipe it off?'

I spit onto the sleeve of my woollen cardigan, and holding her head steady with my left hand, I wipe the chocolate from around her mouth like some scornful mother with her child. I say to her, 'There you are, it's all gone now' and we hurry in through the canvas flap that provides the door to the tent. Inside many of the smaller children are sitting cross-legged on the ground in front of what looks like a big cinema screen. Lisa and I sit on some chairs at the back, eagerly awaiting what we hope will be a child's movie or something. The volunteer teacher then walks in, and without even thinking Lisa jumps to her feet and is about to give the Hitler salute and shout 'Heil Hitler.' I manage to prevent her just in time – shutting off the years of Nazi indoctrination is not an easy task. The teacher fumbles around with a projector which has a roll of film on a circular spool above it. He then walks to the front and begins a lecture. He starts with a tirade against what the Nazis are responsible for in Germany and Europe, that Hitler and his propaganda had filled our heads and hearts with the fire of hate which would have to be extinguished if Germany were to fulfil a new role within a new European community.

'What you have been taught and all that you have known in the past years is a lie, fabricated by a clever devil and his evil disciples to deceive the masses in Germany, to profess that Jewry was the downfall of Germany, when the truth was many Germans were the downfall of their own nation, not the Jews. Germany had become the destroyer rather than builder of nations. Now, do you understand? If your elders are not already able to accept the consequences of what Germany has done, then you must be their moral conscience. You are Germany's future; it is up to you young people to ensure that the mistakes your country has made are never repeated in future.'

At that he again fiddles around with the projector which stands on a table near the back of the room and says, 'I am now going to show you what became of a proportion of the people that vanished from your communities from the year 1934. It is not pleasant and some of you will be physically sickened by what you are going to see, but you need to see to both believe and understand the sheer gravity of what Germany under the National Socialists is responsible for. We can't allow this to ever happen again.'

He then switches on the projector; the screen flickers momentarily as numbers flash up, a countdown to zero and then a scene reminiscent of hell itself unfolds. Human skeletons barely able to stand, piles of rotting skeletal corpses, piles of clothes, suitcases, shoes and valuables, small mountains of gold teeth which had been extracted from the mouths of the murdered. Lisa and I look at each other with shocked expressions, as we have never really seen the evidence of what the camps were like, but here it is laid bare before us. Some children begin to cry at the sight of emaciated beings glaring wide-eyed at the camera. We have seen dead bodies and body parts countless times during the war, but these on the screen are the living dead; these are Jews, many of whom perished in the camps such as Bergen-Belsen and Auschwitz. We see human remains in the ovens used for the disposal of murdered Jews. We are told many were incinerated while still alive. I sit bolt upright in my chair, my hands on my lap, my eyes riveted to the screen before me. I feel Lisa slide her hand across my lap to mine, and she takes hold of my hand, her fingers hot and clammy. I look at her and ask her if she is okay and she nods and whispers, 'Yes.' I caress her fingers with mine in a reassuring gesture of moral support at the horrors we are witnessing. The screen goes blank, numbers and symbols flash and disappear in an instant and the projector stops. We are told to return home without any romantic or sentimental notions of the National Socialist past, that it is the biggest mistake in our country's history, and that with help Germany will recover and be a better nation. We are also reminded there are countless cultures and races within the world far beyond Germany's borders, all of which will be open for us to experience with time. Hatred, prejudice and war are not the ways of any civilized society; such ways are the path to destruction as we ourselves have witnessed. We are then told to stand and say a prayer for all those who died as a result of Nazi aggression, to ask the almighty for his forgiveness. Afterwards we file out of the hot stuffy tent into the August sunshine.

Lisa turns to me and says, 'Shit, I can't believe all of that, but it's all true as we saw it with our own eyes.'

We head back home arm in arm saying very little, stunned into silence. As we take one of the many shortcuts through walls of rubble and twisted metal, we come upon a group of *Wolfkinder*, a group of children orphaned by the war, dressed in torn and dirty clothing with dirt-stained faces. They stand around a small pile of burning wood, yet one little girl has discovered the body of a dead rat. She tosses the rat up into the air and one by one the other children peel themselves away from the fire, joining in her game. We stand and watch them play with the rat's corpse, which one of the boys throws high up into the air; as it sails down, its tail flailing in the air, one of the girls shrieks with delight as she catches it in her hands. The group then gives chase as she runs through burrows made by collapsing masonry, desperately trying to hold onto her prize. When she is caught, she stands staring angrily at the boy who has tagged her yet hands him the rat's corpse which is promptly thrown into the air again and thus their game continues.

These *Wolfkinder* that Tia and Lisa came upon had nothing to their name, no parents and no home, just the cold embrace of the Grey Lady – Berlin. These were the dispossessed, brothers and sisters of pain, sharing the same emotional wasteland. They were too young to be in the possession of an adult's anger, yet each shared that common bond of misery. Together they played in the post-apocalyptic landscape of Berlin. At night they huddled together for warmth, their sleep fitful, disturbed, fraught with the demons of the past six years of war. It was as if they were sleeping upon the sepulchre of some failed mass social experiment, of which they themselves had served as the guineapigs, some form of splayed specimen in a biology lab, pins restraining each limb, awaiting evisceration, alive, aware and struggling violently at the caress of the scalpel. Sometimes during the evenings their sleep would be disturbed, by twin silhouettes: one that of a woman, the other a male, most likely an Allied soldier, only just visible against the grey walls in the darkness. The *Wolfkinder* would watch curiously as the woman gave the soldier head, yet innocently unaware of what was happening. After some minutes of play, the couple would leave the building as suddenly as they had appeared. The *Wolfkinder* barely stirred, much as a pack of wolves after feeding on a kill. To these children the world and its vices meant nothing.

> Lisa and I feel so sorry for these children; they will remain as they are, feral remnants of the disaster that was the Third Reich until any surviving relatives come to find them. The authorities are desperately trying to resolve the problems of repatriating these children, though it is a slow process as many of these children don't trust anyone and scatter like wary animals when any adults try to approach them.

As we make our way back home, we see more American soldiers walking around with their cameras. We guess they must be off duty to be carrying cameras with them, although they have rifles slung on their backs. We see some of our friends talking to them and we go and see out of curiosity as things are being handed out to them, candy or whatever it is. We want a share! After a few minutes of haggling for things we don't really have much use for, we end up with a pair of silk stockings. Our women just love these as they are considered luxury items. The women of the rubble gangs would steal these off us in no time if they saw us with them, so we hide them inside our clothing. One of the Americans hands me a glass bottle containing this bright red fluid.

I look at him, puzzled, and I ask, 'What is this stuff? Medicine or something?'

He laughs at me and says, 'Hell no, it's that stuff your women, or rather our women, paint their nails with. There's a brush inside that you use to paint it on with and it kinda looks pretty.'

Lisa is given a lipstick which she is very happy with. Under the Hitler government and the BDM – Bund Deutscher Mädel, the League of German Girls or Band of German Maidens – makeup and beauty products such as these were banned. We were never allowed to wear this stuff or wear perfume as such.

We are quite excited to get home and try these things out but don't want our parents to find out. We go back to Lisa's house and when we arrive, her father is busy in the backyard repairing broken window frames. The house is standing yet is pockmarked by bullets and shell fragments from the fighting. Lisa and her family lived in the cellar below the house for the last two years of the war, as it was the safest place to be. The house is relatively unscathed other than broken doors and window frames that enemy soldiers smashed through. We run upstairs to Lisa's room and she quickly removes her skirt and socks, tearing open her packet of silk stockings.

She slides them over her feet and legs, pulls them up then asks, 'What do you think?'

I reply, 'Oh my god, they do look very nice.' I am very keen to try my pair on so take off my trousers and socks and then proceed to feed the stockings onto my feet, unrolling them up my legs. It is no easy task for a girl that has never worn them before, and yes, I manage to put a hole in them. I curse loudly, while Lisa howls with laughter.

She then tells me to stand up so she can see what I look like. She turns me around, tugging bits here and there then stands back admiring her work. 'Hmm,' she says. 'Oh yes, these do look very lovely.'

I begin to make model poses like the women in those magazines that the Americans sometimes leave lying around.

Lisa smiles to herself before saying, 'Right, we had better take these off and hide them because if my mother or father finds them, they will get mad at me.'

We help each other remove the delicate silk stockings and both pairs are stuffed unceremoniously inside the pillow on Lisa's bed. Then the bottle of nail paint is opened; we are both very excited by this amazing little commodity we have been given.

I say to Lisa, 'Here, put your foot up here and I will do you first.'

She places her foot in my lap and I then endeavour to paint her toenails with the liquid, trying hard not to get any on the surrounding skin. It takes me around fifteen minutes to do both her feet and I fan them with my hands to try and get the paint to dry as quickly as possible.

Lisa then stands up and, admiring my workmanship, she asks, 'Well, what does it look like to you, Tia?'

'It makes you look so different; it looks so pretty and feminine. I love it.'

Then it occurs to us both: how are we going to get this stuff off her toenails? I spit onto some cloth and rub away, but the paint won't budge.

In the end Lisa says, 'Oh bugger it, leave it. I will keep my socks on, and I will worry about getting it off tomorrow.'

I have to get back home so I give Lisa a hug, telling her I will call for her tomorrow as it is Saturday. Often, we had to help our mothers with washing clothes on weekends, a laborious job which we hated with a passion, but I would go and help Lisa and her mother then she would come and help me and my mother do ours. If there was time after, we could go off out for a while; if not we would sit in our bedrooms talking and maybe play a board game.

Saturday morning, and I want nothing more than to sleep in a little longer. I kick off the bedclothes and stretch. I have a wash, get dressed and tell my mother I will be back shortly. I make my way to Lisa's home. When I arrive Lisa and her mother are already busy doing their washing. God, I hate this work. It seems to take hours to do even the smallest amount. Lisa's mother has a large metal tub full of water that must be heated on a small stove, but not so it is boiling. When the water is ready, it is poured in and mixed with a long wooden implement which has what look like chair legs on its end. The clothes are thrown in and turned over and over, and the water turns to a grey colour. When Lisa's mother is happy the clothes are clean, she takes them out of the tub and places them on a flat stone in the yard, scrubbing at them with a hard brush. She then puts them in another tub of water and the process is repeated before the clothes go through the cursed mangle. I have the job of helping Lisa turn the mangle, putting each piece of clothing through it. You have to watch your fingers: if you get one caught in this thing it will break it like a twig. Once this dreary task is complete, the washing can be hung out on the line where it will soon dry.

Now our work is done here, we then go back to my home to help my mother with her workload. Thankfully, my mother was up much earlier, and she has done most of the work by the time we get back. All we have to do is put the clothes through the mangle and peg out the washing on the line in the backyard. It doesn't take us long, and once done, we wash our hands which are by now beginning to prune. Then we head off out. Mother tells us that we are not to wander off too far. She is terribly paranoid about the Russian forces in the city, though her worries are not without foundation. We would never have attempted to cross outside our zone anyway. We would sometimes see Russian soldiers walking around but they were never impolite or aggressive toward us. We promise mother we will obey her wishes, that we will not go too far and be back in two hours.

She shouts to us as we walk off, 'Two hours! If you're not back, I will be sending your father and brothers out to look for you.'

We wave at her and continue up the road. We don't go far on this occasion. There is a small bridge with a stream running beneath it. Some boys are already messing around in the water below. The water is only around two feet deep, but on a hot day like today the cool water is inviting to paddle in. We climb down the steep bank to the stream. The boys ignore us and don't bother us. We have seen them lots of times, but we don't really know them and don't even know their names. We sit down on a large, grey boulder at the edge of the stream. Taking off our shoes and socks, we test the water with our toes. It's very cool, and even in this heat it still takes your breath away a little. Soon we are walking underneath the bridge. The boys are under there digging around the silty bottom.

One squeals, holding up something in his hand, '*Splitter, splitter* [shrapnel, shrapnel]!' he cries out with joy. He has found a piece of bomb or something similar.

I take Lisa's hand and we squeeze past the boys who now resemble lions around a kill, each digging furiously with his hands in the hope he too will find shrapnel.

I turn and say to the eldest boy who is around 12 with dirt all over his face, 'Why don't you go over there to that pile of rubble there?' I point toward a bombsite across the road. 'There is lots of shrapnel over there and it is easier to find there than here under this water.'

He stands looking at me for a few seconds before barking, 'Oh, go away; we don't want to play with girls here.'

I screw my nose up at him and we continue along the stream for a few more yards. I step on something sharp and quickly pull my foot back. Sure enough, Lisa bends down and picks up a jagged piece of shrapnel. It's everywhere, it seems, evidence of a steel rain which once fell over Berlin. Lisa holds onto the shrapnel as we want to go back to get our shoes which we left near where the boys were playing. When we get back, the boys have run off but not before throwing our shoes and socks into the stream.

Lisa complains, 'Those little bastards … if I catch them, god help them. My mother will go mad. Look at my shoes! They are soaked!'

We decide to go up and sit on top of the bridge to let our shoes dry out in the sun for a while before going home. As we walk home, our shoes make those funny squelching noises, and we laugh all the way back to my house. We explain to mother what the boys did, and we are so sorry. The shoes will be fine – they just need time to dry properly. Boys can be such beasts to girls; that doesn't change no matter where you live in the world. It's always the same. I ask mother if Lisa can stay at our house for the night,

She says, 'Lisa must ask her parents if it is okay first.'

So we run all the way to Lisa's house and excitedly ask her mother who says it is fine and even gives us a few treats to take back with us. I love having Lisa round for the night, as we can read each other stories and discuss ancient legends and tales which we also like. Strange thing is we never talk about the war or any of the horrible experiences we had during its course. In fact, few people mention the war; it's almost considered rude to talk about it, and Hitler is a taboo subject. You must never mention his name: it's like a swearword, though his name is occasionally whispered in quiet conversation, but never out loud.

I dream of a huge oceangoing factory ship,
a floating abattoir searching the open ocean for mermaids.
Harpoons with large explosive heads are ready and poised to kill.
A blonde is harpooned, and she is dragged aboard,
her belly is slit, and her innards spill out.
They squeeze the caviar from her uterus.

Tentative Steps

A prayer is said before they consume her edible parts.
The rest goes overboard.

I stirred from the puzzling imagery of the dream. Lisa was still sleeping beside me. I didn't wish to disturb her. I carefully leaned over her with all the stealth of a cat, and reaching with my arm, I grabbed my little diary-cum-scrapbook, writing down the details of the dream for later analysis. It was probably something to do with all that weird legend stuff we'd read the evening before. We'd read until our eyes became blurred and we started to feel very sleepy. We'd slid beneath the covers and were asleep in an instant, both entering our own independent gateways of fantasy: how I adore dreams, the good ones anyhow.

It was Sunday morning, and the sun was shining, breaking through the curtains of my bedroom window. Lisa was stirring so we both got out of bed and went downstairs to wash. We were eager to meet up with our group of close friends we used to call the 'Berlin Gang'. The Berlin Gang consisted of me, Lisa, Katrin and Ursula, plus eight local boys we were friendly with. If it was safe, which was not that often, we used to go out scavenging whenever we could. The end of the war didn't change our friendship, for a while at least, and so we met up when we could to go out on little adventures. There were many disused German army barracks dotted around our area, and we used to get inside looking for things we could take home to eat. Many of these military barracks had now been taken over by the Americans, so it was now not so easy to gain access to them.

We found a hole in the fence and it looked quiet, so we all crawled through into the compound. We were walking toward one of the buildings which had its door propped open when suddenly this big American came out. He was wearing a green uniform; for a split second we froze, then turned and ran for the hole in the fence. He gave chase, shouting at us to stop but we ignored him. We were as quick as rabbits, and there was no way he was going to catch us. What we didn't see was this American MP [military policeman] running toward the fence to cut off our escape. Two of the boys made it, running off, but we were trapped. The MP told us to come and stand against the fence, which we did. He then asked all the obvious questions like 'What are you doing here?' and 'What are you looking for?' I explained that we regularly came here to look for things to eat, that's all. I was being honest with him and I think he sensed that. He just shook his head at us saying we were not to come here again as this was now US military property not German.

He then said, 'If you want something to eat come with me.'

We followed him rather sheepishly to a parked vehicle. He pulled open the back, taking out several cans of peaches, corned beef and this sweetened milk stuff, the name of which I can't remember. He distributed the cans among us, ensuring we had two of each and then said something like, 'Now go on, scram. Take it home. You're lucky your folks don't get to hear about this.'

We walked off down the road vowing we wouldn't do that again. The two boys who had made their escape were watching from some trees down the road; they had seen everything and were now wishing they had stayed with us. We couldn't help but laugh about it on the way home, while the two boys sulked for the rest of the afternoon. When we arrived back at my parents' house, we dropped the cans on the kitchen table telling my mother and father, 'Look what the Americans gave us!' My parents were suspicious how we came by our little bounty but accepted the story that they were simply given to us by a sympathetic American.

Lisa went home in the early evening after having some sandwiches and peaches with us. As it got dark, I went to my room and lay on my bed just reflecting on the day's events. Mother came up telling me I must get to sleep, that proper schooling would soon begin again. I heard that one of the schools near us was opening soon and we had been invited to attend. It was more compulsory than an invitation though. I thought to myself, *It can't be any worse or any harder than before, surely?* I climbed into bed with all kinds of thoughts on my mind and the next thing I knew my mother was calling me to get up. She was taking me to work with her and said the work would do me good until I started school again. I wondered what the work was and hoped it wasn't anything to do with the rubble women we saw most days.

I was downstairs washing in the sink when I heard my mother's angry shout of 'What is this here, Tia?' I stopped, my hair dripping water everywhere, my heart pounding, wondering what I'd done wrong. I ran upstairs to the scene of my mother holding the pair of silk stockings and nail paint I had thought I had hidden in a safe place in my bedroom – not so, and now I had some explaining to do, yet my words just came out as babble.

'We will discuss this later with your father. Now come on, dry that hair and get dressed,' she barked.

I had most the day to think of an explanation, but I knew there would be some trouble over this as they felt I was too young for such things, and they were the kinds of things only loose women wore. My fears of helping mother at work were founded as, sure enough, we were assigned to a rubble gang, spending most the day just handing buckets of stone down a line of women. I thought I'd rather be at school than doing this; it was a horrible task. The Allied occupation forces didn't want any idle bodies, and all women and girls could be called upon to help clear rubble. The local administration saw that everyone complied with the rules – there was no getting out of it. 'The rebuilding of your country depends on you and starts here,' they said to us.

That afternoon I walked home with my mother, concerned about what might happen over the stockings and nail paint. She had guessed Lisa had been involved, but I kept quiet, reluctant to drop my best friend in the shit, as they say. When we arrived home, my mother showed father the stockings and the nail paint. He wasn't pleased about it. I expected to get a thrashing for my misdemeanour; instead, I was given a lecture on how these types of western things were the hallmark of prostitutes and loose women, and that the Americans were perverting our young women by bringing these things into our country. I was told to never again bring anything like it back home. It was a case of 'not under our roof' – that was one of the rules mother and father laid down. Mother didn't stop there – she could see no traces of nail paint on my fingernails, but insisted I take off my socks so she could check my toenails. I felt like a rat in a trap as I slipped off my socks which revealed my crime.

Mother just said, 'Right, we must get that stuff off,' and spent the next thirty minutes torturing me with a scrubbing brush, trying to scrub the red nail paint off. All I can say is that it was not pleasant, and the nail paint proved very difficult to remove. Bits came off in places while in others it remained firmly attached. Mother grumbled to herself as she scrubbed away but eventually she admitted defeat.

Next day we returned to the rubble gang and Lisa and her mother were also there. I told Lisa about the discovery of our contraband, reassuring her I had not mentioned her name as I didn't want her to get the same treatment as me. After a while we were able to laugh about it and it all soon blew over.

A few weeks later we bumped into more cosmetic-touting young Americans, and again we were offered this stuff they call nail varnish.

I told them, 'No, no, no, as once it's on, you can't get the bloody stuff off!'

One of the Americans then said, 'Yes you can but you have to use this stuff,' passing us a small bottle of clear fluid. The Yank went on to explain that when you needed to remove the varnish you wiped your nails with it then the varnish came off without leaving a trace.

We looked at one another with glee, but I was not convinced, so I kicked off my left shoe and removed my sock, saying, 'Okay, I want to see if this works.' I got Lisa to paint my big toenail with the red varnish then allowed it to dry. I touched it and it was dry and didn't rub off even when I used spit on it. Then I allowed a trickle of the fluid to drip onto the painted nail and rubbed at it with the sleeve of my jumper. The red varnish disappeared in an instant, leaving no trace. Again, we looked at one another with a broad grin and we grabbed the nail paint and remover off the Yank before he gave it to one of the other girls.

Lisa said, 'We can wear it when we go to the lakes at aunt Schiefer's place.'

I used to go with her to her aunt's in late summer on a kind of holiday to the lakes at Schlachtensee and we swam and sunbathed there. We both felt we had scored something of a victory, deciding we would hide the nail paint and remover in an old stone wall near my house – no one would ever find it there.

The rubble-clearing continued for some months and it was a task which the authorities felt would keep the women of our community occupied. Machines were later brought in for the various rebuilding projects, though this was a very slow process as buildings are not rebuilt overnight. Large accommodation blocks had to be built first to house huge numbers of people whose homes had been bombed during the war. They were the priority in most senses, and this was right, I thought. Many thousands of Germans had been expelled from the east which added to the problems of food and shelter for people.

We were soon relocated to a temporary school about a quarter of a mile from where we lived. The building had been a school before, but it needed a few basic repairs before it could be cleared to open again. It was a totally new experience for me and Lisa as this new school consisted of both boys and girls in one big mixed class. Our last school was different and only girls attended until it was forced to close due to the war situation. Kids from the surrounding areas went to the new school; some we knew, others we didn't.

I recall these two boys: they were the 15-year-old Sauerstond twins, Erich and Ernst. These two young buggers were Aryan pride in overdrive; they had short, blond hair with blue eyes, and would have been the pride of their Hitler Youth troop, no doubt at all. Oh yes, they were gorgeous-looking boys what with their high cheekbones. All the girls fancied them. We used to walk home from school with them and Ernst became my first ever boyfriend, though we were both nervous and awkward with one another. Ernst was the first boy I had kissed in a romantic sense, though the kissing was not exactly what you'd call proper kissing, more smooching with closed lips, the art of proper kissing, or 'snogging' as it's referred to, would be learned later. Ernst never came to my house and I never told my parents that I had a boyfriend at the time for fear of what they'd say or that they might not approve. It was easier to just keep things quiet for the sake of peace and quiet. We would walk around acting as friends; as much as I yearned to hold his hand, the thought that someone would see us and tell my parents prevented me doing this. We sometimes went out into the fields; Lisa would be with us and I would hold Ernst's hand then, and occasionally we would stop to peck lips in brief acknowledgment of each other's presence but that would be all. It was hardly the pre-coital passion I would later enjoy – perfectly understandable considering I was still too young at the time for that kind of emotional burden.

The romance, if you can call it that, soon ended when Ernst and Erich played the classic twin's trick on me. We were out the one day running around by the bridge with the stream running beneath it, when Ernst came running up to me and planted a kiss on my lips – only it wasn't Ernst, it was Erich! Lisa noticed this deception as she had spotted the only distinguishing feature the boys had – a mole that Erich had just behind his ear.

Lisa shouted out, 'You buggers, stop this now!'

I asked her, 'Lisa, what is it?'

Then she told me of their deception. I didn't find it funny at all, telling them both so and told Ernst to bugger off in no uncertain terms. He left with his brother like a dog which has just been scolded by its owner.

I sat with Lisa on the bridge and cried for a few minutes, 'How could they be so cruel?' I asked.

Lisa just put her arm around me, saying, 'Look, boys are dumb and do dumb things to amuse themselves. Bugger them. Don't let them make you cry. I don't like seeing you cry.'

We walked back and before parting to take the different roads to our homes, we hugged each other. Lisa kissed me on the cheek, saying, 'See you tomorrow, Tia. Don't worry about those two fools. You are better than what they are; all girls are better, that's what they don't like.'

The sun was setting and there was a slight chill in the air. I stood watching Lisa until she disappeared from view. I gazed at the sunset for a few minutes. I took a deep breath and felt a single tear running down my face. I wiped it away with my hand before hurrying on home.

Watch the sun as she is shot down wounded,
uterine orange in colour,
and the sun always appears,
an insect-attracting glow upon the horizon.

Germany, 20 November 1945, drew the attention of the world press and media as the Nuremberg war crimes trials began. The trials were a series of tribunals convened by the Allied authorities under international law. Most of the leading Nazis who stood trial at Nuremberg were more or less resigned to their fate, yet former Reichsmarschall Hermann Göring, once the second most powerful figure to Hitler, attempted to orientate the tribunal proceedings as if they were some ghastly theatrical show.

Lisa wrote in her journal:

> The war crimes tribunals have started today. They will go on for months, it's the talk of the town naturally. Most of the characters, all leading figures within the Third Reich, who once presided over so many areas of our lives, are now little more than shambolic figures of their former selves. If you want to find out all about it, you just go into any of the cinemas in operation in the city, where you can sit and watch it all, or you can tune into the radio broadcasts. Me and Tia went to one of the cinemas to see what was going on; what we saw were men resigned to the fact that they were now on

borrowed time. Ribbentrop cut a pathetic figure, hunched over, dressed badly and appearing to have aged overnight; Hess [Rudolph Hess], the one-time deputy Führer, sat rocking like an imbecile in an institution. Yet, I did argue on Hess's part: what was he doing here? Hess flew to England on what we now know was an abortive attempt at peace negotiations. Apart from the very early years, Hess played no part in the genocide of which he stands accused alongside the others – that is just my view. Göring is the main stage attraction; he appears alert, coherent, able to counter every accusation laid against him with all the finesse of a fox leaving a hen house. Of course, he will hang; most of them should hang for what they did. I remember some of these high-ranking figures calling for every man, woman and child to fight the invaders of our nation, yet where were they when that time came? They did not stand shoulder to shoulder with the Wehrmacht and fight, did they? No, of course not; instead, they filled their pockets with the gold teeth from the skulls of Jews they were responsible for killing and fled or hid away in dark underground bunkers, hoping for some divine salvation. We did not receive that salvation: the people paid the ultimate price – they always do in war. The atmosphere is strange in the city now; it's like 'don't speak to Germans' all over again. With all the press revelations, the hatred and anger toward us seems to be revived. Some Allied soldiers arrogantly ask me, 'Were you a follower, a supporter? Were your mum and dad followers of the regime? Did they have oil paintings of Hitler hanging in their living room?' I say to them, 'Why don't you ask them? Why don't you go and see for yourself? As for me I'm hardly a model fascist, I can't recite one passage from *Mein Kampf*, I barely attended the BDM or even school because you were dropping bombs on us twenty-four hours a day, seven days a week.' They didn't know what to say to me, but I thought if this is how it's going to be from now on, we might as well just say, 'Fuck this!' I met up with Tia who was always a soothing presence, a voice of reason in times like this. Tia's opinion on the opening of the Nazi war crimes trial was, 'In a few days it will blow over, passions will calm, the focus will be on the bad guys, the real monsters of our society, then maybe we can carry on with our lives again as normal.'

> *Dictators standing centre stage,*
> *all with their own roles to play.*
> *Justice finally will prevail,*
> *for those who took the coward's way.*
> *Monsters exit centre stage,*
> *lying on their bed of sin.*
> *Personas built on blood and death,*
> *facades discarded show evil within.*
> *On with the Show* AV III

In school the girls would find that debate on the tribunals was openly encouraged as part of the denazification process that the Allied authorities were keen to introduce to all German children as part of the new education ethos. Lisa continued:

> Our new teacher was a stern-looking German man, He explained he had taught children before the war, but had been driven from his beloved profession by the fascists that had taken control of our society. He explained how he fled the country, vowing to return once the fascists had been destroyed. He exclaimed that our society was as much to blame for allowing it all to happen; then he asked us one by one how we would prevent such terrible things happening again. We examined the whole rotting corpse of National Socialism; class work became one long autopsy on National Socialism and its evils. We as the young of this country were entering a new era, we all had a moral obligation to ensure that fascism was never allowed to prevail again. I understood everything that the new education system was saying but was eager to learn about other cultures of the world. In time all these things were revealed to us, but maybe for me and Tia it came a little too late, as we weren't kids anymore – we were teenagers and with hindsight we had missed out on so much, we had been conned by the Nazi system. The world was a

huge place; all you had to do now was learn about it all. We had a fantastic library which built up from just a few books to a few hundred. Many were written in English which were a little harder to understand. I had wanted to learn English, though. Tia and I would take books home, books on subjects like wonders of nature, cities of the world and books on the arts and music, all the kind of things that the Nazis denied us from reading in favour of German-only publications. We both spent hours looking at these books, writing down notes, vowing to visit some of these places when we were old enough to go travelling. When Tia stayed over at my house, we would go through the books together, often using the light of a candle as we were often up way past what our parents termed as bedtime. The weather was colder now and as we lay on our bellies side by side thumbing through the pages of the books, our breath was visible in the light of the candle. Tia said, 'Winter is coming. I can feel it in the air, even here in your room.' We would carefully extinguish the candle, pulling the blankets over us. We'd lie there talking for a few minutes comparing hand sizes and silly things like that. It was as if we didn't want this moment, this relaxing carefree part of the day, to end. Often Tia would fall asleep with her head on my chest, her left leg across my thighs and her arm across my midriff. Sometimes Tia would wake me up with her snoring in the night, and I would gently squeeze her nose which always did the trick: she would grunt and grumble for a few seconds then would be sound asleep again. Yes, no matter what the world outside was doing, we had each other as friends. I couldn't think of ever being without Tia. I adored her. I often lay awake in the early morning thinking, *What do we do when we get married? We might lose touch and steadily drift apart, and all of this will be a memory someday, a memory we might reflect upon among the pile of excreta-stained nappies of married bliss, where the demands of a husband and crying child drive us both fucking mad.* I don't know if Tia feels the same way as me as I have never asked her, but I can imagine she does, as her plans to travel around the world always include me and never anyone else.

Chapter 2

On Jaundiced Pages

December 1945 found Tia and Lisa attending another school. The school was one which had been in operation during the war but had ceased its educational activities after suffering bomb damage. It was subject to hasty repairs in the hope that as many local children as possible would attend, Tia and Lisa included. Lisa recalled:

> I couldn't say we were over the moon about going back to school again, but it was either that or working on the rubble gangs. We could not have just got ourselves jobs, as no one would have employed us at that time. So, school was better than being on the rubble gangs with the older women or just doing nothing. The women of the rubble gangs felt their work was more of a punishment. We believed school had to be better than that – well, so we thought anyway. The problem was neither of us had a clue what we wanted to do after school. We didn't want jobs where we could end up wiping the bums of old former Nazis, neither did we want jobs looking after children or babies. The thought of ending up in some factory as part of some mass production line also filled us with dread. I guessed we would end up working in shops, *Brauhäuser* [pubs] or cafés. Only the future could determine our fate and whether or not we were worthy of any future at all.

To the backdrop of the continuing Nuremberg Trials, the girls began school again.

> *Medusa writhes on the ground,*
> *she resembles a fish out of water,*
> *she is crying blood,*
> *with all five fingers inside of herself,*
> *she flashes a grin down on Adolf Hitler Strasse.*

Tia wearily rose from the comfort of her bed; it was Monday morning and she had to meet Lisa for what would be the first day of full-time education for them both since the strategic bombing of Germany had begun to affect all educational activity. She grabbed a pencil, scribbling down the cryptic vision as presented in the evening's dream in her notebook – dream or nightmare, she could not decide. She sat pondering for some moments, trying to interpret its contents. Her thoughts were interrupted by her mother shouting up the stairs for her to get ready to leave for school.

> I get dressed and manage to drink a cup of acorn coffee; it's lukewarm with the taste of cigarette tar. How I have come to loathe acorn coffee; it's all we can get, it is merely a coffee substitute – *ersatz* – and yes, it is made from acorns. How anyone can start their day on this stuff I don't know. I pick up my bag which contains nothing more than two bread rolls – the rolls have a slither of meat fat in them. It's disgusting but when you get hungry you will eat most things you previously would have spat out. It's cold outside and I grab my warm coat, wrap a scarf around my neck before leaving the house.
>
> I call in at Lisa's house and we make the journey to school in the cold drizzle which seems to always start as you leave the relative comfort of home. We walk arm in arm to the school, just a quarter of a mile or so, but in the drizzle, it is a miserable affair. We walk quickly with our heads hanging down as if this would keep the drizzle off us. Passers-by are merely ghosts to us. We don't acknowledge anyone: the goal is to get to school, get in the dry, maybe learn something interesting and not be lectured like the previous school years that we had to contend with under the Nazi government.
>
> We arrive at the school three minutes late. Everyone stares as we knock on the door. A voice from within the classroom bawls, 'Enter!'
>
> I whisper to Lisa, 'Enter? What is this? A checkpoint or something?'
>
> I go in first and we come face to face with Horse Teeth and Onions as we later nickname him. This is Herr Gottfried

Wilhelm, the teacher who epitomizes the style of many post-war teachers in Germany. The nickname explains it all. He is a tall, thin man in a black suit, with white shirt and black dicky bowtie. His polished shoes shine so you can see the reflection of the room in them. He has a long, thin face with large teeth that protrude slightly, hardly an Aryan specimen we think to ourselves, and typical of pre-war non-sympathizing teachers that the Nazis ejected from our country. He also possesses a peculiar onion-like odour, a sweaty armpit smell he has all year round. In summer he stinks twice as bad.

'Well, well, well. What do we have here, two late arrivals, I see?'

We are questioned as to why we are late, and we can give no clear explanation. We are warned about being late again and told to take our seats. We look around the classroom, heading to two vacant places side by side in the middle. The other kids look at us, and, as we look back at them, two faces stand out: the Sauerstond, twins, the two boys who fell foul of our tempers not so long back. For the moment, they are a familiarity, an ally in a class full of kids we have never seen before – ours is a huge neighbourhood, education has a premium value after the Nazis, so kids from far away come here to learn.

Then comes Herr Wilhelm's opening speech, delivered with all the ferocity of Joseph Goebbels in his prime: 'You are the tainted generation which I have undertaken to educate for the better of this devastated country of ours. To avoid uncertain paths, we have to lay down new foundations from which to walk upon. There will be no talk of Hitler or National Socialism in this room or on these premises. If I hear of anyone breaking this rule, they will incur my greatest wrath and receive a lashing from this [brandishing a long, whippy cane].'

He stalks the rows of desks, intimidating each child by swishing the cane over their heads. He comes along our line of desks and as he whips the cane over our heads, we barely flinch. I see Lisa stifle a smile; she fights to prevent herself from bursting into laughter, but luckily Herr Wilhelm passes us by and does not notice. This old man doesn't intimidate us. Who or what does he think we are? We shall judge whether his education is worthy of our attention, and until then he is held in somewhat silent contempt by many of us in the classroom. We are not thinking like this out of arrogance: we have been through much, have experienced many unpleasant things. We have seen death and destruction, body parts, blood, fire. Yes, we have seen it all, so much so that no cane wielded by an old man could ever possibly instil fear within us.

After the speech Herr Wilhelm's attention turns to the blackboard at the front of the classroom. He then bellows, 'What can any of you tell me about other countries of the world?'

One young boy raises his hand and when granted permission to speak, he says, 'I know that in Africa there are lions and crocodiles.'

There are some stifled sniggers before Herr Wilhelm roars, 'Silence!' Then he says, 'Ah, yes, Africa, full of negros quite uneducated, unlike us, no?' Just as some of the boys are beginning to smile and nod their heads in agreement with what is obviously a trick question, Herr Wilhelm roars, 'No, that is quite incorrect! Africa is rich in culture, far more diverse than ours, with far less of the privileges we might enjoy. I see I have habits to break; many of your heads are still filled with the rubbish of what was a doomed regime. I see I have quite a task but learn you will.'

So, we start with a geography lesson focusing on the cultures of the world about us, and how the people, their customs, cultures and traditional way of life are not so different from ours. We are told that the Aryans, so beloved of the Hitler regime, are in fact not a race of white Europeans but Asian. The race issue is one of the first taboos to be destroyed. No race is any greater than any other we are told. We are all children of this world who can learn and experience much from one another.

> A recess is called and after being given permission to leave the classroom for the playground in an orderly fashion, we head outside into the chill wind and drizzle to what is nothing more than an area of concrete. The other children huddle around in groups. The Sauerstond twins join us. Our chatter is nervous, but as familiar faces we are glad of them for moral support in this arena of strangers. They apologize for their behaviour of the past and soon we are quite relaxed standing around talking about the events of the day so far. For twenty minutes we stand outside talking. We tell Ernst and Erich the nickname we have given Herr Wilhelm. They think it is very amusing and their old charm begins to make an impression on us. I still like Ernst even though the swap trick he did on me with Erich really hurt. I felt maybe in time I might allow him a second chance if the opportunity arose.

Lisa recalled that first day back at school and the truce with the Sauerstond twins:

> Those two were rogues, but so good looking they would melt your heart. They apologized for being nasty to us, a time which seemed so long ago but was merely months. We decided to forgive and forget so long as there was no repeat of their antics of the past. Tia still liked Ernst as she told me so and I actually liked Erich, but the thought of us two being involved with identical twins as boyfriends seemed so weird. At that first day back at school those two were a welcome sight. The second half of that day wasn't too bad. The focus was on geography and history and how other races, however primitive, all serve to enrich the world. Of course, Herr Wilhelm was right. I can see how his education formula devised by the Western Allies was working. It made you curious to learn more and made you realize just how cheated you had been under the Nazis. The day went well in all, apart from us being late. We had a second lunchbreak, the drizzle stopped and the sun battled through the clouds. Herr Wilhelm sat at his desk eating a meal and drinking a

glass of water. We had peeked through one of the windows to see what he was doing.

As school finished we departed after reciting prayers and then made our way home. The twins walked with us before going their separate way, telling us they would see us tomorrow. Again, Tia and I walked home arm in arm. Soon we were back among the hustle and bustle, seeing the now familiar faces of Allied servicemen. Tia came back to my house to say hello to my parents before going home.

I spent the evening reflecting on the day: maybe school wasn't so bad after all. I told my parents about the day and what was being taught. I think they were happy and understood that the past had to be left in the past, that we all had to move forward. What we learned now in the few remaining years was critical to our futures. Tia and I would never make university; we understood that we were in many senses just 'mongrels', working-class girls destined for menial jobs who would find boyfriends, maybe marry and have children. That thought troubled me greatly, more than anything else, I didn't want that kind of a life, I wanted some excitement, I wanted to travel, to see things beyond our borders. I know Tia felt the same way, but to do things like that we would need money. The key to earning reasonable money in this country was to learn to speak English fluently. If you could master English, you could work as a translator or something. Learning as much as you could to further your prospects was important along with learning to type and write shorthand. School did not always teach these things so you had to find someone who would. That was not easy. My mother had a friend who agreed to teach me and Tia English, how to use a typewriter machine and dictate in shorthand. We decided we wanted to try and find work within the German or Allied press/media. Yes, we had big ideas but at least we had a plan other than starting work at a factory as would be the case for many girls in post-war western Germany. We would do our best, work together as friends, to see where life could take us. We had ambitions beyond that of just becoming pregnant housewives; we wanted to go as far as we could. Settling down just didn't feel right to either of us … it was just something we both felt.

Lisa's mother Hedrun approached her good friend Klarissa Bergmann on the possibility of her teaching the girls English language, typing and shorthand. Frau Bergmann agreed on the principle that if she did the girls could help her in recompense with a few chores around her house. It was a modest-sized house, typically German with its whitewashed exterior walls with roses which would paint the garden with their characteristic red blooms in the summer. A few ground rules were laid down by Frau Bergmann: there would be no 'monkey business', the girls would turn up on the allotted time for their lessons and they would be smartly dressed while in her company. Hedrun agreed to the terms which appeared somewhat draconian, but she understood that her friend's teachings could prove of high value in a Germany where the West would now be a primary social and political influence. Tia recalled her and Lisa's first English tuition with Frau Bergmann:

> We had to wear these white dresses; we didn't have many dresses so wore what our mothers could find. I walked to Lisa's house and together we made our way to Frau Bergmann's. We felt a strange sense of humiliation wearing our dresses, like a couple of well-to-do girls on their way to religious confirmation. Yes, we were embarrassed having to wear these white dresses under our heavy winter coats. To make matters worse it started to rain halfway to Frau Bergmann's house, so we were relieved to get there. There was this large ornate brass door knocker in the shape of a ram's head. Before Lisa even touched the knocker, the door opened to this rather stony-faced, middle-aged woman who exclaimed firmly, 'I am Frau Bergmann. Please come inside.' We shuffled in through the doorway, glad to be out of the rain. Frau Bergmann led us along the hallway into a small room out the back with a table and chairs. She said, 'Please take a seat' then put some water on the stove to boil for some cups of tea, saying 'I hope you didn't get too wet on your way here, but a good cup of tea should warm you

both through. Hot drinks are good, yet you can still catch a chill you know.' We both sat gazing around the room at the pictures and portraits decorating the walls. Once the water boiled, Frau Bergmann made us a cup of hot tea. She apologized that there was no sugar, besides she didn't take sugar in her tea or coffee. As we sipped from ornate china cups complete with saucers, Frau Bergmann sat opposite us at the table and said: 'I will teach you English. It's not quite the devil's language that the National Socialists so proclaimed; quite the contrary, the English are a very cultured race of people, much in the same way as we Germans. In fact, many English customs are similar to those of our own. English is not too difficult a language to master, and it is universal, spoken over much of the world now, you know.' The first things we started to learn were just basic sentences such as 'Good morning sir or madam', 'How are you today?' and 'My name is so and so, I am pleased to meet you'. Frau Bergmann gave us each a piece of paper and a pencil to scribble down the things we had learned in each session and this helped us to practise back home. There was much emphasis on the actual vocalization and pronunciation of the words too. If we got them wrong Frau Bergmann would immediately interrupt and say, 'No, no, no no, that is completely wrong, child. Try again, and please concentrate on what I have told you.' Frau Bergmann just rolled the words and there were times we thought *Christ, this is bloody impossible.* As frustrating as it was at the time, we were very keen to learn and after a few sessions, we did start to improve, our English becoming more coherent.

After each session, which was usually on a Saturday afternoon, we then had to return Frau Bergmann a favour. Most of the time we helped her with dusting the house and moving bits of furniture around. The garden was delightful, but we were not permitted to help there because Frau Bergmann did not want us to dirty our clothes. As we began to master the English language, Frau Bergmann began to show us how to dictate in shorthand script then how to use a typewriter, typing in both English and German. She would dictate what we had to type, and we had to type it correctly. Lisa and I took turns on the typewriter as there was only the one machine. If we made an error, she would scold us and tell us off for wasting paper – yes, she was strict with us for sure. Though, I feel, had she not been strict with us, we might have taken the mickey out of her.

Our schooling was becoming somewhat strained, as we grew bored with the lessons and were getting restless in class. Herr Wilhelm had the habit of slapping you around the back of the head if he felt you were not paying attention. One morning in class, he did this to Lisa. It wasn't that she was not listening to him or not paying attention, she just didn't quite get what he was saying. He often spoke like he was reading a piece from Shakespeare or something – he could be a real middle-class dick sometimes. This one occasion he slapped Lisa round the back of her head; it wasn't hard, but I felt a sudden gush of fury, and the moment he hit her, I jumped to my feet, glaring angrily at him. He spun around in surprise.

'Well, what do we have here then?' he barked.

'I don't want anyone hitting my friend, sir.'

'Oh, you don't, do you? Get here now to the front where we can all see you.'

I walked to the front of the class.

He said, 'I am in charge of this class and this school. What I say is final, and not you or any other child here in this room can say otherwise. As an example to any other would-be buccaneer, I will now administer the punishment.'

Lisa stood up from behind her desk and shouted, 'No!' Her shout echoed through the room just as Herr Wilhelm was brandishing his cane which he had taken from out of a cupboard behind his desk. 'You are not hitting her with that!' she shouted.

I was shocked by her verbal attack upon the man. I knew we were both in trouble, my mind frantically wondering how we were going to reverse this predicament.

Herr Wilhelm barked at me, 'Give me your hand now!'

'No!'

Becoming increasingly frustrated, he again shouted, 'You will give me your hand this instant, you obstinate girl!'

Again, I said 'no', putting my hands behind my back. By this time giggles were erupting in the class, Herr Wilhelm shouted at the class to shut up or everyone would receive a beating for insolence. The laughter grew. I recall a boy sitting at the front with big buck teeth grinning to the point where he resembled a chimpanzee. I started laughing myself, I couldn't help it. It was then that Herr Wilhelm grabbed me by my arm, trying to pull my hands from behind my back.

Lisa stepped forward and shouted at him, 'Get your hands off her, you fascist pig!'

For several seconds a deathly silence hung over the classroom, Herr Wilhelm's eyes bulging from their sockets, almost foaming at the mouth with rage. The silence was broken when he shouted at us, 'Get out of here, and don't come back!'

We both left the room, out the door, down the corridor and out the school into the sunshine. It was like we were moving from one alternative reality into another. We stood outside for a moment looking back at the school building, as if a friend was departing unexpectedly from our lives. Arm in arm we walked down the road, in silence at first. There was a churchyard with a wooden bench outside and we sat down.

Lisa said, 'I can't believe that has just happened. What are we going to do now? What do we tell our parents?' She rested her head on my shoulder as we pondered our situation. She suggested we went back to apologize when the other kids had gone home. She looked at me with concern in her eyes, saying, 'It may be our only chance to salvage the situation, other than that we are going to be in the shit with our parents if we can't sort this out.'

I said, 'You called him a pig, not only a pig but a fascist one. I don't think he appreciated that very much.'

We both laughed and hugged each other. We waited for the school to empty then made our way up the steps back inside, walking along the corridor to Herr Wilhelm's class. We both bit our lips in anticipation as Lisa knocked on the door.

A voice within commanded, 'Who is there, who is it?'

Gingerly we turned the handle, entering the room. Herr Wilhelm was at his desk writing; he looked up, but before he could say anything, we both blurted out, 'Please forgive us, Herr Wilhelm, sir; we are so sorry for what happened earlier. We promise it will never happen again.'

He looked across at us and asked us to take a seat. He then said, 'Do you understand what a fascist is? Isn't that what you called me? I should be visiting both your parents and maybe explaining your conduct to them would be better for you both?'

We shook our heads. 'No sir, that would not be good for us.' We promised we would never do anything like that again and would accept any punishment, even his cane, if it would resolve the crisis.

After considering a suitable punishment, he declined to use the cane, telling us he admired our spirit, but we needed to understand what respect was about, how only unruly societies functioned without respect. We were told we would have to give a talk about respect to the class the next day and do a few extra chores in school rather than going out into the playground at breaktimes. We both agreed, realizing we were very lucky not to have been kicked out for good and have him visit our parents. Our parents would have killed us if he had come to our houses and told them what we had done. Herr Wilhelm explained before we left how some of his family had faced persecution under the Nazis. He then told us that three of his family had been murdered by them. We wanted to know more, but were dismissed.

'Another time, maybe. I have work to do now. Off with you both and I'll see you tomorrow morning – and don't be late.'

With that we thanked him and apologized again and we walked out the building down the road as we had earlier, yet happier that word of this would not reach our families.

What Tia and Lisa hadn't bargained on were the jungle drums of their neighbourhood. It was typical for any child to go home telling his or her parents of the kind of day they had at school, the drama of that afternoon, and Tia's and Lisa's escapade was soon the subject of local gossip. News was passed from garden fence to garden gate, soon reaching the ears of the girls' mothers. As the girls reached Lisa's house, they were met by her mother who they knew from her expression was not pleased.

She simply said, 'You have something to explain to me, I believe? You had better both come inside and tell me what happened at school today, or at least your version of it.'

The girls sheepishly went inside, feeling the best policy in this case was honesty. After explaining what had happened in class that afternoon and the fact that they went back to apologize, even agreeing to take the cane if it would resolve the problem, Lisa's mother was satisfied, but still angry at being the subject of the local gossips. She turned to her daughter and said, 'I am not sure how to explain this to your father; he won't be pleased.' She then turned to Tia and said, 'You had best go home now as your mother will probably have also heard the news. Go on, off you go.'

Tia recalled:

> I kissed Lisa on the cheek, telling her I would see her in the morning. I said sorry to her mother for my part in the afternoon's altercation, that it would never happen again. I then made the short journey home, petrified of what my own mother and father were going to say. When I got home and walked through the door, mother was in the kitchen. Father was asleep in his chair. Mother was preparing the evening meal, a one-pot stew consisting mainly of vegetables. I walked into the kitchen, sat down at the table and watched as she washed up.
>
> Drying her hands on her apron, she then said, 'Right, what's this I have been hearing from every gossip in the street, especially from Frau Sauerstond's sister-in-law?'
>
> I thought to myself, *I should have known those fucking twins wouldn't keep their mouths shut.* So, I sat there and explained everything all over again. I promised her I was sorry, that I had offered to take Herr Wilhelm's punishment and had also said sorry to Lisa's mother.

Mother then said, '"Fascist pig" Herr Wilhelm was called, was he not?'

I answered her quietly, 'Yes mother, it was, and we are both so sorry.'

Mother then explained to me, 'Do you understand what that poor man who is trying to teach you children some form of an education went through? He was a teacher before Hitler; yes, as a young man he taught children. When Hitler became Chancellor, he had to leave. Three of his family remained behind in Germany while he left with his wife to go to America. Do you know they put his remaining family into a camp because they were of Jewish blood, and they did not survive? My punishment for you both will be the cancellation of your English lessons for a month. You must pray to god your father does not hear of this – he does not know about it. We shall say no more about it and you can help me around the garden to try and make amends for what you have done too. There will be no going off out on the weekends until I decide otherwise. Now do you understand?'

I again told my mother I was sorry for causing her trouble and began to feel tearful. She could see I was now getting upset. She drew up a chair opposite me: 'Look, I know you have been through a lot, we all have. It is honourable to defend your friends, but you can't behave like a delinquent in school. You must try harder to not become involved in anything that may disrupt what could be a good education for you and Lisa. You are getting too old to thrash with a belt; things like that should not be happening now. Soon you will be leaving school and looking to work. It's not an easy world out there, Tia, believe me. It's even harder for us as we are women.'

She leaned forward, kissing me on the forehead then told me to go and wash before the evening meal was served. It was one conversation with my dear mother I always remembered. Had my father found out he would have strapped me for sure; fathers were still very strict, even after the war. The next morning on our way to school Lisa and I discussed how in future we had to avoid trouble at school. Once we left school to find jobs and get our own places, life would be easier – we could enjoy more freedom, couldn't we?

> *They called us the tainted generation,*
> *yet we were the beginning of a new dawn.*
> *Blank pages on which to be written,*
> *overlaying an ingrained scorn.*
> *We believed in a better future,*
> *embracing all that life had to give.*
> *Just beyond that faint horizon,*
> *we finally learned how to live.*
>
> *New Dawn* AV IV

Christmas of 1945 was not entirely devoid of joy as it had been over the previous years. There was no shortage of Christmas trees or decorations with which to embellish them. Under Hitler the Nazi authorities attempted to rid Christmas of its Christian origins, as they believed their own ideology could not be reconciled with the teachings of Christianity. Tia recalled:

> I remember Christmas 1943 was the gloomiest on earth; it was horrible. We had this small tree which was virtually bare. Due to the war, the production of decorations for Christmas had ceased completely. All there was that year was hunger and despondency and Christmas 1944 was worse. Christmas 1945 was a little better as we had the Allied soldiers here and they brought in lots of things like decorations and treats for the children. We now had plenty of things with which to make our own cards and presents for friends and family, so it did feel more like Christmas with these things and the extra food supplies being brought in. Christmas morning 1945 was characteristically cold, yet I went out later to visit Lisa to give her a small handkerchief I had made for her. Lisa had knitted me a brown scarf which I thought was lovely. I sat in the kitchen of her home with her family and we huddled around the large black stove. We each had a cup of that stinking acorn coffee and heard

stories of how the American and British soldiers would be having turkey for their dinners. We couldn't complain though: we were all alive, our future a work in progress as Lisa's father proclaimed happily. Lisa's father had been with some local men procuring alcohol from somewhere; they were not drunk, but you could tell that alcohol had buoyed their spirits. Before I left to return home, I gave Lisa a hug. I always gave her hugs and a kiss whenever we parted. I loved her so much; she was the best friend anyone could have. As I walked home in the cold, I thought how I could never imagine life without my best friend. I found myself in an emotional mood once home. I thought back on the year that was rapidly coming to an end. What would 1946 be like? I remember spending the remainder of that Christmas Day with my parents listening to the radio and reading. As evening drew near, it became ever colder so I went to bed early. I lay wrapped up in my woollen blankets trying to imagine summertime. Once spring returned, it would not be long until the carefree days of summer. This summer, arrangements were in place for me to go with Lisa to her aunt Schiefer's at Slachtensee. Oh, it's beautiful there and we were both so looking forward to those two weeks away. I lay dreaming about Schlachtensee, falling into a deep sleep.

1945 was a year of both pleasure and pain, a vomit pile of conflicting hopes and emotions. Christmas Day passed by peacefully. The chill air of New Year's Eve 1945 gave way to the frost-laced dawn of New Year's Day 1946. The past was still painfully too close for many, yet the winter sun attempted to pierce the gloom. Soldiers in their greatcoats were in good spirits, a few now on first name terms with the locals. There were smiles and greeting of 'Happy New Year' – where there are smiles and greetings, there is hope.

It is as if the Grey Lady has cast aside her bouquet of thorn. The buildings where the *Wolfkinder* once sought refuge were now empty, the children gone – no one was quite sure where. In one of these ruins lay a discarded, dirty, torn child's teddy bear, its ears and eyes missing, its sawdust filling spilling out. On one of the walls appeared the typical scrawl of a young child who had scratched the words 'I want to go home. I want my mother and my father', probably with one of the many rusty nails that lay scattered on the floor. The building, like many others in Berlin, would soon be demolished with another built in its place.

Lisa recalled the last day of school prior to Christmas 1945:

> Herr Wilhelm gave out bibles to everyone in the class. Before wishing everyone a happy and peaceful Christmas, he told the class, 'Germany's fate is now a matter for god himself to decide. I am sorry that the bibles I am now gifting to your care are old and not new. I am hoping that within the jaundiced pages that you will discover not only comfort, but the courage to rewrite your own history.'
>
> We were all in a sense rewriting our history from jaundiced pages, the now-stained and yellowed pages of books which had for some years been consigned to damp cellars, or buried in metal trunks in the hope of seeing the light again someday, when the madness which had consumed our nation had somehow abated like some medieval plague. Either way, Herr Wilhelm's words seemed poignant for that time, enough for me to write them down in my diary: 'We are building our hopes upon ghosts.'

Chapter 3

When the Owls Sang at Schlactensee

*Doesn't feel like Christmas Day,
the festive spirit still far away,
No ornaments to grace the tree,
it's difficult to rewrite history.
The bitter cold still sets within our bones,
men fell hard from their gilded thrones.
A work in progress we may be,
but joy arrives so subtly.*

Hope's Promise AV V

New Year's Day 1946 for many Germans was spent quietly in the confines of their homes. There was little celebration to be had the night before, in contrast to other cities around the world, particularly those of the victorious nations – it appeared as if somehow a New Year had passed Germany by.

Tia woke around 9 am. As she yawned, she could see her own breath as it met with the chilled air of her bedroom. She dressed, making her way wearily down the stairs to the kitchen where her mother was busy cleaning. The small fire in the stove had only just been lit, the fuel provided by the remains of a broken-up rocking chair. Although the flames flickered within, they exuded little in the way of warmth. Tia wrapped the woollen blanket which acted as her bed cover around herself, drawing her legs up onto the chair to relieve her cold feet of the stone flooring. She sat shivering. Her mother looked at her, telling her she should dress soon before passing her a cup of hot coffee. Of course, the coffee was still not the real coffee she had been dreaming of – it was the much-hated *ersatz* acorn coffee – but it was hot and warming to the soul; as bad as it tasted, she gulped the hot liquid down, staring into the flames of the small kitchen stove. It was a time of quiet reflection. She sat deep in thought, drifting to the war years. The dystopian empire of which she and many of her friends had once been the pawns, had been as real as the yellow flames that now began to emit a little warmth into the chilly air. She sat for some minutes, mesmerized by the flames as they took hold upon the wood and few pieces of precious coal within. Then came the flashbacks, the whistle of falling bombs, explosions, the whine of flying shrapnel as it traced a deadly trajectory through the air, sometimes hitting masonry, other times a human being with a sickening *thump*. She began to tremble so badly that her grip on the cup of acorn coffee became feeble.

Tia's mother noticed her shaking, near trancelike, before the stove, 'Tia!' she shouted, immediately shaking the young girl out of her stupor. A splash of coffee hit the stone floor. Tia apologized, offering to clean the mess. Her mother smiled at her reassuringly and said, 'Look, why don't you go upstairs and dress and get yourself ready for chapel.'

> *Each memory a nightmare I long to forget,*
> *haunted by faces we couldn't protect.*
> *Fierce flames enshrouded innocent souls,*
> *one step to freedom as another head rolls.*
> *War-torn Berlin hangs her head forlorn,*
> *ragged and wasted on a cold winter's morn.*
> *Took all they wanted,*
> *left her stripped and bare,*
> *another heap of rubble but no one left to care.*
> *Living Nightmare* AV VI

Tia's parents were not exactly of a religious disposition, but they did attend church at Christmas and on New Year's Day. Under the Third Reich religious practice was discouraged; many hard-line Nazis were atheists including Hitler himself, with many of the opinion that 'what is good enough for our Führer, is good enough for us'. Now there was a sense of freedom in the air and for many it felt good.

Having dressed, Tia waited for her mother to get ready. They then put on their coats, hats and gloves and set off for the Kraus household. Tia and her mother would call for Lisa and her mother, and together they would go to the chapel. The men of course had other ideas of how they should spend their time, Tia's and Lisa's fathers were with other local men, indulging in alcohol they had procured, the alcohol being US bourbon which was in ample supply for the Allied soldiers celebrating Christmas and New Year thousands of miles away from home in Germany. What bribes the young American servicemen took in return for the bourbon remains unknown. The chapel service itself was an uncomfortable affair, as much as the winter weather that day. The hour-long service seemed an eternity. Both Tia and Lisa felt their feet steadily going numb as they stood rooted to the spot on the cold, ornate-tiled flooring. The priest asked for a final prayer of salvation for all the people of Germany on what was another day of hope, a step further away from a nightmare which would take many steps to escape. As the small gathering of mainly women and children bowed their heads in prayer, the priest offered his blessings to all in attendance. With the service over the girls were keen to get home. As the gathering exited the parabolic curve of the chapel doorway, some stood outside chatting while others hurried home. Tia asked her mother if she could go for a walk with Lisa – they wouldn't be long, they would have a walk around the block to regain the circulation in their feet. Tia's mother agreed and, with a nod of approval from Lisa's mother, the two girls walked off arm in arm up the road. As soon as they were out of earshot of the others, Tia recalled:

> We were glad to be out of that chapel. It was bloody freezing, my feet were an agony of icicles, they felt like blocks of ice, and a walk around the block seemed a good excuse to warm ourselves up and to see what everyone else was getting up to. As we walked up the road, an American Jeep drove by beeping its horn, the driver and his passenger waving and shouting something which we were sure was 'Happy New Year Frauleins'. Our English lessons were proving invaluable but if only the aliens in our neighbourhood would talk just a little slower, we might understand them more easily.
> We decided to go down an old alley we knew at the back of some houses a couple of blocks away from our street. There were some old sheds down the alley, and we thought we would have a snoop around if no one was about. In the first shed there was nothing more than a dead chicken which had begun to smell, even in the cold. Lisa asked if it would

still be edible and I told her, 'Urgh no!' We looked in the next one, working our way down. We were second from the last one when we heard peculiar noises coming from within. It sounded like there was a pig in there dying, a weird noise neither of us was sure of, so we decided to creep up along the side of the shed to see what it was. I went first, working my way along, looking for a hole to peer through. Lisa followed, holding onto the back of my coat-tail. Finally, I found a split in the wooden panelling and, closing my left eye, peered through with my right. For a few seconds I could see nothing. Then a pair of heaving buttocks became visible in the gloom, positioned between a pair of very white legs which splayed with each thrust. I pulled away, covering my mouth with my hand as I desperately fought to stifle a laugh. Lisa was saying, 'What is it, let me have a look.' I moved away still covering my mouth, fighting to stifle my fits of laughter. Lisa peered through the split in the wood. For a few seconds she said nothing, then all hell broke loose as I could stifle my laughter no more. I shrieked with laughter. Lisa pulled away that instant with a shocked expression on her face. I grabbed her arm and we ran just as a male voice shouted, 'Who is it? Who's that out there?' We almost fell over one another at the top of the alley as there was this gate and we fumbled to open the catch. We looked back to see some man standing outside the shed fastening his trousers.

'Fuck off! Don't ever let me catch you around here again!'

We managed to open the catch on the gate and ran like hell out of the alley onto the street. By the time we stopped running, we are out of breath from a combination of exertion and laughter. I said to Lisa, 'God, did you see that, did you see it?'

'Yes, I did. They were fucking in there.'

We laughed about it all the way back to my house. My mother was preparing dinner. She kept asking what we found so amusing, but we couldn't tell her, could we? We said it was just a joke someone had told us that we thought was really funny. Lisa came up to my room and stayed for an hour where we giggled like a couple of small children. Lisa stayed for some dinner.

I say dinner, though dinner was really nothing more than a stew with more vegetables than meat in it. Times were still tough, and we often ate what my father referred to as 'pig's swill', the one-pot meal many German families had become accustomed to during the lean years of war. It was better than nothing though and the Western Allies ensured supplies came into Germany at regular intervals, but it was nowhere near enough. In the Soviet zone things, we were told, were not good. We heard rumours there was little food and something of a crisis was looming there. Of course, we didn't know. It was just what we had heard from people supposedly in the know.

Although the anti-fraternization laws drafted by the Allied powers in Germany had initially proved effective in the immediate aftermath of the war, they were soon being openly flouted by Allied soldiers.

Perhaps of greater concern, particularly in the Berlin area, was the flourishing black market in everyday goods and food items. This was proving very lucrative indeed for Allied troops and was construed by some of their superiors as representing a breakdown in discipline, and showing a lack of respect for the inhabitants of the city. It is quite true that the sale in black market goods benefited certain individuals to the extent that they began earning substantial amounts of money. Usually wealthy Germans were targeted; if nothing else, they often had goods of high value which they could then trade for some otherwise unavailable commodity. The poorer areas of German society had no money and often nothing of value which they could trade for worthwhile goods. Women fared the worst in these black-market deals: if they didn't have money, they were asked for sexual favours in return. As a result, sexually transmitted diseases almost became an epidemic. Although not immediately obvious to senior Allied commanders and their officers, the burgeoning black market which began to spread throughout Germany posed a serious public relations problem and was an admission of both a breakdown in military discipline and moral conduct. The finger of blame was pointed firmly at the American troops based in Germany, although all Allied military personnel took advantage of the situation, profiting in one way or another. Lisa recalled:

> Tia and I were only 15 years old in 1946, way too young for some big Allied soldier to openly proposition. It does not mean that we were not propositioned, because we were. Often it was the very young soldiers who would ask you if wanted this or that. You would tell them, 'I don't have the money to buy these things' to which they would gesture that a fuck, blowjob [as they called them] or hand relief would be enough. With these guys we just walked away, disgusted. We were not interested, and we didn't want anything that badly that we would totally throw away our morals. If we were going to do that, it would be on our own terms, no one else's, certainly no foreign boy soldier's terms. Oh no, we were used to going without and going without things didn't bother us like it probably did them.

Tia recalled her own thoughts on the situation:

> It felt like we were being exploited at one stage; it was not nice. New soldiers were arriving in Berlin on and off as the months went by. It was the new soldiers who wanted souvenirs the most; the ones who had been here during the fighting already had bags full of things to take back home. The new soldiers were easier pickings for us. They wanted Nazi stuff, Iron Crosses, medals, badges, flags, anything at all. If you knew the right places you could still find a lot of these things although many of the cloth items such as flags with swastikas on them had been burned. Our little 'Berlin Gang' once found a cellar beneath a house where a lot of Nazi stuff had just been tossed. There was a lot of stuff in there – uniform jackets, discarded weapons, bayonets, belts, packs and medals. We kept the stash to ourselves and any of the British or American soldiers who wanted something would tell us what they were after and we would go and get it. We did pretty well and were able to get a lot of quite high-end goods this way, but this did not

go unnoticed by our parents who put a stop to it, despite the fact we were bringing home some good stuff. Our parents felt it would lead to trouble and we were warned to pack it in in no uncertain terms. My father told me, 'If I discover that you have disobeyed me on this, I will fetch the strap to you.' My father was like that – he didn't want his daughter getting into anything she might not be able to handle. He had heard of young German girls having sex with young Allied soldiers for favours or other things, and he was just concerned and didn't want anything going wrong. I did not wish to end up being kept inside the house, so I obeyed.

Nothing really big happened in 1946 that I can really recall other than the denazification process being handed over to the new post-war German authorities. My mind was firmly set on the summer and going to Lisa's aunt's house at Schlactensee for two beautiful long weeks. It was barely an hour from where we lived but, god, we looked forward to going there. We had missed out a few years of going there due to the Allied bombing when it was too dangerous to travel anywhere, so we were really excited about going in the summer of 1946 and the fact that it would be in peacetime, not wartime. We couldn't wait.

I dream of her soft sand caressing the skin of my bare back,
her blue skies, cool waters and summer sunshine.
Oh Schlachtensee, how I long for you and your summer's
embrace.

As spring of 1946 arrived, leaves slowly began to appear on the trees, the sun regained its strength, bathing Berlin in its inviting warmth. Another long, dark winter had passed, bringing forth a sense of wellbeing, a unique atmospheric quality that only nature can sometimes provide. Berlin, like many parts of Germany, was still under occupation and would remain so for some years, but with the spring sunshine came a feeling of hope. There were still ruined houses, piles of rubble, buried corpses and unexploded bombs to contend with, but with hard work Germany would slowly rise from the ashes.

The girls continued with their schooling and their English tuition with Frau Bergmann. Both were now proficient at speaking English, often to the bemusement of the Allied soldiers they encountered in and around the city, who did not expect two pretty young German girls to be able to address them in their mother tongue. The two girls became familiar with one young American, a 20-year-old private named Joel, from a Connecticut farming community. Lisa recalled:

> Joel was garrisoned nearby with a US Army administrative unit saying he was just an office boy who ran errands for people he referred to as 'The Brass'. He used to laugh at our English, the way we would pronounce certain words. I guess to him we sounded funny. It was Joel who first introduced us to the habit known as Chewing Gum. All the Americans chewed gum; it was kind of a hallmark, and you weren't a 'Yank' unless you chewed gum, they used to say. The gum was called Wrigley's and it was spearmint flavour. You took a stick of gum out of its wrapper, rolled it up then put it in your mouth. It was meant to keep the mouth moist, helping to relieve tension in times of stress. Tia and I chewed the gum but once the taste wore off, it lost its appeal and we spat it out, much to the young American's consternation
>
> 'Hey, hey! You can't do that. You have to keep chewing it – keep it in your mouth.'
>
> After explaining the virtues of chewing gum, he gave us each a packet which we then put in our pockets. Chewing gum was another thing both our parents despised and thought of as a disgusting, pointless habit. Chewing gum, it was said, was unladylike, just like so many other things in those early post-war years.
>
> Before Joel drove off in his Jeep, he blew a bubble with his gum which burst in a small popping sound. Now, we thought, that was great and we asked him how he did that. He explained how you flatten it out using your tongue against the roof of your mouth and then how you manoeuvre the flattened gum to the front of your mouth and blow. If you got it right a bubble would form; if you didn't the gum would almost slide out of your mouth. On the way back

home, we practised. Unsuccessful at first, we persisted and finally both of us were blowing bubbles. I blew too hard on one occasion, and the bubble burst, leaving gum all over my face – not so pleasant I have to say. Either way, the gum was contraband and like the nail paint, we had to stash it in our secret hiding place. We would collect the gum and nail paint and take them with us to Schlactensee. My aunt was a more liberated thinker about these things than my parents, and I knew she would turn a blind eye to some of these things and not tell them.

Schlactensee was one of the highlights of the girls' summer. The last time they had been to Schlactensse together was in August 1942. Schlactensee is situated in the Steglitz-Zehlendorf borough, between the quarters of Nickolassee and Zehlendorf, on the edge of the Grunewald forest. It was and still is one of the most popular lake resorts in the Berlin area. The quality of the water made Schlactensee popular with bathers during the summertime, the surrounding forest also offering an excellent outdoor experience. The girls were familiar with the lush Grunewald forest as they had been there on many previous excursions with the Jungmädelbund, the Young Maidens' League or young girls' Hitler Youth organization for 10- to 14-year-old girls. For Lisa and Tia, they were as familiar with the area as their own backyards. It was still a huge treat to be able to go to stay there for two whole weeks in August. They had been looking forward to this holiday all through the long winter months, when finally, the time came for them to pack for Lisa's aunt Schiefer's house. Lisa's father would take the girls in his rather battered Volkswagen. It was as well that the journey was just under an hour's drive. Lisa's mother, Katherina, stayed at home as she did not get on too well with her older sister. Whenever Lisa asked why her mother rarely visited or had contact with her sister, the answer was always, 'There is a clash of personalities; we do not get on when we are together.' The girls had a suitcase each which had to be squeezed into the front of the car where the engine was situated on most cars but not the VW. Tia had left her home at 7 am that morning, having said her goodbyes to her parents. Both her parents warned her to behave, not to get into any trouble and to do whatever Lisa's aunt said. Having agreed their demands, Tia set off for Lisa's from where they would then depart. The early morning air was cool and the sky grey like sheet metal but both girls were optimistic of experiencing some hot weather over the next two weeks. It would be two weeks of swimming, camping out, walking and sunbathing. They would meet up with some of Lisa's friends and between them they would have a wonderful time. Lisa recalled:

> My father's car was a wreck, a rust bucket as one mechanic called it. There were several times on the journey I thought the engine would cut out and ruin everything, but as much a heap of junk that old Volkswagen was, it was totally reliable. That said, both Tia and I were relieved when we arrived at my aunt's house. We grabbed our suitcases and ran to the front door which was opened before we had even reached it. My aunt was so pleased to see us as it had been some years since we were there last. We were so happy that we both hugged her at the same time. She marvelled at how we had both grown and she complimented us on how pretty we looked. Then it was father's turn to greet his sister-in-law as we took our suitcases up to one of two spare bedrooms. My father had time to sit and talk with her. My aunt lived alone after losing her husband, my uncle Dieter, who had been on groundcrew with the Luftwaffe when he was killed in late 1943. He was a good man and his loss was still raw. My aunt put on a brave face, but I could tell she was still hurting over her loss. Having us around helped her, I think. Father seemed to enjoy talking with her. I think under different circumstances they themselves might have become lovers. I could tell my father thought a lot of her and was pained by my mother's attitude toward her. I know they rowed over this issue on several occasions. My father stayed for some lunch, then had to return home to mother – no doubt there would be a row when he got home. I don't know if there was, but it was just a feeling I had. We gave father a hug before he left. I kissed him on the cheek, telling him I loved him. He told us to behave ourselves, to have a good time and to look after Aunt Andrea; we promised him we would. He said he would see us both on Saturday morning in two weeks' time.

That first Saturday at Schlactensee was spent talking with my aunt and helping her with things around the house and garden. She told us that she had a young man who came and helped her with occasional odd jobs; we laughed, nudging her and teasing her. She swore there was nothing in it at all. that it was strictly business. Of course, we were just joking with her, but that is what I loved about her so much – we could be ourselves while we were there, different to things at home. It was probably because we didn't see her that much that she treated us differently. We could wear some makeup and nail paint and she wouldn't say a word about it to mother or father. She was lovely, adorable and she spoiled me and Tia rotten. She was much like an aunt to Tia too; she knew Tia was my best friend and treated her accordingly, like one of the family. I know Tia loved her as much as I did. We wanted this to be the best summer break ever and, as it turned out, it was.

The next day was Sunday. There was no church as Aunt Andrea didn't believe in it. Dawn had broken with clear skies and the temperature soon rocketed. We couldn't wait to go swimming in the lake and just sunbathe, something we had dreamed of all winter. We changed into our swimming suits which were two-piece bikinis, collected some towels and stuffed them in a bag. Aunt Andrea had made us some black bread rolls to take for a snack as she knew we would spend most of the day at the lake. All she asked is that we be home by 5 pm, no later. We both gave her a kiss and a hug before we left.

On the way to the lake there was one friend I was so excited to be seeing again. We would call for her on the way and she would come swimming with us. Her name was Himmel Boiten and she was a little older than me and Tia, but she was gorgeous and such a good friend. I hadn't seen her for so long I couldn't wait. Her name Himmel was unusual, as in German *Himmel* means heaven or sky, but I thought it was a fitting name for her. Tia knew Himmel and liked her a lot too, so we were excited at having a wonderful time with her, doing as much as we could together, and catching up on things, as we had a lot to catch up with since we'd last seen one another. We had kept in touch through letters but it wasn't quite the same as actually speaking to someone face to face, was it?

The two girls made their way down the quiet lane to a row of houses where Himmel lived with her mother, father, two sisters and brother. They ran up to the front door and knocked excitedly. As Himmel opened the door, there were whoops of joy, plenty of smiles and much hugging. Himmel then asked her two friends to come in while she put some things into her bag. Himmel's parents and sisters came and greeted the girls, Himmel's brother Walter was out in the back garden fixing his bicycle but shouted a loud 'hello'. Once Himmel had packed the few things she needed for the day's swimming, the three of them left, taking a route through the forest. As they walked arm in arm on the tree-lined path, they talked incessantly about the end of the war, how things had panned out plus hopes for the future. Nearing the lake, the girls could see a fair crowd of people gathered to swim or just relax and take in the glorious sunshine. The girls looked around for a place for themselves, and after spending some time fussing over a suitable location, they threw down some blankets, and put up a windbreaker which was tall enough for them to change behind. Himmel slipped on her swimsuit and then they all charged into the cool waters of lake Schlactensee. They played and splashed around then decided to play a kind of piggy in the middle game with a ball Himmel had brought with her. Lisa recalled:

> We were laughing so much our faces began to hurt. It was just wonderful being back at Schlactensee after so much time. The place was untouched by the war; it was just as I had remembered under Hitler, only there were no soldiers in Nazi uniforms hanging around here now, just ordinary people plus a few Allied servicemen who had come to enjoy the water. It was our happy place. It was great to see Himmel again; she looked stunning and so well, and we couldn't stop hugging each other. Soon some of Himmel's friends arrived with more blankets, packets and food and soft drinks, which were put in the shade of a tree before we charged into the water again. The one thing with Himmel

was her swimming. She could have been an Olympian. She was very fast indeed in the water, a natural as they say. She could dive to the bottom of the lake which is twenty-six feet at its deepest point. She could go the bottom, pick a rock up and swim to the surface. We would have races with her but not one of us could beat her. In the BDM they nicknamed her 'The Torpedo' – she had dozens of competition certificates. Yes, Himmel was quite someone – she was athletic, an amazing swimmer, a proficient lifesaver and to top it all she was a very good-looking girl indeed. She didn't like her photograph being taken, though I managed to get one of her sitting on the sand after a swim.

Tia also recalled the legend that was Himmel Boiten

Oh, she was adorable, she was just lovely. She was so kind and courteous to everyone – yes, we loved Himmel. She was a fantastic swimmer as Lisa has already noted. She was so fast as a swimmer, amazing to watch. We would time her with a ball to see how long she took to get it. She would stand on the shore ready and we would throw a ball as hard and as far as we could out into the lake, then we would shout 'Go!' and Himmel would hurl herself like an arrow into the lake, and within seconds she would have got the ball.

When we stopped swimming to have some lunch, we put all the food on the blanket, sharing it out between us. Our conversation was varied: we talked about the war, the ongoing war crimes tribunal at Nuremberg, Allied soldiers and what we hoped for in the future. Himmel wasn't sure what she wanted to do in life.

Her explanation for this was simple: 'We were educated under National Socialism, so everything we learned under them over the years is now irrelevant, construed as being a lie. So what do we do? We who are no longer at school can't go back to school. We are in a situation where we must re-evaluate. Unless we are very lucky, we will work in shops until we get married have children and become housewives.'

One of the other girls said, 'I'd rather die than become a boring housewife having to look after kids all day long.'

Lisa and I nodded in agreement. We just thought at that time there could be no melancholier an existence than being shut up in a house all day with babies screaming then having to wait hand and foot on a husband the moment he walked in through the door from work.

Himmel then said, 'I don't want that kind of a life, but I don't know what I want either.'

Lisa broke the conversational deadlock by saying, 'Well, balls to the boys, we can all live together if we want to; we can all work and pay toward renting some place and have lots of fun.'

Himmel replied, 'Hmm, yes that would be wonderful but then people would talk about us, wouldn't they? They would think we were either running a convent or sleeping together.'

At that we all burst out laughing and the youngest girl, a girl named Petra [Petrianna Albrecht] said, 'Well, I don't care, it is something we can talk about isn't it?'

Afterwards we all lay down in a line just taking in the sun and staring up at the sky. I drifted off to sleep for twenty minutes or so. When I woke, I noticed the others were all dozing away too. They all looked so peaceful, so I decided to fill one of our drinking cups with some water from the lake and throw it onto them. As I did there were screams of shock as cold water hit warm bodies. They all jumped up as I shouted, 'Last one in the water is a rotten apple.' There was a charge as we all bolted for the lake and dived in.

Lisa recalled the end of that first day at Shlactensee:

We had been in and out the lake all day and decided that we would come out of the water for the day and have one last sunbathe before we had to go back to my aunt's. Himmel was sitting with her legs crossed on a small wooden jetty; she watched as we all raced one another back to the shore. She noticed that the young Petra was taking more time than the others – she appeared tired and kept stopping to tread water. In an instant Himmel leapt into the water, and within seconds she was bringing Petra in by holding her across her chest with her right arm and doing a backstroke with her left.

When they reached the shore, Petra said, 'Thank you Himmel, I was okay, just a little tired, honestly.'

Himmel just smiled and told her, 'You are welcome, Petra.'

For the last hour we lay on the sand before packing up to go. We planned to camp out in the forest near Aunt Andrea's the next night and we all walked back along the forest lane, arm in arm, laughing and joking but very tired from the day's activity. We made sure we walked our friends back to their homes then we walked back with Himmel, I held her left hand while Tia held her right. When we reached Himmel's front door, we had a group hug and kiss and said we would call for her tomorrow to go walking and then camp out in the evening. It had been a magical day. We wished that we could spend every day like this.

When we arrived at Aunt Andrea's, we found she had cooked some food and we all sat down to eat in the small dining area. After dinner we sat in the garden talking until around 9.30 pm when we decided to go to bed. Tia and I shared a room with two single beds, each with a bedside table with a little electric lamp. It was so cosy but very warm, so we flung open the windows. We remembered that we had the nail varnish with us and decided that we would paint each other's fingers and toenails. When Aunt Andrea came up to check on us, she could smell the nail varnish.

'Remember to remove it before you go back home, or your mother and father will be very cross with me indeed. Your mother especially, Lisa – she will make me out to be the devil in disguise,' said Andrea.

We promised her we would remove the nail paint in good time and thanked her. Before she left the room, she said, 'I don't understand the fuss. Is it not a girl's privilege to want to enhance her features; after all, men can't wear makeup, can they?'

We all laughed as she left the room. We turned out the lights, settling down to sleep. Tia then asked, 'Remember what you said earlier, about us all getting a place to live together?'

I replied, 'Yes and what an idyllic thought that is.'

'Well, maybe someday we will do it,' said Tia.

At that we both drifted off into a delicious sleep.

At 3 am in the morning Lisa was startled awake to find Tia sitting bolt upright in her bed almost out of breath, gasping, 'Oh Jesus, oh fuck, oh fuck.' Lisa switched on her bedside light, asking her friend what was the matter?

Tia replied, 'Oh, it's nothing. Just another nightmare.' Then she began to cry.

Lisa recalled:

> I got up and just gave her a hug, telling her it was just another stupid bad dream and not to let it upset her. I then asked, 'What was it you dreamed about?' and she said that she had this terrible dream that Himmel had drowned in the lake. So, I said to her, 'Look at me, look at me now; nothing on earth can drown Himmel Boiten. She is more a fish than any of those that live in that lake, you know. It's just a bad dream now. Forget about it, okay?' By this time, Aunt Andrea came to check that all was alright as she heard us talking. I told her Tia had had a nightmare. Aunt Andrea kissed Tia on her forehead, saying, 'I feel so bad for all you children. War has filled your heads with horrors few can comprehend, but make no mistake – no harm will ever come to any of you, not as long as I am alive.' We wished Aunt Andrea goodnight and settled back down to sleep. I noticed Tia was restless, so I got out of my bed and squeezed in with her and just held her to give her reassurance. We soon fell asleep and awoke to a beautiful dawn of sunshine with the birds singing in the trees.

Monday morning: the girls washed and dressed, planning to meet up with Himmel and Petra to go hiking around Schlactensee. There were many hiking routes around the lake, ranging from easy to hard going. The girls were fit and planned to take one of the more challenging routes through the forest and be back in time to set up their tent in preparation for the night's camp-out. The weather was set to be another day of scorching sunshine, so they were all up early and eager to go. Lisa recalled:

> It was nice to get out into the forest as we had spent all day Sunday swimming and sunbathing. After breakfast we set off down the lane to call for Himmel who was ready and waiting for us at her front gate. The three of us then called for Petra who lived further on down the same lane. The houses were situated in little clusters and I thought how nice it must be to live here all year round. Once we had called for Petra Himmel, got out her map of the area to devise a route that would test us from a physical point of view while enabling us to take in the best Schlactensee could offer regarding views etc. We had all learned how to use maps in the Hitler Youth, a skill that has all but vanished with today's young people.
>
> We each had a quick swig of water from our canteens then headed off up a steep hill into the forest. Once in the trees the atmosphere changed: it was slightly cooler but steamy too. We wore boots, shorts and vests as anything more and we would have been too hot. As we laboured up what must have been the steepest hill in all of the forest, I told Himmel about Tia having a nightmare about her last night
>
> Himmel replied, 'Nightmare … oh, that does not sound very flattering.' She laughed, saying, 'Am I really that bad that I am a nightmare?'
>
> Tia, slightly embarrassed, spoke up and said, 'Himmel, no I had a nightmare that you had drowned while swimming.'
>
> 'That would be as likely as a bird never flying over our heads again,' said Himmel. I told Himmel it had made Tia cry and Himmel just said, 'Oh, that's really sweet.' She stopped for a moment then went over to Tia, giving her a hug and telling her, 'Don't ever worry about me; in fact, look at all of us – we have all seen a major war and here we are, still alive at its end.'

At that we walked on. Tia jabbed me with her elbow, pulling a face as if to say, 'Why did you tell her?' We just smiled at each other and carried on walking.

By the time we had reached the top of the hill, we could see through the gaps in the trees that we had covered a good distance. We found a spot by some boulders to sit down and have some water from our canteens. We shared out some homemade oat biscuits that Petra had brought with her. We had brought along some bread rolls and apple cake, while Himmel had brought some pickled vegetables. We agreed it was a bit too early for lunch at that point so decided to make a rope swing with some rope we had brought along for the purpose. We found a suitable tree and threw the rope over a sturdy, low-hanging bough, tying a kind of loop at the bottom so you could put a foot in it. The idea was you would hang onto the rope with a foot in the loop and one of us would push. We made several adjustments to the swing before we were happy with it. It was great fun. When it was Himmel's turn, she tried to do a Tarzan call, but it came out totally wrong. We rolled around on the floor in fits of laughter, the noise she made echoing around the area. God knows what the other locals thought.

After we had got bored with the swing, we took it down and decided to have some lunch. It was so peaceful up here, a million miles away from the world with all its problems. Himmel sat gazing while munching on a bread roll then said, 'Who causes all of the problems in the world? It's men mostly, is it not? Men like to make war more than they do love, it would seem. I don't understand them … the whole world and its people have to follow, just like we did really.' We all understood what she was saying, nodding in agreement. Petra's cheeks bulged like a hamster as she ate while listening to the conversation; it was a comical sight.

Then Himmel announced, 'I did have a boyfriend, you know, up until three weeks ago. He was desperate to marry and have kids. The thought of marrying at eighteen was frightening though. I didn't want to give him any false hopes, so I told him I was not going to marry anyone just yet.'

Then I told her about the Sauerstond twins where we lived. Himmel asked, 'Have you kissed a boy, I mean properly?'

I sat there shaking my head and told her, 'No I haven't' and Tia said the same.

Himmel then said, 'Oh well, there's plenty of time to learn all of that stuff but you can actually practise with your hand.'

We laughed. 'How do you practise kissing with your hand?'

Himmel replied, 'Look, it's really easy. You make a fist with your hand, then you open your mouth and place your mouth over the side of your fist, then you gently move your head like this.'

We watched in fascinated silence as she demonstrated. I said, 'Wow, that kind of looks nice.' 'Oh, it is, believe me and you will have birds flying out of your arse when you try it for the first time.'

We all laughed, inquiring if there was anything else she could teach us. Tia just came out with it and asked Himmel, 'Have you ever let a boy …. you know?'

Before Tia could finish Himmel added, 'What, have sex with me, you mean?'

'Hmm … yes.'

Himmel replied, 'Well, yes, a couple of times but with the proper boyfriend I had. I didn't just go around doing it.'

We all asked her what it was like, did it hurt, and so on, and she explained, 'Yes, it does hurt a little which is why you must be relaxed and the boy not be in a hurry; if he tries to go in you too fast it can hurt a lot. He must be gentle – that is the key. So, it hurts a little bit as he breaks your cherry but once it's all in, it's like wonderful.'

Petra, who was the youngest, looked at us in horror, exclaiming, 'No boy will ever do that with me! It sounds horrible!'

We laughed again and Himmel said, 'Oh, Petra, you will see in time when you are a few years older, believe me.'

Tia recalled the conversation in the forest over the lunch of bread, pickles and apple cake:

> When Himmel was talking about making love, she looked at me, smiling; there was a kind of sparkle in her eye and she almost winked at me. I just thought, *This girl is amazing; is there nothing she hasn't done?* I was very intrigued with Himmel and this did not go unnoticed by Lisa who began to tease me but in a nice, not spiteful, way. Anyway, we continued the hike back down the hill, exiting the forest along the shore of the lake.
> Himmel then said, 'Does anyone fancy a swim?'
> I said, 'But we have no bathing costumes.'
> 'We don't need those, you know,' she shouted. 'Come on, last one in is a chicken!' She pulled her vest off over her head, and momentarily I noticed her physique, a beautiful flat stomach with perfect breasts. Then she had kicked off her shorts and boots before diving into the water. I was not looking at her in any sexual way; it was more like how one might admire a fine nude painting or sculpture or a fast car or something. Being a girl, I marvelled at how well defined she was, but it was entirely innocent and not a view in how a male might have looked at her at that moment.
> We all thought, *Sod it!* and off went our clothes and we all ran into the lake. The water was so refreshing after the hike. We splashed around, diving under the water before making our way back to the shore. It was a nightmare trying to sort our clothes out as we had thrown them in all directions. It was like, 'Hey, these aren't my knickers, they're yours.'
> Once we had dressed, Himmel had the brainwave of going to see a man she knew named Herr Leitmann who owned a small rowing boat we might be able to borrow. So, we all headed off with her to see this Herr Leitmann. His house was not far. When we arrived, Himmel asked if we could take his rowing boat out on the lake for half an hour. He agreed on the principle we be careful with it, so off we went, back to the lake where the boat was moored. The five of us managed to squeeze aboard and we began to

row out toward the middle of the lake. Himmel was rowing and then she and Lisa began messing around, rocking the boat from side to side. The rest of us were starting to panic as I could sense the boat was going to capsize if they carried on. Seconds later the inevitable happened: the boat tipped too far to the one side, capsizing and tipping us all into the water. At first, we were too busy laughing, but then we tried to right the boat. We all pulled on the same side of the boat which we managed to turn halfway before it got waterlogged. We trod water while we watched in horror as the hull filled up and the boat sank to the bottom.

Petra shouted, 'Oh, shit! Now we're in big trouble.'

Himmel said, 'The water is not that deep here … we can get it out. We just need some rope, that's all.' She then dived down to where the boat was resting on the bottom, around fifteen feet down. We could all see it in the clear water, and luckily, when Himmel surfaced, she said it wasn't damaged. So, between us we recovered the two oars, placing them on the shore where we left them as a kind of marker. Then we went off to Herr Leitmann's to tell him we needed to borrow some rope so as we could recover his boat.

'What do you mean you need rope to recover my boat. Where is it?'

Himmel then explained to him that his little boat was currently at the bottom of the lake in fifteen feet of water, adding, 'If we can just borrow some rope, we can get it out for you.'

Herr Leitmann grabbed some rope and swore at us, saying, 'Just take me to where my damned boat is.'

Himmel led the way back to where we had left the oars on the bank. She disappeared behind a bush, put her bathing costume on and jumped into the water, asking Herr Leitmann to throw her the rope. Diving down to the boat, she tied the rope around the thwarts and, once secured, she surfaced, instructing us all to pull. It was not too difficult and once the boat was in shallower water, we all hitched up our skirts and jumped in to help Himmel drag the boat out.

Herr Leitmann inspected his boat, shaking his head. 'Your bloody horseplay almost cost me my boat. Do you know how much these things cost?' He shouted at us again, 'Go on, get out of here before I lose my temper with you all.'

After Himmel had changed and dried herself off again, we decided we had seen enough water sport for one day and that we had best head back to Aunt Andrea's to change our clothing and collect the white canvas tent we were going to sleep in that night. We had agreed a spot with Aunt Andrea, where she would be able to see the tent from the attic window where her junk room was. We had some things to cook over a campfire and a small portion of real coffee that Petra had managed to acquire, but she wouldn't say from where.

Our camping spot was just perfect. We had enough of a clearing around us to have a campfire and were not too far from Aunt Andrea's house if we needed her at any time in the night. It was a beautiful night. We shared stories from the war, played cards and a few games of chess which we found very relaxing. We also laughed about our earlier drama with the rowing boat; in fact, we laughed so much we nearly cried. We then cooked some meat with a few vegetables in a pot over the fire then made some tea, brewed using local plants. Real tea was in short supply even though the Allied soldiers drank it by the gallon. We sat drinking the tea around the campfire as it slowly died down. It was a warm, humid night and when you looked up you could see the stars through the gaps in the forest canopy.

When we began to feel like we had had enough, we changed into some nightwear before going inside the tent. There was lots of room but what made my heart skip a few beats was that I had Lisa lying on one side of me with Himmel on the other and Petra at the end. It felt as if Himmel had purposely wanted to sleep next to me. It was dark inside the tent and as we lay there, relaxing with the odd giggle, we heard an owl fluttering up in the trees above the tent. Then a short distance away another owl joined in, hooting. It was as if they were singing to each other. We quite enjoyed their little show in the trees up above our tent.

I turned to Himmel and remember saying quietly, 'I shall always remember this, being here when the owls sang at Schlactensee.'

Himmel smiled at me and then moved closer, putting her arm around me. We drifted off to sleep. There was some light snoring that night plus a few shrieks from the owls who were continuing their courtship in the treetops but otherwise it was a slice of pure heaven. I remember waking up early in the morning just as it was starting to get light. I found that Himmel and I had our legs entwined and she had her head on my chest. In fact, by morning we would all be so tangled up that none of us knew whose legs were whose. I remember smiling as some of the others were snoring and then I went back to sleep.

Oh, how those owls did sing at Schlactensee.

Chapter 4

Alternate Fatalities

I left behind a part of me,
on the tranquil shores of Schlactensee.
Purest peace and serenity,
time stood still as the wind blew free.
On the placid lake the children of war,
became innocent once more.
You made a woman from this haunted girl,
now this beautiful flower in time will unfurl.
Summer in Schlactensee AV VII

The two weeks at Schlactensee passed by in a blur of swimming, hiking and sunbathing. For Lisa and Tia, leaving was not the easiest part of these holidays. On their last day they had to pack ensuring that nothing would be left behind, the nail paint on their fingers and toes was removed and the contraband stashed at the bottom of a suitcase. All that remained was for the girls to quickly pop down the bottom of the lane to say their goodbyes to Himmel. There was much sadness. Himmel didn't want her friends to leave and begged them to come back soon and, if they needed to, they could stay with her family. Himmel reminded Tia to 'Please write to me as much as you want'. As the girls parted and made their way back up the lane in the afternoon sunshine, they said little. The journey back to reality was now just an hour away – school, home and their neighbourhood beckoned – and for the time being they had no choice. They would be leaving their full-time education soon to seek employment; how fat their oyster would grow depended largely upon the kind of employment they could procure. Both girls felt confident that with English, typing and shorthand in their educational repertoires they had a better chance than most at that time in Germany.

Lisa remarked to her friend, 'You really like Himmel, don't you?'

Tia replied, 'Yes, of course I like her, but I like you just as much.'

As they approached Aunt Andrea's house Lisa's father's car came into view. A few backfires ensued which made the girls laugh. They went inside to collect their suitcases before squeezing them into the VW. The girls thanked Aunt Andrea for having them for what had been a wonderful holiday. They got into the VW, soon disappearing down the lane in a cloud of black smoke which obscured the diminutive figure of Aunt Andrea as she stood waving them off.

The one-hour drive back to Berlin seemed a long one. Tia and Lisa were both engrossed in their own thoughts. Lisa's father chirped away but neither of the girls was listening to him properly. 'For goodness sake, cheer up you two; you look as if you have both returned from a funeral,' he remarked as he looked at the two of them through his rear-view mirror. A flicker of a smile but clearly the girls were suffering from post-holiday blues. Tia recalled:

> Lisa's dad dropped me off home first. I took my suitcase out of the car, kissed Lisa and told her I would see her at school Monday morning. Then I went inside. My mother and father asked if I had had a good time and I told them it was heaven at Schlactensee. I didn't feel like talking much so I took my suitcase upstairs to my room to unpack my things. The minute the bedroom door was shut, I got out a pen and paper to scribble a letter to Himmel.

She wrote:

> I am missing you and Schlactensee like crazy already. I know that you are not that far away, but it feels like you are a thousand miles away from us here. Lisa and I had such a great time. It had been so long since I last saw you, and you've not changed in the slightest and the fun we had in the forest and swimming in the lake were some of the best times I can ever remember. If we can we would love to come and find work at Schlactensee sometime. Though saying this will make you want to run away. I think, we would both drive you crazy, I am sure. I am going to post this to you on the way to school on Monday. I just wanted to let you know we arrived home safely and missing you so much already it hurts.
>
> Love always from Tia xxx

On the way to school on Monday morning, Tia posted her letter to Himmel. Lisa teased her and said, 'You haven't wasted any time, have you. She is great though, isn't she?' Tia just laughed in nervous agreement with her friend. School that day seemed to last an eternity in the hot stuffy classroom with Herr Wilhelm pacing between the rows of desks, observing everyone like a hawk might a mouse before falling upon it. Tia sat with her head resting on her hand, chewing on the end of her pencil. She was so detached from the proceedings that Herr Wilhelm felt compelled to inquire.

He walked stealthily up behind her and shouted, 'Something on your mind, young lady?'

Tia almost fell off her chair, as the class erupted into laughter. Lisa, sitting behind her friend, tried to stifle her own laughter. Herr Wilhelm called silence in the class and all fell quiet as he again addressed Tia, 'Would you like to tell us all of your wonderful holiday; it must have been quiet an exemplary break as you have not been here with us all day. That is the problem with going away to places of wonderful unfamiliarity – we forget ourselves and forget we have to come back.' He turned to Lisa and asked what the two of them did during their time at Schlactensee. Lisa recalled:

> I wasn't much for standing up for class talks but, on this occasion, I wanted to. I told the class how we had swum with a friend who could easily become an Olympic champion, then how we went up into the forest above the resort, hiking then making the swing in the tree, how we had camped out and cooked dinner over a campfire and spent nights out in our tent in the forest with the owls calling out in the trees above. Oh, and yes, we sank a boat that we took onto the lake. There was a roar of laughter until Herr Wilhelm called for silence again before asking Lisa to explain how they managed to sink a boat. Lisa explained it was horseplay, but all ended well, and the boat was recovered undamaged. Herr Wilhelm announced that he was pleased to hear that the girls' foolishness had not been too costly but warned against horseplay on the water as a dangerous undertaking. There were a few kids in the class who had never been on a holiday, and who were soon going to Schlactensee themselves. I told

them they wouldn't want to come back. After my brief talk Herr Wilhelm gave a lecture on the history and geography of Schlactensee. It was a nice way to round off a first day back at school.

As the girls walked home, the Sauerstond twins accompanied them. Tia admitted she was not in the mood for them, but Lisa agreed to meet Erich the following weekend. Ernst did make a concerted effort to get Tia to go on a date with him, but as hard as he tried, he failed miserably on this occasion. When Tia got home, she again scribbled a letter to Himmel:

Dear Himmel,

Sorry if I am being a pest but just had to share some more news with you. Head has been in the clouds all day long, could not concentrate in class and to make things worse the two twins we told you about, well, the one wants to take me on a date. I told him no as I just don't feel up to it at this time. Am I being stupid or selfish? I don't want to remain like some kind of convent girl all my life, but I don't know. I like Ernst. He is dreadfully good looking, and he is polite and acts like a gentleman. I can't wait to hear from you, missing you still so much.

Love from Tia xxx

Tia held onto the letter for three days before posting it, worried that Himmel might think she was being a pest or something. Her worries were of course totally unfounded as Tia received a letter from Himmel just a couple of days later:

My dearest Tia,

Oh, you poor sweet thing, I so feel for you, I really do. If you wanted to come and work here in Schlactensee I could not see it being too much of a problem as you can type, do shorthand dictation and you can speak English pretty well (I'm so envious of you by the way!). You would need maybe to find a job which includes accommodation (would your parents allow that?). Maybe you could both come here when the time is right? You are not being a pest at all, in fact I was so pleased to receive your letter so quickly as was missing you so much too. Please write as much as you like, and I will do same. As for the boy, Ernst, give him a chance and see how it goes. It might be fun, but remember what we talked about, be careful. Must go now as I am writing this to you in the moonlight and I have to go to work in the morning. Will be thinking of you and thank you for being so sweet about me.

All my love and best wishes to you

Himmel xxx

PS. Please say hello to Lisa for me, won't you. xxx

Tia was so thrilled to have received Himmel's letter that she must have read it several times over, like a besotted fan of some iconic movie star. Tia shared the contents of Himmel's letter with Lisa and they both agreed on the plan of going to find work at Schlactensee on leaving school. There were several pluses to their plan: firstly, Schlactensee was becoming even more popular than it was before and during the early war years; secondly; the local economy was gearing up to profit from the masses of Allied servicemen who were coming into Germany for tours of duty, and it was only a matter of time before coffee shops, bars, restaurants and hotels would emerge under this new post-war enterprise. The girls decided for the time being to keep their plans a secret. Tia said she would write to Himmel again, asking for some recommendations for possible employment in the area. Lisa wrote to her aunt and asked if she and Tia could visit her for a weekend so that they could then approach potential employers. There was so much to consider but the girls had made up their minds. They still had some months to go before leaving school, yet both felt better at having this plan under their belts.

As the weekend approached, Lisa talked more about her upcoming date than anything else. Tia felt left out in some ways and decided to take Himmel's advice accepting young Ernst Sauerstond's offer of a date. Of course, both girls did not mention to their parents where they would be going on the Saturday; they just wanted to see how things went first. The twins had decided to take the girls out into the fields, away from the populace and prying eyes of the locals who might inform on their antics. Southwest Berlin possessed some beautiful rural backdrops which were ideal for romantic strolls. As Saturday morning arrived, the girls, fearful of alerting their parents' suspicions, dressed casually for their secret dates. They packed a small picnic before setting off to meet the twins at the bridge at the bottom of the road. The twins were already there waiting. They had made a plan that as soon as they saw the girls coming, they would walk off to the fields and the girls would wait at the bridge for a few minutes then follow them. As they waited at the bridge while the boys disappeared from view, they each took out a stick of Juicy Fruit chewing gum. Five minutes had elapsed according to Lisa's wristwatch and the girls set off, taking the same path as the boys some minutes previously. Soon they were out of earshot of the traffic and climbing a wooden fence into a pasture with knee-high grass. They looked nervously over their shoulders and quickly walked along the track alongside a stream which led to a kind of deep pool in a meadow. The twins were waiting for them sitting by the pool. As Lisa sat down beside Erich, Tia held her hand out to Ernst and asked him to walk with her so as to give each other some private space. Tia recalled the date:

> It was quite pleasant just strolling along the bank of the stream holding hands, but the deadlock of nervousness had to be broken so we stopped, and I turned to face Ernst to experience what was my first real snog. He embraced me and our mouths locked together. I'd forgotten the chewing gum so momentarily pulled away and spat the gum out into the stream before resuming what was like a mouth-to-mouth resuscitation exercise. It felt really nice and I could tell he was enjoying himself. After a few minutes, I felt something hard sticking into my left thigh. Again, I pulled away momentarily to see what it was. As I looked down, I could clearly see the characteristic bulge of what men refer to as a 'hard on'. I just said, 'Oh' and started laughing. I couldn't help myself. Ernst just pulled me close to him again in a feeble attempt to hide the bulge in his trousers. As we continued snogging, I became a little carried away in the moment and I ran my hand down over the bulge in Ernst's trousers. His legs began to quiver and I though he was going

to faint. We ended up lying on the grass with me on top of him. I told him, 'You can put your hands on my arse if you like; I won't bite you, you know.' To be fair Ernst was being a perfect gentleman. I greatly admired his restraint on this occasion and he only put his hands on my arse after I told him he could. That was as far as I allowed things to go on that first date.

After spending over forty minutes alone with him, we walked back to where Lisa and Erich were. As we approached, I could see Lisa getting up and quickly buttoning up her blouse while Erich was fastening his trousers. I was worried for a while that she may have done something stupid, but she assured me with a wink of her eye that she had not 'done it'.

In all it was very nice as we unpacked the picnic and just lay in the grass for a while. It started to rain so we decided to head off home. The boys covered our heads with their coats to keep the rain off us; they were very sweet indeed. We left them at the bridge where we met, telling them we would see them Monday, then we headed for my house. When we arrived, we said hello to my mother and father then went upstairs to my room where we could talk about our dates. As soon as I closed my bedroom door, I begged Lisa to tell me what she had done, and I would tell her of my date.

Lisa then explained in a casual manner, 'Well, I took off my blouse and bra, letting him have a feel. I couldn't help it, the poor sod's cock was going to break out of jail had I not done something about it.'

I asked, 'What do you mean, do something about it … what did you do?'

'Well, I gave him hand relief and that was it. The moment my hand grasped his cock, I could have done anything I wanted with him; he was totally under my spell and it felt great. He did make rather a mess. It was like a volcano erupting, as his semen shot up into the air. I've never seen a boy ejaculate before and I was fascinated by it, and, by the noise he was kicking up, it must have felt wonderful too.' She continued, 'Okay, that's my story done, now what about yours?'

> I told her what happened as I began snogging Ernst, how I ran my fingers over the hard bulge in his trousers letting him feel my arse. Lisa looked slightly disappointed when I told her that that was all that happened. Then we both had a good laugh about it but agreed those boys were very sweet and well behaved.
>
> I asked Lisa, 'Would you let him fuck you next time?'
>
> 'Hmmm, maybe, if he can get some birth control, I don't know.' She asked me the same question.
>
> 'I'm not sure, maybe, maybe not.'
>
> Sex was no big deal to us, but we were not in a rush to be deflowered, yet we felt we were old enough to enjoy sex if we wanted it. Our parents would have gone raving mad had they known, but they didn't know, and we felt it best kept that way. Attitudes in Germany were slowly changing, they had to – how else could we move forward if change did not evolve and freedom take place for everyone?

As the last days of summer gave way to the autumn of 1946, Tia's and Lisa's dual romance with the Sauerstond twins steadily flourished. The twins had taken the girls out to the local cinema and continued their forays into the pasture when the weather permitted. They had come close to deflowering the girls on several occasions, but the girls were adamant that they were still not quite ready for the next level of romance. To be fair, the boys were head over heels in love and were respectful of their girlfriends' decision. It was only after the passing of eight months that the girls announced to their parents that they had admirers. At first their parents were concerned but then realized Germany had changed and the world had changed, and their girls had changed too. When the parents asked who their suitors were, there was some sense of relief. Lisa's parents in particular were fearful their daughter was seeing an Allied serviceman, so were relieved to hear it was one of the Sauerstond boys. Tia's parents only concern was the welfare of their daughter and her getting pregnant out of wedlock. After Tia had reassured them there was no 'monkey business' going on in the relationship, they seemed to settle down. Tia recalled:

> I promised them I was not going to be foolish and would not fall pregnant like some young German girls had.

They understood I was not a young child anymore, that soon I would be leaving school, starting a job and, who knows, even marrying and starting a family. Of course, I had no intention of marrying just yet, but it made them feel better me saying that. It was what they termed as a 'little white lie' and if it got your parents off your back then it was not a bad thing to do.

> *My heart all a flutter,*
> *a frantic pitter patter,*
> *as he takes his hand within my own.*
> *Feelings unexpected, almost rejected,*
> *like no experience I've ever known.*
> *A girl's first kiss,*
> *pure unadulterated bliss,*
> *light years away from Berlin's cries.*
> *So many emotions,*
> *triggered explosions,*
> *that day love's battle was won.*
> Secret Rendezvous AV VIII

With the onset of the bitterly cold winter of 1946, the girls' dating was largely confined to the dances which still went ahead at local church and village halls. These were often frequented by girls with Allied soldiers for boyfriends. Lisa recalled these dances:

> These girls, some of whom we knew pretty well, would swagger in with their army boyfriends on their arms with their noses up in the air as if they were too good to be here. They really thought they were something but everything they had on had been paid for by their boyfriends; they were users really. We would smile at them as they went past and would say hello, but we often thought, *Fucking hell, look at her – what a dog's dinner she looks*. After the dance had finished, you could often go outside around the back of the hall and see these girls with their skirts hitched up to their waists being screwed up against the wall. It was not romance in my eyes, it was more like what a whore might

do, and they were just being used until their boyfriends had to leave to go back home, then they'd find another sucker to take them out and spend money on them. Worse still was they might have a 'bun in the oven' as the British used to say.

Tia recalled the dances with the same pessimism as Lisa:

The dances were shit and the music was shit. We would go with the twins and dance with them and drink our Fanta cola. We would sit and belch and just be bored most of the night and then when it ended, we would all walk back home. It wasn't very exciting at all.

Tia continued her correspondence with Himmel, sharing the details of her romance with Ernst, frequently asking her advice on romantic matters. In return, Himmel would share her own stories with Tia. Recalling their correspondence, Tia reminisced:

There wasn't much we wouldn't tell one another. Himmel asked if I had been to the next level with Ernst and I told her that every time we snogged, I felt that tingle down below and wanted to do more, but it just didn't feel right for some reason. Himmel would say you're still too young for that sort of thing, you are only fifteen, so just stick to the snogging bit and if you feel it's going farther than what you want, you just stop before it does. Our letters were intimate. I would ask her to explain what it was like in detail and she would tell me. I had to hide Himmel's letters because if my parents had found them and read them, they would have gone mad. We always ended our letters with the promise that we would see each other soon.

The winter months in Germany were tough during the early post-war years. The rain, snow and cold made life miserable at times, but at least people had fuel to burn to keep themselves warm unlike the latter part of the war. Tia and Lisa continued their dates with the boys, and they enjoyed having sleepovers at one another's houses. It was during their sleepovers that they often discussed the future and their idea of going to work at Schlactensee. Himmel had told Tia that she was working as a waitress in a café not far from the lake and that business was very good usually until the onset of the winter when trade dropped and the café owner had to lay her off until things picked up again. Himmel would then find work in one of the public houses in the area – the pubs were never short on customers, as the ale houses were a focal point of many communities in much the same way as they were and still are in England.

October 1946 saw the return of the Second World War to the German consciousness. It was in this month that the Nuremberg War Crimes Trials were concluded, and sentences handed down to those found guilty. Lisa recalled:

> Just as were beginning to forget about the ugliness of the past years of war, the Nuremberg Trials become front page news again in the tabloid press all over Germany and the world. The trials were both surprising yet unsurprising in their conclusion and the sentences handed down to those found guilty of war crime and crimes against humanity varied. The biggest fish, Reichsmarshall Hermann Göring, was sentenced to death by hanging but was mysteriously able to commit suicide thus cheating the hangman's rope. SS chief Himmler would have probably provided the second biggest draw, but he had committed suicide with cyanide after his arrest. As for Rudolf Hess, poor old Hess had spent virtually all of the war as an Allied prisoner after his flight to England. We still puzzled over that decision; some say Hitler had sent him on that flight and when it all failed, made it appear Hess had gone insane and that Hitler knew nothing about it. Hess was given a prison sentence; he would remain incarcerated until being found dead many years later, in somewhat suspicious circumstances. Ribbentrop, the man Tia and I used to call the 'Butler of the Third Reich', will hang and what an end for a failed Nazi aristocrat like him. Those who ran the concentration camps, Nazis such as Kramer and Hoess, will all hang too, no way out for them at all. The only one I felt a tinge of sadness for was Third Reich 'poster boy' Joachim Peiper of the Waffen-SS. I knew girls

who had written to him during his unit's campaign against the Americans in the Ardennes – a devilishly good-looking man who has been sentenced to death by hanging [Peiper's death sentence was later overturned and a prison sentence given]. It's just all so depressing what with the cold weather and everything. Christmas is still a long way off and next summer is even further away. I am going out for a walk into the nearby park with Tia and the twins later to break up the boredom. I wish I could bring Erich back to my house, but that is out of the question with my parents being around on the weekends, and in the week we are all at school and by the time we get home my parents are home from work too. A girl can't win, it seems.

Tia also recalled that time of the year where it felt as if everything went into limbo, leaving her with little to do but think and dream about things:

I hate this time of the year; there's not much you can do. The leaves of the trees and flowers all vanish, and it appears as if nature has died. The skies are grey and when they are clear it is very cold. I got home from school the one day and there was this magazine on the kitchen table, one I'd never heard of before, called *Horzu*. It was nothing very exciting, just a radio programme magazine which had flourished in the British sector. It was though the product of a free press, not a dictatorial one, which I thought was good. It is still in existence today. I didn't really listen to many radio programmes at that time, preferring books, and of course writing letters to Himmel. I liked poetry books as they lightened the winter melancholy which I used to suffer with in my early teens. I would pick out my favourite pieces then I would send them to Himmel. I wrote a lot of letters to Himmel that winter and had admitted to her to that I had again dreamt of her, but on this occasion, we were just walking along a beach somewhere. When Himmel replied, she wrote, 'You really must stop having these dreams about me, people will talk, ha, ha!' It felt as if we were not so much in some kind of alternate reality, but in some kind of alternate fatality. That night my dreams were filled with a strange eroticism, alternating between Erich and Himmel. When I woke in the morning, I was as confused as ever. I had no confusion over the thought of making love with Erich but making love with Himmel was just so weird a dream. I pondered the normality of it all, yet I felt no shame in it either – I just thought weird, weird, weird! A couple of days later I scribbled a letter to Himmel, but halfway through I stopped. I began chewing on the end of the pencil, unsure of whether to proceed and reveal the contents of my dream to her. After some minutes I finished the letter by writing, 'How on earth do I say this without you thinking I have gone completely crazy?' At that I stopped again, rubbed it out and just wrote of the dream I had about Erich. I couldn't tell her, not at that time and besides, it was childlike, I thought.

As Christmas of 1946 approached, people across Germany knew they would again not have very much to offer by way of gifts other than things they could make themselves. Tia and Lisa were skilled at making traditional corn dolls, handkerchiefs and scarves and set about the task of making these things which they could then give as gifts to family and friends for Christmas. Tia wanted something better than a corn doll or handkerchief to give to Lisa and Himmel and besides, dolls were for children and scarves and handkerchiefs for old people, she reckoned. Tia had seen a couple of small wooden carvings which had been locally made, one of a bear, the other an angel. She desperately wanted to buy these two small items for her friends but the problem was she did not have any money. In true entrepreneurial spirit she decided to drop the dates with Erich on the weekends in favour of knocking on doors and offering help with cleaning and clearing of snow, anything where she could make a few marks to buy her friends the presents. Lisa was disappointed that Tia had for some unknown reason stopped accompanying her on their double dates, making excuses each time the weekend came. Lisa thought for a while that Tia had lost interest altogether until the week running up to Christmas when, finally, Tia excitedly handed Lisa her small, wrapped present and told her, 'You better like this. I had to work my tits off for this, you know.'

Lisa said, 'But why didn't you say? I could have helped you.'

Tia replied, 'If I had told you and you helped me, it would hardly have been a present or a surprise, silly.' The girls hugged and then Lisa gave Tia her present with the strict instruction it was not to be touched until Christmas morning. As soon as Tia arrived home, she sat down to write a letter to Himmel which would be the last one of that year:

My dear Himmel,

1946 will soon be gone and another year here! I am writing this letter to send you all my love and best wishes to you and your family for this Christmas. We won't have much again, but we are at peace and we have the love of friends and family. That is priceless. I wish I was there to give you a big hug and please find enclosed a greetings card which I made all by myself (honest!! no help from Lisa, ha, ha!). As soon as spring arrives, we will visit to see about finding work and maybe somewhere to rent. We may have to stay with Lisa's Aunt Andrea for a couple of weeks, but that would be delightful. Two weeks' pay between the two of us should be enough for a deposit and first rent payment on an apartment of some sort. Either way we will see what we can find once there. We both plan to leave school this summer so everything should work out fine.

Sending you lots of love for Christmas and the New Year.

Your friend always,

Tia xxxxx

The letter was carefully folded then sealed in the envelope to be posted the next day. Tia hoped her friend in Schlactensee would receive the letter and card in good time; it wasn't far away, she told herself. As she settled down to sleep that evening, with the rain lashing against her bedroom window, she again thought about how herself, Lisa, Himmel, life, love and growing up seemed to be those alternate fatalities.

Chapter 5

Velvet Purses and the Bruised Violets

*Oh, Wolf, when you made your way to me through the chill dark forest,
guided by the stars and fireflies,
I felt your lips as they caressed my neck,
your course hair against my soft belly flesh.
Oh, Wolf you seduced me well.
Your shadow decorates the wall,
we beneath that cold radiant glow that is the Black Sun
deep within my girlhood.
Yes, yes, I feel you come.
I throw back my head in ecstasy I cry,
we are a forbidden union of devils – you and I.*

Never have I been so glad to see the end of 1946. Christmas was another dull affair of homemade gifts which wasn't so bad, but the food is driving many of us mad. Potatoes, vegetables, pickled vegetables and preserves – the food is monotonous to say the least. Much of Europe is the same though. Before things can get back to normal, farming infrastructures and labour requirements have to be met. We are living on 1,000 to 1,250 calories; occasionally we can get decent titbits courtesy of our Allied soldier friends. We help our parents grow as many vegetables as we can to help supplement what we have. It's still pretty shit though and no comfort that the rest of Europe, including England, is in the same boat. I just think to myself, *Oh, that fucking war!* What is maddening is I heard that Allied servicemen have been told they are not to give us any food items they may have or may have surplus to their own requirements. But why, for god's sake? I heard recently that twenty litres of cocoa was tipped down the gutter when it could have been used in a clinic to help make the sick stronger. How does one defend Allied democracy when things such as this are allowed to happen? It does nothing for good German–Allied relations. All I can say is thank god for the American and British soldiers we know who do give us anything they can spare. We know they could get into serious trouble for ignoring their politicians. How long this will go on for, no one really knows; it could go on for years. Fuel for our fires has been very hard to come by this winter. You go out scavenging anything that can be burned, or you even burn some of your own furniture. you get that desperate. You sit in the house and it's as cold inside as it is outside and all you have are the clothes you are wearing and any blankets you might have; yes, you sit around wrapped up in blankets. When you breathe you can see your breath in the freezing air. You sit and shiver in the freezing cold until you can get some fuel for your fire. Many are starting to say, 'Things weren't as bad as this under Hitler. The war is over, and we are even worse off.' The Allies are wary of uprisings or riots. There are rumours that General Eisenhower wants as many Germans to die of the cold as possible. I know many have died through this winter which has been murderously cold, but I'm still alive, though I've felt like death many times, I know Lisa feels the same but at least we have our boyfriends. Yes, I am glad 1946 is dead and gone and spring is approaching now; the sun gathers her strength and when she is out, she sends us her warmth, and, better still, we don't have to suck dicks or lie on our backs for it. It's free, from Mother Nature herself. Blackmarketeering and exploitation are still rife, but fuck them! I've told them I'm not trading my cherry for anything.

Tia's words as the spring of 1947 approached were equally caustic. The winter had been very bad, a measure of pain aggravated by inadequate food, shortage of fuel and the spectacle of Allied forces destroying decent food supplies rather than allowing it to go to the Germans. Lisa's opinion was much the same as Tia's:

> For every step forward, there were ten backward, it seemed. Through the winter we did see our American friend Joel every now and then. He wanted to give us stuff to help us out but feared being caught and the possibility of having to face a court martial for disobeying orders. We understood, of course we did, but we were very fucking angry. Tia and I just thought, *Wait until spring, then it will be summer, then we'll get our arses out of school and go and find those jobs we dreamed of at Schlactensee.* It was dire there that winter, but we didn't care about that – we'd get by, we knew we would; we just wanted to get away from that shithole. 1946 was one great summer but was hell in winter and one I won't forget easily. If we made it in Schlactensee, we could be seeing out the winter of 1947 in a cosy inn, a café or a bar; any would do as long as we got paid for it.

During 1946 and 1947 relations between the West and the Soviet Union began to inexorably decline: it was a political falling out of bed accelerated by the Truman Doctrine, which was announced on 29 March 1947. The Truman Doctrine was a foreign policy, the stated purpose of which was to counter Soviet geopolitical expansion during what soon became known as the Cold War. Tia recalled:

> Well, that Truman Doctrine really ripped the condom off the cock, didn't it? We always suspected this would happen though. It is a worry having the Soviets so close in the east of Berlin. There is that fear that one day they could just steamroll their way in and take the whole of Germany. Stalin must be pondering his options, weighing things up, yet is hesitant because America has the atomic bomb and he doesn't. Whoever has the biggest stick can to a degree dictate policy in Europe now. An atom bomb is one big fucking stick with which to hit someone with – just ask the Japanese, they will tell you that. I still don't trust Stalin. To me he is the man in a dirty overcoat, who sits down in

the park near the children, give you sweets and then shows you his cock. What a relief we aren't stuck in east Berlin, as I can see trouble looming there. Some people both me and Lisa know have already moved out of east Berlin; they are fearful of more conflict or becoming trapped there with the Russians. I couldn't think of anything worse than being stuck under a socialist regime. Fascism was bad enough but socialism ... I'd rather die than live under that. The socialists attempt to paint a picture of a people completely at harmony, as equals, when that picture is painted with excrement – it's a lie; everyone is starving, living off dogfood and none of them are smiling much, are they. No, fuck that. I can't wait to go to Lisa's Aunt Andrea's, and we don't have much longer to wait. I really hope we can get something sorted out there at Schlactensee. I really do.

Scared if I should fall asleep,
the nightmares they claw away at my skin,
Burrowed deep within my bones,
the howls of anguish haunt my soul.
Fighting to remain one step ahead,
but monsters reside beneath my bed.
A little girl lost so long ago,
searching for a future she is still to know.

Monsters AV IX

During a flurry of letter writing throughout the spring of 1947, Aunt Andrea agreed that both Lisa and Tia could stay with her at Schlactensee, provided they completed their final term of schooling. It would mean the girls would not arrive until the July, but both were so excited at the prospect of moving to Schlactensee they felt the concession that Lisa's aunt had insisted upon was perfectly reasonable. The parents of both girls were not happy when the plans were first revealed, but even they understood that there were better prospects at Schlactensee than in the suburbs of a ruined city. Tia recalled:

> When I first tried discussing our plan of going to live and work at Schlactensee, my parents were not happy at all.

They felt I was too young to be leaving home unless I was getting married. I argued the difference, and in the end I won. They knew Berlin was a wreck and that getting jobs was difficult at that time. That doesn't mean that there weren't any jobs, just a lot of competition for the ones that were going. Leaving home after the war was no big deal. When you have lived through a war, it changes you, and it changes your parents and their attitudes to life. I hastily a wrote a letter to Himmel to inform her we would be finishing school and heading down in July. She wrote back saying she was over the moon and that her father was asking around about available rental accommodation in the borough, while she was asking around about possible employment prospects. In all, Himmel felt we had a good chance as we both spoke English as well as German.

Lisa remembers:

My parents knew how I loved Schlactensee. It wasn't far away yet it was beautiful in comparison to where we were living at the time. The best way I can describe it is that, say for example you are living in England and you live near the Lake District, yet you can't see it as it's twenty or thirty miles away from you. You love it and yearn to be near it and will do what you have to do to achieve being nearer. Tia and I had always wanted to go and live and work there. Our parents were just worried about how we would cope and things like that. It was a joke really; we were far more independent than what people gave us credit for. We had gone through a war, the Hitler Youth, the capitulation and we had survived off our wits on many an occasion. Their minds were soon put at rest when Aunt Andrea spoke with my father about it. She said she would keep an eye on us and that we would come to no harm in a place like Schlactensee. Aunt Andrea warned us we would have to take whatever jobs were on offer and that could be doing housekeeping, kindergarten work, or working in a canteen or something similar. We might even need to travel to nearby towns for work. She warned us that things might not be as easy, but we agreed to her demands. I think we would have agreed to anything at that point to convince our parents and Aunt Andrea that we were ready to go out into the world, a very different one to when we were at war.

As the spring gave way to early summer, the girls were still courting the Sauerstond twins, Ernst and Erich, and resumed the rituals most young courting people at the time were engaged in. In the week school and studies were the priority; on weekends it was love and having some fun. Lisa recalled that time:

> We'd felt like hens who had been cooped up all through the winter. It was great to head out into the green pastures in the warm sunshine once again. Tia and I always went out as a pair with the boys but once we got out into the fields, we would go off separately to share some privacy with the boys. The boys always looked forward to it, as boys do. This time I felt biologically different when Erich and I kissed, if that terminology makes any sense. I don't know what it was but when we snogged, I felt immense butterflies in the pit of my stomach, and I felt a nice tingling sensation deep between my thighs, I could feel myself becoming moist. I just thought, *Oh my god*. When Erich slid his hand below the waistband of my skirt, I didn't stop him. His fingers slowly travelled further until they were caressing me between my thighs. The feelings he was producing with his fingers just made me lose control. I didn't care if anyone saw or heard us; I was really enjoying what he was doing to me. My breathing became heavier as he ran his tongue around the insides of my mouth, then he suddenly stopped and pulled out this small silver packet. I asked him, 'What is that you have there? What are you doing?' He told me it was a condom, birth control, and asked me if I wanted to go further with him. I was so hyped up from the kissing and the feelings that I agreed. I lay down, watching him as he fumbled excitedly with the sheath. Once he had rolled it over the length of his shaft, which was neither huge nor small, I remember taking a deep breath as

he moved in between my thighs, lying down on top of me. I felt his fingers as he positioned himself and began to enter me. I remember shouting out, 'Ouch! Fuck, that hurts!' I felt a kind of popping sensation then he slid all the way inside me, and it was one of the nicest feelings I had ever experienced. I could tell he was enjoying it, but he was very gentle; he didn't go at it like a rabbit. In that field on that day I gave him my velvet purse; he bruised my violet and I experienced my first orgasm. I remember I was shouting out all manner of obscenities: 'Oh, yes, oh fuck' – all the usual stuff that flows freely from your mouth in the throes of sexual ecstasy. It was only a matter of minutes before Erich blew his load and, when he did, it felt like I'd been given both barrels of a 12-gauge shotgun. I recall his expression, a face contorted in that single act of gratification, his flood of sperm now captive within the confines of a rubber sheath. We lay there motionless for a minute, just looking at one another, then Erich withdrew and removed the sheath from his now shrivelling manhood. Tossing the contraceptive aside, he announced, 'That was really very nice.' He kissed my lips, stroking the side of my face as I lay there looking at him. Then it was a case of bang! it occurred to me that I was no longer a virgin, I wasn't what they called 'pure' anymore, yet did I care? No, I didn't. Nothing can remain pure, untainted forever, can it?

Tia recalled the experience of her first visit to the meadow since the previous summer:

I knew Lisa had been up to things. Ernst and I were not that far away and we could clearly hear all the moaning and groaning that only a couple making love can make. It was a right rattle they were making too [laughs hysterically for some minutes]. It is lucky that no one had come along at the time. Ernst and I had a good time but there was no way at that point I would let him have his way with me, but I knew if we were going to be a proper boyfriend-girlfriend thing, at some point I was going to have to let him, wasn't I? I did give him hand relief which he was happy with.

The boys asked us to go with them the following weekend to the meadow, but it was then we had to tell them we were going to Schlactensee for the weekend. When they asked us why, we had to tell them of our plans to move there. There was an icy silence for a few minutes; the boys looked pretty hurt.

Erich asked Lisa, 'And when were you planning on dropping this bombshell? Why didn't you tell me?'

Ernst looked at me as if to ask the same question.

Lisa just replied, 'I don't have to tell you anything. You don't own me, so what's the problem? Besides, it's not that far and you can visit, and I can visit you.'

There was much huffing and puffing from the boys who were visibly very annoyed, but the cat was out of the bag now: the boys knew our plans so that was it. We said to them, 'If you want to end it, we understand.' The boys replied that they didn't want to end it at all.

Then Lisa announced that her parents were going out to a dance that evening, suggesting the boys come round to her house at 7 pm and we could all meet there. This seemed to perk them up and they were once again full of enthusiasm.

The evening turned out to be quite a night and was planned with military precision. As soon as Lisa's parents left and had vanished out of sight down the road, I came out from behind a wall and over to her front door where she let me in. We had told the boys to hang around by the brick wall opposite Lisa's house; if it was all clear, we would whistle which was their signal to come across to the house. We knew time was not on our side, so we all rushed upstairs into Lisa's room. Lisa drew the curtains and began to take her top off.

I asked, 'What about us? Where can we go?'

She stopped momentarily. 'Across the landing … my brother's bedroom; you can go in there, but don't make a mess or he will know.'

I took Ernst by the hand, leading him into Lisa's brother's bedroom. I shut the curtains then we lay down on the bed and began kissing. As we kissed, I ran my hand down over the hardening bulge in his trousers. I pulled the zip down and after fumbling for some time, managed to extricate his twitching snake from its confines. As I ran my hand back and forth along its length, he began kissing and biting my neck. I don't know why but I just jumped up, took off my clothes and said, 'To hell with it. Let's do it.'

But we were faced with a problem: Ernst had no birth control so one of us was going to have to interrupt Erich and Lisa and ask if they had a spare condom. Ernst was too embarrassed to go so I had to. I walked naked across the landing and tapped on the door. 'Do you have a spare condom as we need one?' As I opened the door, a small silver packet was thrown through the gap then the door slammed shut. Ernst was waiting for me. I waved the packet in the air with a big smile on my face. He snatched it off me like a child would a chocolate bar, as he put the condom on. I was lying there with my legs open, waiting for him in nervous anticipation. I told him to be careful as this was my first time and I didn't want it to hurt. He squeezed between my thighs and with a grunt he began to push inside me. I felt a sharp. stinging pain and cried out, 'Ouch, no, no, this is hurting. Please stop.' He restrained me by holding my wrists down above my head, and at that instant the sensation changed from pain to one of the most luscious pleasure. Oh, it was wonderful, and I was seeing stars for the ten minutes or so that Ernst lasted. It was fantastic even though it didn't last very long. I recall hearing noises coming from the other bedroom.

Afterwards, we dressed yet began to feel paranoid that the neighbours might have heard us fucking. The boys wanted to leave as they didn't feel safe and were worried Lisa's parents and brother would be back and catch them there. So, they hurried off home then Lisa gave me a kiss and said, 'Told you it was nice, didn't I?'

'Oh, yes, it sure was nice but hurt at first too,' I replied.

As I walked home, I thought about how I'd lost my innocence just half an hour before, but then thought, *Oh fuck, did Ernst get rid of that used contraceptive?*

Did I leave any blood on the bed? Did I open the curtains? Just things that would have alerted Lisa's brother and parents that something had been going on in their house in their absence. It was too late to go back to check so I hoped my fears were just me being paranoid. I later learned that Ernst had thrown the contraceptive out the window and it had landed on the outhouse roof next door. The woman next door saw the condom on the outhouse roof and complained to Lisa's mother about it. Lisa's brother somehow became prime suspect and we had to bite our lips. Ignorance is bliss under circumstances such as these. Had the truth come out, god, we would have had some explaining to do.

It was a weekend in mid-June 1947 when Tia and Lisa were again off to Schlactensee to stay with Aunt Andrea for the two days. The girls would use the time to cycle around Schlactensee with Himmel to try and find work prior to their planned move. Tia recalled:

> I had written to Himmel and she wrote back saying she could borrow a couple of bicycles from some friends once we arrived and we could use these to get around the area to look for jobs. She would come with us and help us. Himmel's father had many local connections and was negotiating with the owner of an empty hunting lodge, asking him if we could have it rent free for a few months until we were on our feet. The owner of the lodge was a good friend of Himmel's father and knew him as a man of his word. Himmel's father offered to act as a kind of guarantor for us which was so kind of him. It made us feel more optimistic that we could succeed with our little adventure. The main thing was to find work; if we could not find a job within a sensible distance, it would be a problem and we might have to go back home. The thought of that was too horrible to comprehend, so we steeled ourselves to make a determined effort.
>
> The Friday before the weekend away, I packed what I needed. My mother watched me. She began to sniffle which then made me want to cry. I consoled her, reassuring her I would be fine, and Lisa would be fine, that we would both

be very happy. I said, 'You and father can visit anytime you like.' I was creating all these wonderful, dreamy scenarios of a life we hadn't even started or could guarantee at that time. There was so much we had to do, and we only had one full day in which to try to find work for ourselves.

That night I couldn't sleep. I tossed and turned, everything tumbling around inside my brain. I thought about Ernst and felt sorry that I was leaving him behind and would not be seeing him as much. I thought of mother and father, the Berlin Gang, then Himmel. Somehow when I focused on Himmel, everything felt different, everything made sense and had reason. We would be alright, we had Himmel to help us and we would have many good times. How long they would last, I couldn't say; we were growing up and we might all have a fantastic summer then all drift apart as some friends do. Somehow, I could never imagine that happening, not to us. Either way I was glad when dawn broke as it signalled the end of my night of agonizing mental activity.

At 7 am, I was up saying my farewells to my mother and father and going out the front door with suitcase in hand. I walked to the end of the path, opened the gate and looked back. I remember looking at the house, saying to myself, 'You have been standing here for a long time. The war didn't destroy you as it has many others; you are home and you will still be here if I ever need you.' I felt a pang of sadness that I could soon be walking down this path for the last time. I then headed off down the road to Lisa's house. I looked back again to wave at my mother who was standing in her bedroom window; she waved back. Father had left for work earlier; he used to work a half day on Saturdays for some extra income. He had come into my room before he left for work. I pretended I was asleep and felt him kiss me on the head before quietly creeping out of my room. He had never done that before and I felt a pang of guilt for not having acknowledged him. As I walked down the road, I thought of Himmel again. I could see her pretty face, her blue eyes and her full lips as she smiled. I thought of young Petrianna

Albrecht too, a young girl yet so mature beyond her years. I thought of the boat sinking episode and I couldn't help but laugh out loud to myself. The few passers-by I encountered on my way must have thought me a fugitive from an asylum or something.

I arrived at Lisa's house. Her father was waiting to put our cases in the car, that dreaded VW again! Lisa knew the VW was her father's pride and joy, yet after ten minutes, the engine overheated and he had to stop to let it cool before continuing. What was wrong with the car he didn't know, yet every time Lisa moaned at him: 'Father, why don't you fix this thing?'

He retorted, 'Fix it? And how might I do that, girl? I'm no bloody mechanic.'

I'm sure Lisa used to say this on purpose as every time she found her father's reaction amusing. It meant the relatively short trip to Schlactensee took us almost an hour.

Lisa grumbled that we could get there quicker on bicycles. She grasped my hand and smiled excitedly, saying, 'This is it. I know we have to find some sort of work before we can move, but it's exciting all the same.'

We arrived at Aunt Andrea's house at around 8.40 am. Lisa's father greeted his sister-in-law but had to leave straightaway, so we grabbed our suitcases and dragged them into the house. We had a quick breakfast of toast before we headed off to Himmel's house, to get the bikes and set off to recce the area for employment. My stomach began to churn with butterflies, a sensation I would experience every time I was in her presence or about to enter it. The feeling grew as we approached her house, reaching its zenith as we neared the front door. When it opened, there was Himmel, wearing a pair of black sporting shorts and white vest. Lisa hugged her like she hadn't seen her for years, but in the excitement stepped on her toes, the barefooted Himmel crying out, 'Ouch, Lisa, you're standing on my toes,' yet the hugging continued.

When it is my turn, Himmel smiled at me warmly, wrapping her arms around me. I put my arms around her lithe waist as we hugged, feeling the warmth between our bodies. It was an almost spiritual connection. Himmel kissed me on the cheek whispering into my ear, 'God, I've missed you so much, I really have.'

We went inside as her mother and father greeted us, asking us to join them in the garden while Himmel changed. Himmel's father, Friedrick Hans Boiten, who originally came from the Netherlands, explained his family had settled in Germany well before the First World War. He was a tall, handsome man, immaculately dressed and who wore this peculiar pin in his suit lapel. I recall he often wore it; it was a black enamelled pin with a kind of gold sun symbol at its centre, the gold rays radiating outward. He was an accountant by profession and now worked for a local firm. As we sat down in the delightful garden, Himmel's father proclaimed, 'I have found a suitable property for you; it belongs to an associate and he is a good friend of mine. If you would like to have a look at it later, I can arrange this for you. Be warned, it is nothing much and it is sparsely furnished, but there are people who would pay handsomely for a place like it. I have assured the owner of your good character and he has agreed to let you have the place rent free for a period of three months, after which the situation is to be reviewed. If you are happy with this arrangement, I can contact him.'

We were both so excited we nearly jumped up and down with joy. We told him, 'Yes please, Mr Boiten, can you please tell him yes!' to which he laughed, replying that we had to see it first. We didn't really care at that moment; it was the first part of the plan coming together for us.

Himmel had soon dressed and joined us in the garden. 'Right, come on, we have lots to do today, she said,' before grabbing us by the hand and leading us back through the house. Parked along the side of the house were three rickety-looking bicycles. Himmel took the one and Lisa and I fought over the remaining two.

'I want this one as it's taller and I am taller than you.'

'Yes, but the saddle is wobbly on this one.'

The argument continued until Himmel cycled off, shouting, 'Come on you two, there's no time for arguing.' She was laughing, amused by our infantile bickering.

We jumped on the bikes, cycling after her, but we were not as fit as she was and were soon red faced and puffing like an old couple in a marathon. Himmel looked back at us, laughing so much she almost fell off her bicycle. We stopped for a minute as we needed to get our breath. Himmel was still taking the piss out of us but told us, 'I do love you two and we're going to have some great times here.'

We ended up at Wansee outside a small cinema house. Himmel told us, 'Here, we have to go in here. I know the man who runs this place and he needs some fit, reliable young people to work for him. The pay is not that good but it's a start. If the two of you can get in here, you will be fine.' She told us to wait outside and that she would be back in a minute, before disappearing through the front door. I admit we were both nervous; we had never worked before let alone in a cinema house full of people. We stood outside shaking like sheep at the prospect of being thrown into the bottomless pit of the post-war employment world. Himmel was gone five minutes before reappearing in the doorway, calling us to come inside. We propped up our bikes outside. Inside it was kind of dark and dank with that familiar scent that old cinema houses have. The floor was white marble with black patterns in it, the ceiling quite ornate with plaster flourishes that would not have been out of place on some fancy wedding cake. As we stood with Himmel, nervously gazing about us, a man came shuffling down the stairs. Holding out his hand to shake ours, he introduced himself as Mr Schirner. He told us he was not the owner of the premises but managed it for the owner who was currently away on business procuring some films. He explained the area would soon be back on its feet as a prime recreational area, not just for the Germans who lived here but the Allied troops stationed in Germany.

He went on, 'We intend to profit well from our future venture here, but we need new films, gripping films, which are current and to the liking of the occupying forces in particular, who will pay good money to come here with their sweethearts to watch a good film.' He then asked if we had worked anywhere before and how old we were. When we told him, he placed his hand under his chin and said, 'Hmm, well, Miss Boiten here has told me that you are both good characters and that you are prepared to work hard. I am prepared to give you a chance and see how you both progress, but you must both understand that you will be required to work some evenings and that it is not always easy: there will be ticket office work at times and also cleaning work to do before and after screenings, but if you're happy with this then I will be happy to give you a chance.'

We were again so excited, promising him we would work hard and not let him down. Himmel looked thrilled too; she didn't stop smiling. Mr Schirner then asked us to follow him to his office where he asked us for our home addresses, parents' names, dates of birth and all the usual pre-acceptance stuff young people today are subject to prior to commencement of employment. He told us he would write to us within a week to confirm a starting date and time. We explained to him that by that time we should be living in the area within cycling distance. Himmel nodded in confirmation, telling him her father had made some arrangements for us regarding accommodation. Mr Schirner smiled and said, 'Excellent, that's very good. I will write within one week and see you both again when you start work.' Before we left, Mr Schirner showed us the type of uniform we would be required to wear. Once issued, they would be our own personal responsibility and if lost or damaged, we would have the cost deducted from our pay. We were happy with that; in fact, at that moment we were happy with anything. We didn't care. Mr Schirner then shook our hands again and wished us well as we walked from the subterranean gloom into the brilliant sunshine outside. We all jumped for joy and hugged.

Himmel then said, 'Right, we go back to my house next. My father will take you to look at the lodge; it really is very quaint and in a lovely setting, though you will need bicycles to get to work from there, which will take you around twenty minutes. You should always leave early and arrive at work at least ten minutes before you are to start, maybe even earlier on your first day.'

So, off we went again on the bikes, heading back to Himmel's house. We marvelled at the beauty of the place and the fact that we would soon be able to enjoy all this on our days off from work. We just hoped the lodge would be suitable for us. Back at Himmel's house we had a cool drink made from berries that Himmel's mother had collected from the woods. Lisa and I were so happy. I couldn't stop smiling to myself. Himmel said from across the garden table, 'Look at you both, the cats who ate the cream!'

When Himmel's father returned from what he said was a business meeting with colleagues, he joined us in the garden and poured himself a glass of juice. He then asked us how things had gone that morning and was very happy to hear that we had jobs all sorted out. He then said, 'Well, all that remains is show you the lodge. Are you both ready?'

We couldn't move fast enough we were so excited. Himmel came with us and sat in the front of her father's car while we sat in the back. The red leather seats felt cool against our backs; it was so comfy that I felt myself dozing off, my eyes becoming heavy, closing intermittently as I fought against nodding off.

Himmel looked back at me and laughed, 'Ah, you're going to sleep back there, but you're missing all the scenery.'

It seemed like an endless summer's day in some other universe, yet we were soon shaken from our fatigue as Himmel's father said, 'Here it is, just up here by these trees.' We drove up a narrow lane in some woods and could see the lodge up on a slight rise. We looked at one another in disbelief: it was beautiful and the thought that this could be where we would be living really excited us, bringing home the reality of it all. We pulled up outside and couldn't wait to get inside to see what it was like. Himmel's father had the keys and opened the front door. As we walked inside, we were met by a large boar's head mounted on the wall. Himmel's father remarked, 'Don't let him bother you; that's Alfred and he's been up there for nearly thirty years.'

Inside there was a living room, a small dining area and a kitchen. Out the back was a washhouse, with a mangle standing in the backyard. We knew we would be using all of this yet doing our own washing was no trial for us. The cooking stove was fuel fired but as Himmel's father explained, there was plenty of wood to be found locally. A short spiral staircase led upstairs to two large bedrooms; both had double beds that needed a clean but were perfect for us. The view from the windows was sublime; through the woods you could see one of the lakes from the front bedroom window.

'This is fantastic, Mr Boiten, we would love to stay here; thank you so much and please tell the man we would like it,' we said.

He smiled at us, saying 'Good, then our previous verbal agreement is binding. Leave the paperwork to me. I will take care of things for you and as soon as you are ready, you can move in.'

With our minds made up, it was time to go. We jumped into the car and headed down the lane back to Himmel's house. It was sad we couldn't have spent more time with Himmel, but we had a lot to do over that weekend and were relieved that we had sorted everything out. Before we left Himmel's, we thanked her mother for the drinks and her father for being such a great help to us. We really didn't want to leave but we had to get back to Aunt Andrea's and help her with a few things before dinner. We both gave Himmel extra hugs before we left. I didn't want to let her go and I think she sensed this, saying, 'It won't be long, Tia. You will soon be here and we shall have great fun.'

Lisa said, 'Come on you two, we can't stand here all night.'

At that we reluctantly broke our embrace and began our walk back to Aunt Andrea's house. I kept looking back at Himmel, waving to her before we turned the corner. I blew her a kiss just as we rounded the corner. I saw her blow a kiss back. Lisa began laughing and when I asked what was so amusing, she said, 'You two, you really like her, don't you? And she adores you, but I guess you're aware of that.'

I pretended to be casual about it all, shrugging and saying, 'Of course we adore each other; we are the best of friends, just like I adore you as my best friend. We are all best friends and that's how it is.'

Lisa was still smirking to herself as we continued walking. Was I infatuated in some way with Himmel? No, I don't think I was infatuated with her at all; it was too real for that. Infatuation implies a degree of falsity due to hormones coupled with the youthful mechanics of immaturity. As young as we both were, neither Lisa nor I were immature: the war had ensured we had grown up fast and the Hitler Youth, now a long dead entity of our past, had made us strong and independent.

To change the subject, I spotted a caterpillar inching its way along the ground. I picked it up and showed Lisa who recoiled in disgust. I then started to chase her with it. She ran, squealing like a little girl, terrified that I was actually going to throw the creature on her. When we arrived back at Aunt Andrea's, we were both laughing and out of breath at the same time. As we stumbled through the front door, Aunt Andrea was eager to hear how we had got on.

We sat down after helping to prepare the evening meal and told her everything about the day. She was very pleased that the Boiten family had been so helpful to us; in fact, she said, 'That young Miss Boiten, a wonderful young lady she is; I really like her.'

Lisa chipped in, 'Everyone either likes or loves Himmel, most of them anyway.' She looked at me and winked, to which I mouthed a 'shut up'.

After dinner we were so weary that we went up to bed. Lisa sat up talking for some time, but I was so tired I wasn't really listening, grunting 'yes' or 'no' without fully understanding what she was saying.

It must have been 5 o'clock in the morning when I woke, startled from a nightmare. This one was about the war again. I heard the siren go and was running down a road to a shelter. When I looked up, I could see the bombers even though the sky was black and bombs coming down toward me, I felt the weight as one struck me on the shoulder. Then I woke. It took me a while to calm down as it always did. I lay there for what felt an eternity. When I looked at the clock again, it said 8 am. I decided I was going to get up and go and see Himmel as we would be leaving before lunchtime. I jumped out of bed, dressed quickly and went downstairs. Aunt Andrea was sitting outside in her garden, so I popped my head round the back door and told her I was just going to say goodbye to Himmel. Aunt Andrea asked if Lisa was awake yet and I told her she was still sleeping, and I didn't want to disturb her. Aunt Andrea remarked with a smile, 'That girl will sleep all day if she's not roused.' I told her I wouldn't be long and would just say bye and come straight back.

I ran up the road to Himmel's so was out of breath by the time I got there. I knocked on the door and Himmel's mother answered. She asked me if anything was wrong, and was I okay.

'I have just come to say bye to Himmel,' I told her.

She smiled. 'You said that yesterday though,'

I blushed just as Himmel came running down the stairs and saw me at the door. Her mother said, 'Your friend is here to say bye to you.' Her mother was lovely; she patted the side of my face, saying, 'Until we meet again,' then left us to talk.

Himmel was in her black shorts and vest explaining she did gymnastics every morning to help keep fit for her swimming. It felt strange us being alone. I said, 'I wanted to say bye again. I couldn't leave without seeing you, just for a minute, to say bye.'

At that she embraced me. 'You are just so sweet. Do you know that?'

I loved Himmel's embraces; she held you tight and made you feel loved and all warm inside. My stomach was in knots and I felt lightheaded. Himmel noticed and made me sit down on the grass. She was very concerned, stroking my face, saying, 'Are you okay? Do you want to come inside and sit down?'

I reassured her I was fine, that I was just so excited about everything. Himmel looked into my eyes. Her eyes were beautiful; I'd seen many blue-eyed girls before, but none as beautiful as hers; they shone like crystals. She held my hand for a moment then leaned forward, kissing me on the lips. 'Right, I will walk back with you to make sure you are okay.' She quickly went inside to get some shoes, came out and took my hand and said, 'Come on, Tia, I will walk you back.' As we walked it was one of those moments you felt you didn't want to end. I even tried walking a little slower, but Himmel kept saying, 'Come on, Tia. Lisa's aunt will be wondering where you've got to.'

As we approached Aunt Andrea's house, we stopped, looked into each other's eyes and embraced again. I told her, 'I can't wait until we move here, Himmel; it will seem like an age.' She told me to be patient, that the time would come soon enough, and she asked me to write as soon as I got back home. Subconsciously I still held onto her hand as she said goodbye, and as she slowly walked away, our connection was broken. It was that feeling you get when you pull a plug from its socket and things go dead. Our fingers brushed momentarily then I watched her walk off down the road. She turned and waved and before she was out of sight, she blew me a kiss and I blew her one back. I felt happy and sad at the same time, then I noticed Lisa leaning out of the bedroom window at the front of the house.

She was smirking broadly. 'Oh, Himmel, I *do* love you.'

I shouted up at her, 'Just you wait ... the next worm or caterpillar is going down your neck, Lisa Kraus!'

On the journey home both Tia and Lisa were absorbed in their thoughts. They recollected the events of the past year with a smile, hoping that the years to come would be filled with happiness and prosperity. They knew they would have to talk with the Sauerstond boys. Interrupted as usual by the VW overheating, Tia turned to Lisa and said, 'I don't think I can go on with Ernst anymore. It's just not there for me, if you get what I am trying to say. It would be different if we had planned to get married, but I don't want to marry him. I don't want to marry anyone at this time.'

Lisa reassured Tia that she would respect her for this, then said, 'For me it's not just velvet purses and bruised violets ... it's different ... I think I love Erich. I want to keep seeing him even when we move. I just hope he understands all of this.'

Chapter 6

Breaking the Black Mirror of our Past

I find myself walking barefoot through the forest dawn,
I wear its mist as if a burial shroud,
the wolf's breath it smells of cadavers.
I can taste them as his tongue enters my mouth.
He abandons me with love bites upon both breasts,
his seed deep within my womb,
a heart-shaped coffin in which to rest,
the darkened passage that is birth,
yet another howl in the dead of night,
a subtle agony that love once was,
seduced with all the softness of a knife,
the velvet throes are stained with blood,
my tears have long since dried.
Yes, I've cried a thousand times for you my love,
yes, I have cried a thousand times.

When the girls arrived back home, they became restless, they felt like circus animals in a cage with little to do to consume the time on their hands. Tia immediately ran up to her bedroom and wrote excitedly to Himmel. She thanked her for helping her and Lisa to find employment and asked her to pass on her sincerest regards to her mother and father for all of their hospitality and assistance. She wrote: 'I or rather we are now petting the wet dog of boredom; it permeates the soul. I feel restless and I just hope those letters arrive soon.' She closed the letter by drawing a heart with an arrow through it with the words 'With all of my love and wishes to you, Tia xxxx'.

Lisa also wrote a letter to Himmel, asking her to thank her father for arranging the accommodation for her and Tia, and her mother for being so kind to them over the last weekend:

Dearest Himmel,

Tia looks upon you as the brightest star in her heaven. Don't tell her I told you so, as she will be mad with me (ha, ha), but it is true. She is going to break up with Ernst, but she may have told you this. If she hasn't, don't let on that I have told you this, okay?

Love always, my dear Himmel,

Lisa, xx

Tia had the difficult task of informing Ernst of her intention to end their relationship. She had asked him to meet her at the bridge, their childhood haunt, where she would break the news. She recalled:

> It was not the most pleasant of things to have to do. I could have asked Lisa to tell him, but I felt it wasn't right him hearing the news via my best friend, so I would tell him myself. When I told him, he was shocked and began asking me questions. He asked if I had met someone else in Schlactensee and I told him that I hadn't. I just wanted to be on my own, that I wasn't ready to settle down, marry and have children. He didn't take it very well at all; in fact, he cried, and I felt awful about hurting his feelings so much. I didn't know what else to say to him and after a few minutes, he just said, 'Okay, I'm going home. Please don't bother me again,' and at that he walked off. I sat on the bridge for some minutes feeling totally miserable and began to cry myself. I wished Himmel was here to make it alright as she somehow always did. I walked home deep in thought and when I got home, I wrote a letter to Himmel telling her about it all. I knew she would write back with words of comfort which would tide me over through these miserable times. I told Lisa the next day what had happened, and she just said, 'Well, it's done now; it's sad for Ernst but he'll live.' Erich told Lisa a few days later that Ernst was angry about me and said I was a cow. She told him off for it when she saw him next and reminded him that I didn't

belong to anyone, that I was free to choose what I did in life and that he must get on with it. I thanked Lisa for her support, hoping it would not put a strain on her relationship with Erich. She reassured me everything would be alright and not to worry over it.

In town the next day we bumped into the young American, Joel. We stood chatting with him for some minutes, telling him that we were leaving soon to live and work in Schlactensee. He asked us if he could have our address as he would come and visit us, saying it was a beautiful part of Berlin. He pulled out a notebook from his pocket and wrote down the address of the lodge we would soon be calling home. We liked Joel as he gave us news about what was happening. He told us things were becoming strained with the Russians, that the brass, as he called, them were not happy with certain proposals they were trying to implement. He told us the brass would prefer it if the Russians pulled out of Berlin, but there would be no chance of that ever happening and they would maintain their encirclement of the city. He told us not to worry about them, that they'd be stupid to try anything with the USA and England, but it did concern us. Joel told us not to repeat a word of what he had said to anyone, and that if the brass found out he had talked he might be court martialled for it. We promised him we would not say a word to anyone then we said if we didn't see him around before we left, he mustn't forget to visit us. He seemed really happy and said, 'I really like you girls; you girls are alright, aren't you?' Naturally, we nodded in agreement then he drove off up the road.

Every day was an agony of waiting for the mail to arrive and sometimes we didn't get mail on time due to certain factors. Finally, our day of reckoning arrived: a letter enclosed in an official brown envelope popped through the front door. My mother intercepted it, shouting up the stairs, 'Tia, there's a letter for you, probably what you have been waiting for.' I almost fell down the stairs in my haste to get it. I tore it open on the spot and sure enough it was from Herr Schirner, the manager of the little picture house at

Wansee. The starting date was in one week's time, on the Friday evening. I quickly put my shoes on and with letter in hand ran off to Lisa's house. She must have received her letter as I bumped into her halfway there. We both jumped for joy and hugged each other.

'Let's just go, let's go now, just pack what shit we need and go,' Lisa said.

I had to calm her down. 'Look, we must send a telegram to Himmel's father first, tell him we have our work confirmation letters and we will come down this Saturday, then that way he can arrange to collect the keys of the lodge for us.'

As we walked back to my house, we bumped into Joel again. We told him we needed to send a telegram so he told us to jump in his Jeep and he would give us a lift. It was wonderful driving along with the wind in our hair in an American military Jeep. Joel took us to the mail office where US servicemen sent telegrams from and came in with us. We were just about to pay for the telegram when Joel said, 'I will pay for this.' He was just so sweet to us and we thanked him for his kindness. The telegram would reach Himmel's father much quicker than a letter. I think it was a few days later I received a telegram back from Himmel telling us everything was in place for the coming weekend and to calm down. Oh, it was an amazing feeling; we were both elated, so much so we began packing. We wanted everything to be in place in advance for the Friday morning. We would then be ready for work at the cinema for 6 pm that evening. I felt like writing another letter to Himmel, but at this stage it would be pointless as we would be seeing her before the letter arrived. Instead, I scribbled a note in my diary: 'It's finally happening. Lisa and I leave for Schlactensee this Friday morning; we have literally packed all that we need and all that remains is to say goodbye to the Berlin Gang, give them our new address and beg them to come and stay with us.'

I will miss them, as we went through school together, the Jungmadelbund together and the Second World War together. They are like sisters and it feels as if we are leaving a part of ourselves behind in the city. I can't wait to leave though and am so excited that we will be able to see Himmel everyday if she doesn't get bored with us. I hope everything goes smoothly and mother and father don't get too tearful when I go – that will be hard for me, but they understand that both Lisa and I are young but we are not getting any younger: if we are to do well in this world, we have to go out there and work for the privilege.

Over the last two days prior to the girls leaving for Schlactensee they visited all their friends in their neighbourhood, saying their farewells to the Berlin Gang. It was an emotional time which stirred mixed feelings in the girls, yet it was also exciting, a new beginning for them both. When the Friday finally came, Lisa recalled:

We had nothing to do as we had everything packed and ready. I was up at 7 o'clock waiting for Tia to arrive. We were set to meet Himmel's father at the lodge for 8.30 am as he had work that morning. My father took time off specially to take us to our new destination. I had said my goodbyes to mother. She was very emotional, but I promised I would be over to see her regularly and she and father could come and visit anytime they liked. My father had borrowed a car from a friend, so there would be no hiccups on the trip. When Tia arrived, I could see she was emotional: there had been tearful farewells at home before she left, and her eyes were red from crying. I hugged her and we both got in the car.

As we drove off, we passed through many areas of our childhood in western Berlin; we were saying goodbye to the familiar landmarks, or what was left of them, quietly in our minds. Within forty minutes we were at Schlactensee and giving my father directions to the lodge. As we drove up the lane, the lodge came into view and my father said, 'Oh my god, what a beautiful place! How did you manage to get this? This is fantastic!' Himmel's father was there waiting by his car. We jumped out, grabbed our bags and cases and dropped them at the front door of the lodge. Himmel's father was busy greeting my father, shaking hands and deep in conversation. We were so excited it was all a blur. I can't recall what they were talking about.

Himmel's father told my father, 'Don't you worry about these two. We'll keep an eye on them and see that they're alright. This is a nice quiet place here, with no rascals anywhere around.'

We knew we were in good hands here and Himmel's father handed us the keys. Of course, my father wanted a tour of the place and was impressed with the boar's head trophy on the hallway wall. When he left, Himmel's father told us, 'On Sunday you can join us for dinner. It will not be much, but we would like to welcome you and hope you will join us.'

We had to work that evening, and the Saturday afternoon as the cinema was showing a matinee, then we would work the Sunday afternoon for the matinee again, plus weekdays. We would then get the following weekend off so that things were fair for everyone who worked there. We were happy with this as it meant we could go to Himmel's for dinner on the Sunday.

As soon as we were alone, we began cleaning and dusting. There were furnishings in the lodge, not much but adequate. We each had a large bed which was very good. Originally there had been two double bunks in each bedroom so the lodge could sleep eight in total, mostly people on hunting trips. We knew little of the history of the building other than it had once been the property of a Nazi Party official, though we had never heard of him. By mid-afternoon we had the place clean and dusted to our preference and had made the two beds with linen that Himmel had given to us. We both felt tired and sat down in the living area and ate some sandwiches, the only food we'd had that day.

Before we knew it, it was time for us to change our clothes, grab the bicycles which were still on loan to us and set off for the cinema. We were both very nervous when we arrived but were greeted by Herr Schirner who reassured us with a broad smile and welcomed us inside.

I was shown how to issue tickets and take the money and Tia was given the job of serving small cups of non-alcoholic cold beverages during the interval. The film that evening ran for around an hour. I don't remember what it was called but it was basically a short US comedy import or something, so I was told. The clientele were mostly young Allied servicemen who were dating German girls. I don't think many of them were really there to watch the film, as they were too busy snogging with their tongues down each other's throats. We didn't know any of these German girls and they eyed us with contempt. We just had to smile at them, making them feel they were royalty. Most of the films at that time were imported by associates of Herr Schirner, and only in December did German films begin showing alongside western ones. In all, our first shift at the cinema went by without any serious problems other than our nerves which soon abated as the evening drew on. The great thing was we had helped clean up the stalls, sweep the stairs and mop the floors with the other workers and were home before 9.20 pm.

We were so tired we both ate another two sandwiches, locked all the doors of the lodge and went straight to bed. It was June at the time and the weather was pleasantly warm. The idea of separate bedrooms didn't work for long. Tia got a bit spooked with her first night in a strange place, asking if she could come in with me. I said, 'Of course you can, sweetheart. Come on!' She didn't hesitate and jumped in. We both lay there wondering all sorts of things. Was the place haunted? Did it have a ghost? All the kinds of things that go through your mind in an old unfamiliar building like this in the dark. As it happened, we had an owl fly onto the roof in the middle of the night; it began its characteristic hoots and shrieks which woke us both up, but we soon dozed back off.

We woke to a bright sunny morning, greeted by the most beautiful scenery. Oh, it was stunning, and we were very happy. We had arranged to meet Himmel that morning as she was taking us to get some food supplies at Wansee – we didn't really have anything apart from half a loaf of bread, a small amount of butter plus some locally sourced milk that Himmel's father had left in the pantry in a jug for us. Himmel arrived on her bicycle at 10 am, and we were already waiting for her out on the front doorstep. There was much joy as she came up the lane. We grabbed our bicycles – both had baskets on the front handlebars – and off we went to procure what supplies we could. Rationing was still on, so we went to a local farm to get some eggs. The farmer knew Himmel, so he gave us some ham too. By the time we had finished doing the rounds with Himmel, our baskets were that full and heavy we could barely peddle our bikes back to the lodge.

When we got back to the lodge, we invited Himmel inside, put some wood into the bottom of the stove and lit the fire to make some coffee, acorn coffee, of course. Tia remarked, 'This stuff is hot, which is good, but it's barely palatable and tastes like piss.' She pulled a funny face and Himmel laughed at her. Those two together were so amusing. It was great when you got them together. After we had finished our coffee, Himmel had to get off to work and we had to be at the cinema for the afternoon's matinee, but we would all have the late afternoon and evening off. Himmel kissed us both and off she went.

After a busy morning with Himmel attempting to fill their pantry, the girls then prepared a meal, before setting off for work and the afternoon matinee. The meal was a stew with vegetables and some of the ham the farmer had given them earlier. It was a one-pot meal that would last a few days. Tia recalled that second day in Schlactensee:

> I felt a pang of guilt. I hadn't even thought about my mother or father. Things were happening so fast with so much to do during our first few days that we could barely focus on anything. We both chopped up some vegetables for the stew, throwing in some ham to give it flavour. We had to be very sparing as food was still in short supply and you had to rely on locally sourced produce and make what you could

yourself. Once the stew was done, we left it in the pot in the pantry to cook it after work later that afternoon.

As it turned out, the matinee was quite popular and there were more people in there this time, probably because it was a Saturday afternoon. Many people who worked had a half day on Saturdays and came to watch films. It was a US-made drama production this time – no subtitling back then, so unless you could understand English, which Lisa and I did, you just had to watch without knowing what was really going on. There were a lot of English and American soldiers in there and I recall the very first African American soldier I ever met. During the interval he called me over as he wanted a drink. They didn't know I could speak English.

Some swine shouted out, 'We don't serve niggers in here.'

I turned to where the remark came from and said, 'Everyone in here is a customer and has the right to be served. Now who shouted?' There was a deathly silence as whoever had shouted out the derogatory remark was obviously shocked that a young German girl knew English so well. Some white soldiers shrunk into their seats as if trying to hide. I guessed it was one of them and glared at them angrily. I went over to the African American soldier, served him his drink and apologized to him.

He was so sweet, and said, 'That's quite okay, ma'am, that's just how it is. It's alright.'

I begged to differ and told him, 'No, it's not alright. What was the last war all about if it were not for the freedom of the people of this world?'

He just smiled and said, 'It's okay, ma'am, really.'

'Please call me Tia. My name is Tia,' I said. I held out my hand and he seemed surprised, but he shook it and smiled at me.

Before Lisa and I set off for home at the end of the matinee, Herr Schirner asked if he could talk to me in his office. I had no idea what he wanted to see me about as I had done nothing wrong that I knew of. When we were inside his pokey little office, he slumped into his chair behind his desk asking me to take a seat. I sat down, bewildered by what he wanted to see me about. One of the other girls had witnessed my altercation with the off-duty Americans and their abuse of the African American soldier.

Herr Schirner said, 'I appreciate your concerns about the young man in question, but in future you must not get involved in any of their arguments or anything regarding their policy. It is their business, not ours. Our business is to attract business, not to drive it away. Therefore, I am asking you in future not to get involved. Just do your job and say nothing. If there is any trouble, I will sort it out, okay?'

I reluctantly agreed, but only because we needed the money at the time. I just thought to myself that maybe this was not the work for me if Herr Schirner was happy to allow such behaviour. As we left the cinema, we grabbed our bikes and set off for home. Lisa could tell I was angry about something. I told her all about it over the stew that evening. Himmel called in and we gave her some stew and I told her about the African American and what Herr Schirner had said. She told me what I had done had been very noble and brave, yet segregation was still a part of American policy regarding African Americans in general – soldiers and civilians alike. We didn't think it was fair at all, but agreed politics were one of the greatest evils of mankind as we had borne witness to it through the years of the Second World War.

I was still angry. 'Bloody men, fuck them and fuck their politics!'

Himmel laughed as she'd never heard me swear like that before. She then jumped up and said, 'Right, my two sweethearts. I have to go, but I will see you at my house for dinner tomorrow, so don't you forget, okay.' She kissed us both and walked out the door. I got up to see her off as I always did. As she rode off, I heard her shout, 'Don't forget tomorrow!'

'We won't,' I shouted back.

Sunday morning was blissful for the girls: they both had the luxury of a lie-in as they didn't have to be at work until mid-afternoon. The sun was shining through the windows of the lodge, and birdsong filled the air. Lisa woke around 10 am and went to rouse Tia. She lit the small stove and put some water on to boil to make two cups of *ersatz* coffee. Tia came down the stairs and sat at the small kitchen table, still half-asleep and wearing nothing more than a nightgown. Lisa made the coffee and suggested she throw it in Tia's eyes as it might take effect more quickly. Lisa recalled that Tia always took an hour or so to fully wake up and was grouchy until properly awake. Lisa made some eggs on toast and then they washed themselves and dressed, ready to go over to Himmel's for the lunch at 1 pm. As they cycled down the lane, two American MPs were walking up and waved for them to stop. Tia recalled:

> I just said, 'Oh fuck, what do these two want with us?' We hadn't done anything we knew of.
>
> The MP's greeted us with a '*guten morgen*' but were shocked when we replied, 'Good morning.'
>
> They said, 'You both speak English?'
>
> 'Yes sir, we do.'
>
> They asked us if we had by any chance seen a certain man in the vicinity, then showed us a photograph of the young American they were looking for. We said we hadn't They asked us that if we saw him, a report should be made to the local Allied military authority.
>
> We asked, 'Why are you looking for him? Is he a criminal? What has he done?'
>
> The one MP replied, 'It's nothing to worry about, miss. He's not wanted for murder or anything; he just failed to return to his unit after his few days' leave.'
>
> This reassured us as the thought of a maniac on the loose in the vicinity would have been just too much. We told the MPs we would keep an eye out and report it if we saw the young man. They thanked us for our time, then we continued the ride to Himmel's. When we arrived, the smell of meat roasting met our nostrils as we walked up to the front door. Before we could knock, Himmel had opened it and was standing there in a light-yellow blouse with a dark-blue skirt and with no shoes or socks on. I remember thinking to myself, *God, you're so pretty*. Himmel embraced us and led

us into the dining room where she arranged where everyone would be sitting. I was more than disappointed when I discovered Himmel would not be sitting next to me; she'd chosen to sit opposite me. She went and fetched a pitcher of berry juice, pouring us each a glass before sitting down at the table. As I began to tell her about the American MPs stopping us on the way, I felt a foot brush my leg. Thinking nothing of it, I continued talking. Then I felt a toe brushing up and down my leg. Himmel had her chin resting in her hands; she was listening but had a cheeky kind of smile on her face at the same time. I felt myself blushing slightly. Not wishing to be outdone, I used my left foot to remove the shoe on my right and attempted to do the same back to Himmel. Here we were about to have a Sunday lunch – dinner or whatever you call it in England – and Himmel and I are playing footsie beneath the dining table. As we jostled for advantage, Himmel slid her foot beneath mine and it tickled, which made me squirm in my seat.

'What are you two doing? What's so funny?' Lisa asked.

Himmel and I immediately pulled our legs back under our chairs as Lisa looked under the table to see what was going on. She sat there shaking her head like a headmistress might with two naughty children. 'You two, you're both crazy.'

Himmel's mother brought in a pot and her father followed with some bowls and bread rolls. He served us each a helping of a kind of thick vegetable soup with some diced pork meat in it. Afterwards Himmel's mother brought in a cake which was cut into slices and everyone had a piece. It was absolute heaven, very similar to the Victoria sandwich cake enjoyed by British families. Where Himmel's mother was able to find all the ingredients we didn't know.

After this lovely meal it was time for us to get to the cinema. As usual Himmel saw us off. She embraced Lisa and gave her a peck on the cheek, while I received a sneaky kiss on the lips. We set off with full stomachs, wondering what the afternoon matinee might bring. When we arrived, we propped up our bikes along the side of the building before going inside. Again, the cinema was full, meaning I was in demand during the interval to serve soft drinks. There were American soldiers with German girlfriends in there again. I was hailed by one of them who held his hand up to me like a kid in class at school shouting out, 'Miss, miss, over here please.' Negotiating my way along the row of seats and tangle of customers' legs was no easy process. As I neared the American, I caught my foot on one of the girls' feet, falling forward and unloading the contents of my tray over the lap of the American serviceman. His German girlfriend went berserk, shouting, 'You stupid girl, look what you've done. Look at the mess you've made of my clothes!' I began apologizing profusely but she would have none of it.

The American was actually alright, saying, 'It's alright, miss, it was an accident. Don't worry, I can clean my stuff up later.' His girlfriend was not so easy to appease, continuing to complain and hurl abuse at me. The American began to lose his patience with her and told her to quieten down as she was causing a scene.

At that she got up, pushed me out of her away with the parting shot of '*Du dumme Kuhe*' ['You stupid cow'] and stormed out of the cinema.

I quickly picked up the spilled cups and returned them to the service area. I then carefully returned to the American with a fresh drink. He asked me what my name was and I told him, 'My name is Tia, Tia Schuster.' We shook hands, with him introducing himself as James Conolly. He said he would ensure I wouldn't get into any trouble with the manager as the spillage was not my fault. He then asked whether he could take me out sometime.

I replied, 'Yes, of course you can.'

He then said, 'Well, miss, I will see you soon then, but where can I find you?'

I told him I lived with my friend at the lodge, giving the directions. He said he knew where it was, so we left it there. By the end of the shift, I was glad to get out of the cinema. I waited for Lisa who had been in the ticket office again. We jumped on our bikes and set off for home.

On the way I told her about what had happened and hoped that Herr Schirner wouldn't pull me into his office again next shift. As it happened, the American made a point of seeing the manager, explaining what had happened and gave Herr Schirner a few marks as a tip which he was very pleased with. In fact, Herr Schirner told me on the next shift, 'Maybe you should spill refreshments on more American servicemen in future,' but quickly adding, 'I am only joking with you, Miss Schuster, but please do be very careful in future as I don't wish to get sued for someone's ruined apparel.'

That evening Petrianna Albrecht called round to see us, introducing her eldest sister whom I had not met before. Lisa had already met Kirsten Albrecht whom she described as 'crazy' but in a nice sense. I liked Kirsten Albrecht. She was 16 years old, average height, brown eyes, brown hair, attractive and very charming, very intelligent yet mischievous. I was warned by Lisa and Petrianna that I should never dare Kirsten to do anything as she was mad enough to do it. We sat outside the lodge on the back step chatting about work and things when Kirsten announced she had heard that some man in her street had been found dead in bizarre circumstances. When we questioned her about it, she said, 'They found him dead, sitting bolt upright on the toilet in his backyard.' We asked what the hell had happened before Kirsten continued, 'Well, he was sitting there with his trousers around his ankles. They said that his straining to defecate had triggered an aneurysm.'

Petrianna screwed up her face. 'That's disgusting. What the hell is an aneurysm?'

Kirsten explained, 'It's a swelling of a blood vessel; basically, they call it subarachnoid haemorrhage in medical terminology, but don't worry – you won't have one.' Petrianna looked at us, rolling her eyes. Then Kirsten got up and said to Petrianna, 'Right, we have to go. It's nearly your bedtime, and you have school in the morning.'

Petrianna argued her case: 'It's not my bedtime, I hate school and I'm not a baby, you know.'

Kirsten added, 'You are a baby and school is good for you.' They set off home and we could still hear them arguing even after they were out of sight around the corner.

I said to Lisa, 'I really like those two; they're chalk and cheese – one'd never think they were sisters.'

We went inside, bolted the door and turned the key in the lock, spending the remainder of that Sunday evening chatting. Lisa remarked, 'We need to get a radio; the winter nights here will be long and at least we can listen to some music or something.' I agreed though we'd both have to save up to buy one. We sat up late talking as we had the following Monday and Tuesday off. I said we needed to find something better than the cinema: I didn't like doing the evening shifts, I'd rather be home like everyone else.

Lisa replied, 'Ah well, at least we have work and we can always look around for something better. I know it's a pain but for the moment we have to stick it out.' At that we turned out the lights and went to bed.

We both woke around 8 o'clock the following Monday morning. I leaned out of the window and the skies were slightly cloudy, the air reassuringly warm against my face. Lisa made some coffee and we went and sat outside on the back step as we called it. The lodge had a lawn area which ran from the back step down to the woods which surrounded the place; it was beautiful. We sat and talked as we drank our coffee, still in our nightclothes, nothing more than shorts and one of our fathers' shirts. We decided to walk down into the nearby town to visit the café where Himmel was working. After coffee we ate some toast, washed and got dressed then headed off to the town.

It was blissful walking down the treelined road accompanied by the birdsong. The town was much like any other in Germany, with many old buildings and surprisingly a lot of little shops selling vegetables, bread, meat, clothes and shoes. We vowed to return on payday to treat ourselves. We found Himmel's café and decided to sit outside. She saw us and came out and we ordered two orange soft drinks. I thought Himmel looked lovely in her little outfit and

I remarked that she looked like a dairy maid which made her laugh. We told her to come around to the lodge when she finished work and she promised she would. We didn't have that much money, so we didn't spend too long in town, but it was a nice walk. We did buy a ball so at least we could pass some time back at the lodge playing ball games.

For our next weekend off we planned to go to the lakes with Himmel, Petra, Kirsten and some of their friends. So far it had all largely been work, with little time for play, so we looked forward to going swimming. Back at the lodge we played ball on the back lawn until Himmel called in around 4 pm. We had just started to play 'piggy in the middle' when we heard a vehicle coming up the lane. We dropped the ball and went to see what it was.

We were delighted to see it was Joel pulling up. He remarked how lovely the place looked then said, 'I have a few things for you that you might like.' He pulled this green sack out of the back of the Jeep and handed it to me. I put it down and opened up the bag with Himmel and Lisa excitedly saying, 'What's in there? What is it?' We couldn't believe it: there was a full tin of cocoa, some butter, some hard sweets as we called them – these were actually boiled fruit-flavoured sweets or candies as Americans called them – plus two tins of what he said was corned beef and a tin of milk powder. We were like kids on a Christmas morning. I asked Joel if he wanted us to pay him any money as it must have cost him a small fortune. We couldn't even get some of this stuff in the shops, especially the cocoa and milk powder – it was like gold dust.

Joel just said, 'Don't worry, there's tons of this stuff where this came from and they won't miss it.'

We guessed he had got it from the back of a lorry as they say but we didn't care. Joel told us to take it all inside and hide it somewhere safe, so Lisa took it in and put it in the pantry in the kitchen. With the goods safely stashed away, we invited Joel into the back garden. He was impressed with our little abode, looking around with admiration. We then introduced Himmel to him as he had never met her. I could tell he liked her by the look on his face, that kind of look that you'd see on an antique dealer's face when confronted with something priceless. Himmel then suggested we play ball and Joel joined in: he didn't need asking twice! Next thing Petra and Kirsten arrived – they just walked through the trees around the back to announce their arrival. We stopped the ballgame to introduce Joel, and I think Kirsten really took a shine to him as she kept wanting to be on his side during the games. When we began to tire, Joel asked if he could have some photographs taken with us, so we took it in turns to have our photograph taken with him. When it was Kirsten's turn, she put her arm around him and cuddled him. We all sat down to chat for a while.

Joel then announced some news. 'I have been told that I will be going back home soon. I am not sure exactly when, but it will be soon.' It was bad news which really made us all very sad, and for a minute there was this contemplative silence. Joel said, 'Look, don't be unhappy, you will all be okay, and I can come back to visit once I've left the army.'

'Will you promise us you'll come back and see us as soon as you can?' He said he would. Then we began discussing the future, particularly the Russian occupation of Berlin, how the Russians still maintained a ring around the area and the tensions which had become apparent, tensions which had been picked up and dissected by the press in the West.

Joel said, 'All Russian forces are now confined to barracks; these are heavily guarded, and it keeps Russian troops separated from the civilian population of Germany.' I asked when this had occurred, and Joel said during the winter of 1947.

I then said to Joel, 'To be honest we have never encountered many Russians while out walking around. If we did see any we kept our distance as we knew of all the rape stories. We were afraid of them as many Germans are.'

Himmel then asked Joel, 'Do you think they will ever try and come across and take the whole of western Germany?'

Joel laughed and assured her, 'The western military powers would never allow that to happen, so you don't have to worry about it.'

Himmel said, 'What if Stalin orders it to happen, what then?'

Joel then said the words that became a kind of catchphrase for us as we grew up in the yet-to-come Cold War West Germany, 'Ah, knickers to Stalin!'

At that Lisa and I burst into fits of laughter. Himmel and the others didn't understand English too well so didn't get what he had said, so we explained the term to them in German and then they too burst out laughing. Himmel kept repeating, 'Knickers to Stalin, knickers to Stalin' and laughing. It was a wonderful afternoon, but then Joel had to leave. He told us he would come and say goodbye if he could, but if he couldn't then not to be mad with him. We told him to write to us if there were any problems and he assured us he would. We all gave him a big hug and a kiss. Petra threw her arms around him and told him in German, 'You are a lovely boy.' Kirsten asked him to write to her but send any letters to the lodge as she was unable to read English and her parents might get grouchy over it. Then Kirsten took off one of the three silver rings she wore on the fingers of her left hand and gave it to Joel as something to remember her by. Joel was reluctant to take it at first until Kirsten reassured him that she wanted him to have it for his kindness to her friends. Joel told her, 'I will treasure this, thank you Kirsten.' He then gave her a lingering kiss on the cheek. We all watched and thought how sweet a scene this was. We watched him climb into his Jeep, start it up and drive off down the lane, leaving a rooster tail of dust in his wake. We all waved and heard him tooting his horn as he disappeared from sight.

As soon as he was gone, Kirsten became the lovestruck teenager, saying 'God, I like that boy so much.'

Petra teased her, 'But you've only just met him and you're in love.' She laughed at her sister who threatened to kick her younger sibling up the arse. Himmel intervened and called a truce between the two sisters; it is very amusing, but Himmel could see that Kirsten was getting irritated. Himmel suggested we all go for a quick swim as it wasn't too late, so the girls all joined arms and walked off down the lane together, with Himmel shouting 'Knickers to Stalin' and soon we were all shouting it. We only went silent after a resident of a nearby house came out barking, 'For god's sake, will you shut up! I have been listening to your rubbish all the way down the road.' We walked past him sniggering. We were in good spirits as the lake came into view, and we raced off to see who could get to the water first. Himmel beat us to it, threw off her clothes and dived into the cool water. Clothing flew in all directions as we stripped off after Himmel who was swimming out to the middle of the lake. I caught up with her, now treading water, and as I reached her, we embraced for a moment. She brushed my hair back from out of my eyes then kissed me on the lips and winked at me. There were no words. Then there was the race back to the shore. Our clothes lay everywhere, and it took a few minutes to sort them all out.

We were all tired after the swim and when Lisa and I arrived back at the lodge, we locked up and went straight to bed, before we realized we had forgotten about Joel's cocoa. We ran downstairs and with the cocoa and some of the fresh milk, we made this heavenly chocolate beverage. We sat savouring every drop. I recall Lisa sitting there with her eyes closed in chocolate ecstasy again, and she remarked, 'God, this is so good, it's making me wet.' We both burst out laughing and I nearly sprayed Lisa with cocoa. Finishing the last droplets, we both agreed this was a little piece of heaven right here. We then went up to bed and slept soundly. I hadn't had any nightmares for some time now and felt maybe I had seen the last of them. As I lay in my bed, I heard an owl in the distance calling to its mate, then I thought of Himmel and the kiss she'd given me in the water, the sensations as our bodies touched. I rolled over onto my side, falling into a deliciously warm sleep. It was the end of another perfect day. It felt as if, finally, here we were breaking that black mirror of our past.

On the Tuesday morning the girls followed their same routine: the first one up made coffee and breakfast. They were sitting outside in their night attire drinking coffee, eating toast and petting a neighbouring cat that had begun visiting them. The peace was shattered by the sound of a large vehicle coming up the lane. It pulled up outside the front of the lodge and the girls heard a door open then slam shut.

Peering round the corner, Tia broke into a series of expletives, 'Oh, fuck, oh shit, I forgot about him!'

Lisa asked, 'Who, who is this?'

Tia replied, 'It's James who I told you about at the cinema, the American I spilled drinks over.'

Lisa told her, 'Well, you better go and see him then.'

Tia replied, 'But look at us, we are not even dressed.'

Lisa shook her head and replied, 'Oh for god's sake, I'm sure he's seen scantily dressed girls before.' She began to laugh.

Sheepishly the girls crept round the side of the lodge until the young American noticed them. He appeared slightly lost for words and said, 'Tia, it's Tia isn't it? Do you remember me? It's James Conolly. We met at the cinema, or rather you gave me more refreshments than what I asked for.'

Tia replied, 'Yes, yes. I remember. I'm sorry, we weren't expecting visitors and were just having our breakfast.'

The American smiled and apologized then told them maybe he should return later, but as he turned to leave, Tia called him back, saying it was okay, that he could join them in the back garden. She recalled:

> That young man was the perfect gentleman; he was a lovely young man and we soon broke the ice, with him chatting about all sorts of things. He asked us if we had any other regular visitors and we said 'only our friends' – we didn't mention Joel to him at that time. Lisa asked him if he would like some coffee to which he replied, 'Thank you, miss, that would be lovely.' When Lisa returned with a cup of coffee, she handed it to him, and he sat there sniffing its odd aroma. He took a sip, immediately recoiling in horror.
>
> Lisa asked, 'What's the matter? Don't you like it?'
>
> 'Oh, Jesus!' he said, with his face twisted in disgust. 'Is this what you guys have been drinking?'

We explained, 'It's acorn coffee, a kind of substitute – *ersatz* – as we can't find or afford real coffee. You can get it on the black market, but the prices are crazy.'

James put the cup down and, walking off back to his vehicle, said, 'Right, I will sort this out.' For some minutes he ferreted away and pulled out some small sachets and returned to us, saying, 'Here you are: this is proper instant coffee. You just add boiling water to it and it tastes the same as the real thing; even has caffeine in it. I can bring you some more if you don't mind me visiting again, if it's okay, I mean.'

We assured him it was okay. Lisa went back into the kitchen to make some proper coffee for us all. The taste was like heaven, I hadn't tasted coffee like this in a long time; it gave you a real morning boost. We thanked James but said we had nothing to give in return.

He said, 'I don't want anything from you. I don't want you to think I'm after anything, if you get what I mean.' We understood what he was saying and then he asked me if he could take me out one evening when I wasn't working, as a kind of apology for what had occurred in the cinema. He assured me there were no ulterior motives, that he just wanted to take me for dinner. I looked at Lisa and felt guilty that she wouldn't be able to come, before James thankfully asked her, 'What about you, would you like to come too?'

I smiled at Lisa as she said, 'Yes, I would love to, thank you so much. You are very kind.'

So, we arranged this double dinner date for the Friday evening as we had the weekend off. Lisa was going back home on Saturday morning to see Erich and she would return on Sunday afternoon, so it had to be Friday evening. James arranged to pick us up around 7 pm.

He looked at his watch: 'Jeez, I gotta go. They'll kill me if I'm late!' He didn't say where he had to go but judging by the size of the vehicle, he must have been delivering military supplies of some sort. He jumped up into the cab and started the engine, diesel fumes belching out from the exhaust pipe. We covered our noses but managed to wave as he drove off down the lane.

I turned to Lisa. 'Well, that was weird wasn't it' We laughed about it and later on, when Himmel, Petra and Kirsten suddenly appeared from out of the woods at the back of the lodge, we told them all about it.

Himmel teased me about my admirer. I assure her that I was not looking for a date. She asked, 'Hmm, why is that? Do you like someone else, Tia?' I turned bright red, but luckily the others were playing ball and didn't notice me blushing.

'I think I may have another admirer; I'm not really sure at the moment,' I replied.

At that Himmel smiled broadly, a cheeky smile, a smile that always gave me butterflies deep within my stomach. Was I falling in love with Himmel and was she falling in love with me? I think we both knew the answer but, for the time being, we were happy teasing each other, flirting, stealing the odd kiss and enjoying our youth.

When Lisa announced that she would be away for the weekend, Himmel asked what Tia would be doing. Tia told her she would be staying behind at the lodge, so Himmel suggested Tia come and stay with her and her family for the two days rather than in the lodge on her own. Tia agreed and Himmel announced, 'Right, that's settled then. I'm sure Lisa would rather you be with us than on your own while she's away.' Lisa smiled and agreed.

For the dinner date on the Friday James had borrowed a car to pick the girls up. They thought they were going to some small-time restaurant with a menu to match yet ended up at a house as guests of James and some of his friends in the military. Between them they had cooked up the American favourite of hamburgers with cheese and salad and had procured some champagne specially for the evening. The soldiers treated the girls like royalty, marvelling at their English then swapping stories of the war and their home lives. The girls had never tasted American food like this and neither had eaten beef for some time; in fact; they couldn't decide when they had last tasted it. There were also bottles of Coca-Cola which the girls had never tasted before. Lisa recalled:

> We were totally spoiled. James and his friends had 'barbecued' the hamburgers; they cooked them outside

on a kind of standing grill made from what looked like a dustbin. The round bread they put them in was partially toasted. They melted cheese on them, added a salad garnish and handed them to us. We had one glass of champagne each then drank this Coca-Cola, a very popular American fizzy drink. Oh, it was delicious! This was our first but not last taste of this drink. We talked with James and his friends and many remarked how Berlin gave them the blues. I asked them what they meant, and they explained that it was depressing there in the city. Things were becoming tense with the Russians and the Americans believed that soon things would get worse. James asked us if we had been to Hamburg which lay farther to the north. We told him we had never been there due to the war and travelling anywhere had been limited severely. He suggested Hamburg was going to be the place to be. He told us work was plentiful there, there were some beautiful lakes to swim in and there was some good night life starting to emerge with cafés and restaurants opening everywhere. He told us we should give it some serious thought. We stayed talking until around 10 pm when we said we would have to be getting back to the lodge as Lisa was going away the following morning. We shook hands and everyone was so nice to us; we thanked them for a lovely evening of American culture, then James drove us home. We were both very tired and when James dropped us off, he told us he would come and visit us again soon, if it was okay. We told him he could visit anytime, thanking him again for a memorable evening out. When we got in, we put on our nighties and went straight to bed with our stomachs full. Neither of us had eaten that well in a long time – we felt tired and fat and were asleep within minutes.

The next morning Lisa's father arrived around 11 o'clock to pick Lisa up while Tia went off to work at the cinema for the afternoon matinee. She left on her bicycle on her own for the first time; it felt odd without her friend and she began to feel slightly sad. Her spirits perked up when she arrived at the cinema, where one of the other girls would show her how the ticket office was run. She was happy that today of all days she would not be on refreshments duty. Tia enjoyed selling tickets to the moviegoers and at the end of the film she helped clean and sweep up before making her way outside into the sunshine. Himmel was outside waiting for her on her bicycle:

> Himmel said, 'I thought I'd come and meet you; we can go back to your place so you can get some things then we can go to mine.' I was happy to see Himmel and as we cycled back to the lodge I talked about what James Conolly and his friends had said about Hamburg. Himmel said, 'Hamburg is lovely, but it's lovely here too, don't you think?' I agreed with her but then I mentioned the Russians and their geographical desires on Berlin and how it might all get worse. We had all been issued identity cards but as we had never left Berlin proper, we had yet to use them.
> Himmel said, 'We can talk about it later and then speak with Lisa and Kirsten and see what they think.'
> When we arrived at the lodge I quickly went inside, grabbed some night clothes and underwear then we went to Himmel's. I loved going to Himmel's house as her family were so warm and friendly. We all sat in the living room with the wireless on in the background, talking about our lives. Himmel's sister Monica then played some pieces on the piano while we listened, deep in our own thoughts. Afterwards, we all sat down in the dining room for dinner. It wasn't a big meal, but it was enough and by 9 o'clock I felt myself dozing off.
> Himmel's father remarked, 'Poor girl. That Herr Schirner is working her too hard, it seems.' They all laughed then he said to Himmel, 'Take her up to bed; it's been a long day for us all and I'm tired too.'
> Himmel smiled and showed me where I would be sleeping. I had thought that maybe I would be sleeping in one of the other rooms, but my knees began to quiver and my heart pounded in my chest when Himmel said, 'You're sleeping with me tonight, if you don't mind, that is.'
> I smiled, swallowing hard. 'No, really that's fine.'

Above left: The Berlin Gang, probably in 1944. Lisa Kraus is standing at left and Tia Schuster at right.

Above right: Lisa Kraus and Tia Schuster, both aged 16, at Schlachtensee, 1947.

Right: A concerned Petrianna Albrecht after the boat-sinking incident at Schlactensee.

Himmel Boiten, photographed by Lisa Kraus at Schlactensee, 1946.

It wasn't all doom and gloom in post-war West Germany.

A street festival underway near Wansee, West Germany.

Left: Lisa's Aunt Andrea looking out of the rear bedroom of the lodge.

Below: German children run to an aircraft during the Berlin Airlift. (*Photo Dave Sims*)

Above: Twins Ernst and Erich Sauerstond as page boys in this wartime photograph.

Right: The men of Germany fought the war, but the women rebuilt the country.

US armour in West Germany. (*Photo Farley Fox*)

US tankers in West Germany. The mobile canteen in the background was nicknamed 'The Roach Coach'. (*Photo Farley Fox*)

Keith O'Brien (top) and Dave Sims (below) enjoyed relationships with German girls.

Deborah Klinsmann (left).

Roberta Steel (left) and Martina Henderson. Roberta had a passionate relationship with a young German she met in post-war West Germany.

The Tsar Bomba: the sheer size and power of this weapon was terrifying, yet it remained more a political statement.

Above left: Joel in a post-war photograph.

Above right: Kirsten Albrecht.

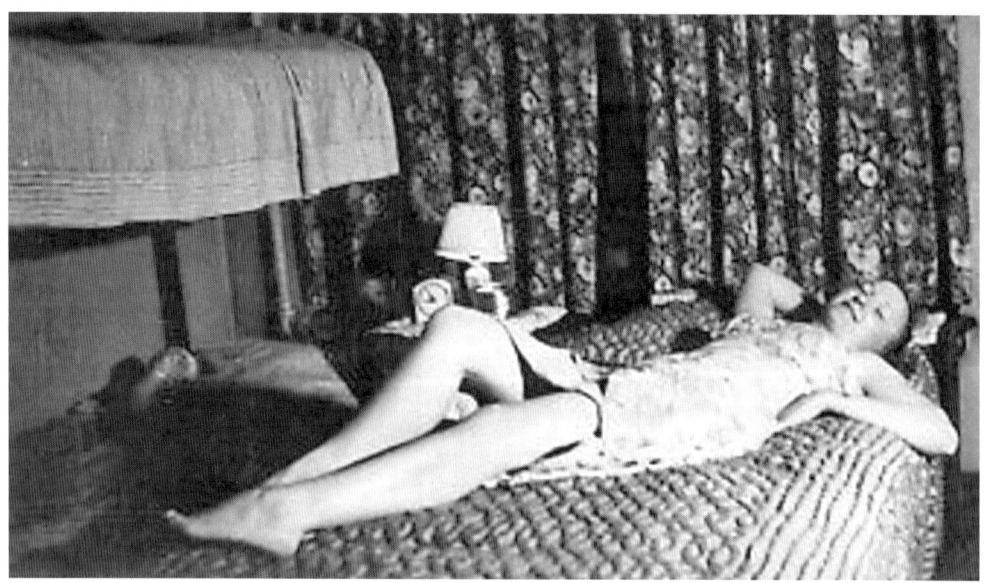

A young Petrianna Albrecht posing.

Above: Christa Hubst playing with children in a Hamburg park.

Above right: Christa Hubst in wartime BDM uniform.

Right: A teenaged Petrianna poses for a photograph in Hamburg.

Above left: German children on their way to school in post-war West Germany.

Above right: Western influences, particularly through music, spawned a youth culture in West Germany that alienated typical German values.

The Hamburg café/restaurant where Himmel, Tia, Kirsten and Lisa worked.

Above: The jukebox became a primary fixture in 1950s youth culture.

Right: The Star Club was just one of many venues in Hamburg which catered to the musical tastes of Germany's post-war youth culture.

Bill Hayley and the Comets performing in Hamburg. The band proved popular with German teenagers and played to packed audiences.

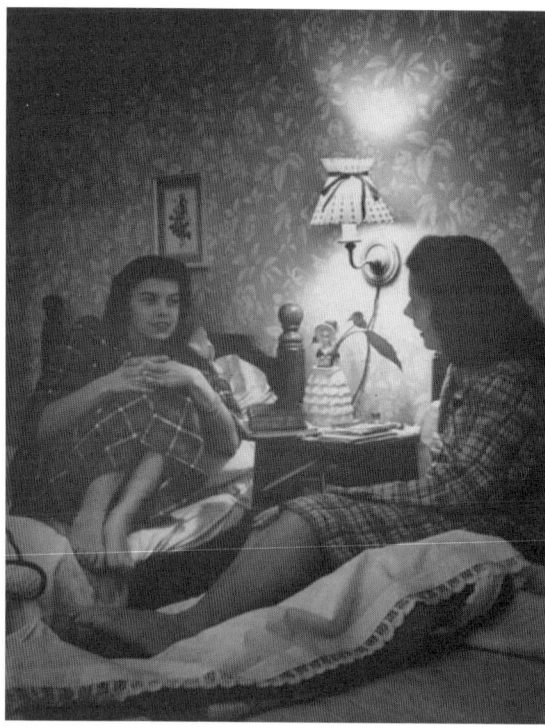

Above: A young Imogen Brietzl in her grandmother's garden.

Left: Sleepovers for girls were the prerequisite to many a cohabitation in the Cold War years. Groups of girls often worked and lived together.

Imogen Brietzl sporting dyed blond hair and American-style clothing sitting in the doorway of a Hamburg house.

Above left: Lisa Kraus with her son Bobbi.

Above right: Daydreaming of a future beyond her borders.

Below left: That derogatory catchphrase!

Below right: The grim effigy that was the Berlin Wall snakes its way along a Berlin street.

Above: Two girls play alongside the hated Berlin Wall.

Left: Ilona Staller releases a dove at a West German checkpoint.

Right: Sharon Tate was butchered along with her unborn child by the Manson Family. Her murder effectively destroyed Flower Power's notion of love and peace.

Below: 'Our affection for one another was nothing to do with lust. Our love just happened to be for one another rather than a man.'

Above: Two girls kiss for the camera. The reality was that rights for gay and lesbian couples was a hard-fought battle.

Below left: Kirsten and Imogen hold hands in a study by Himmel Boiten.

Below right: Two couples in West Germany make their point.

Himmel opened the door to her room and closed it behind us. She switched on the lamp which stood in the corner. It was a warm evening, the soft glow of the electric lamp adding to the cosiness of the scene. She pulled back the bedsheets and began to undress. I watched her, momentarily thinking what a beautiful body she had. I unbuttoned my blouse and slipped off my skirt, placing both on the chair at the side of the bed. I felt so nervous, my mind was racing, *How do I deal with this? I am not going to be able to sleep a wink.*

Himmel must have noticed my quivering body. 'Are you alright? You're shaking, my dear Tia.'

'I'm fine Himmel, really I am,' I said.

Then she knelt down on the bed and asked, 'Tia, what do you think of me, really? Is it the fact you are with me alone that is making you tremble so much? I don't want you to feel intimidated or uncomfortable. If you would like to sleep in another room, I can sort it out for you; it will be no trouble.'

I joined her on the bed. 'The reason I am shaking so much, Himmel, is that I have feelings for you. You will probably think me stupid. I've tried, believe me, I've tried, but every single time I am with you my heart pounds and my knees quiver. I'm so sorry.'

Himmel, still kneeling on the bed, took my hand. 'I thought I had made my feelings quite obvious to you, but maybe I didn't try hard enough. The point is, Tia, I feel exactly the same for you; whether it is right or wrong, I don't really care.'

With that Himmel leaned toward me, our lips touched, we embraced, in instinctive intimacy. The real kisses sent shivers of excitement through my whole body. As we snogged, I remembered how sweet Himmel's mouth and saliva tasted in comparison to that of a male which resembled acid reflux. As we kissed, we caressed each other, we helped each other out of our underwear, casting our bras aside. Himmel lay me down and we continued kissing for some minutes, then she kissed my neck, the circular motions she made with her tongue sending ripples of ecstasy through my entire being. I had never felt this excited before. She worked her way slowly down my body, her tongue flicking the rigid nipples of my breasts, tracing down to my navel. The anticipation of what I knew was going to happen next surged uncontrollably within me as if some form of emotional tsunami. No one had ever gone down on me before, and as Himmel's tongue gently danced about my coin slot, all eight thousand clitoral nerves tingling, I threw back my head, gripping my hair with my hands. I had to fight to stop myself crying out with the pleasure. I was aware of whispering a string of expletives, which included the usual, 'Oh, yes, fuck, that feels good!' In fact, I thought to myself, *Wow! One hour ago we were just friends, now here I am with Himmel slurping away between my thighs.* When Himmel returned to kissing my mouth, I seized the initiative. I turn her onto her back and ran my fingers down between her thighs. I looked down at her and thought, *God, you are so beautiful. Am I dreaming this? Is it real?* I worked my way down her body with my mouth. Only a girl understands how to pleasure another girl. I felt Himmel's body convulse with pleasure. I pray no one heard us, though I don't think I would have stopped had the Virgin Mary herself walked in on us.

Afterwards, we lay on the bed, sweating, in one another's arms, stroking one another's hair and playing with each other's fingers. We didn't need to say anything: we knew we were in love, we always had been. We just wanted to enjoy this moment alone, but knew we had difficult decisions to make in the future, decisions which might affect the way some of our friends and family viewed us.

> *No way to tell where she starts and I begin,*
> *writhing bodies entwined skin on skin.*
> *Her heady aroma blinds the senses,*
> *a deep exploration of hidden crevices.*
> *Bedsheets entangled with ecstasy,*
> *every curve fits so perfectly.*
> *Her touch pure electricity,*
> *burning with fierce intensity.*
>
> *Electricity* AV X

Tia and Himmel made the most of the two nights they shared together. When Lisa returned to the lodge on the Sunday, they were waiting for her outside. Lisa recalled:

> They were both smiling like Cheshire cats. Once we were through the door, we all went out into the back garden and Himmel volunteered to make us drinks. While she was inside, I asked Tia how the two days had been without me. She said she had missed me, especially at work, but Himmel had met her from work, and they had had a wonderful time. She couldn't stop smiling and so I asked her, 'Okay, what did you two get up to at Himmel's. You've not stopped smiling, the both of you, so come on, tell me.'
> It was then Tia said, 'We slept together.'
> 'Hmm, well, so have we on many an occasion; it's no big deal, is it?' I replied.
> Tia then insinuated that they had slept together in an intimate manner. I said, 'You and Himmel, you did it together? I knew it, I knew you two were heading for something, in a way it was pretty obvious to me. It's very sweet, but you will both have to keep this secret for the time being; you know what people and families can be like.'
> When Himmel returned with the drinks, she sat beside Tia, took her hand in hers then planted a full-on kiss on Tia's lips.
> I said to Himmel, 'Yes, I know all about it; you two are so sweet, but as I have said to Tia, you are going to have be careful about this. We need to keep this among ourselves for the moment.' Tia and Himmel nodded their heads in agreement, then Tia mentioned the possibility of us all going to Hamburg together. I questioned the logic; after all, we were happy here, we had jobs, a nice place to live. Why move again when we had just got settled? What James and his friends had told us regarding the tensions in the region and how they might get worse over time made us think.
> 'Hamburg is a beautiful city, with lots to do and finding work there is easy, or at least it will be for us,' Himmel added.

The only thing we could do was speak to Kirsten Albrecht later, to see if she was interested in joining us for a reconnaissance trip. Himmel said she had two male friends there who might let us stay for a weekend, but she would have to write and ask first. We all agreed if things were going to start going backwards with the Allied powers and the Russians, it might be a better idea to move away from Berlin altogether. When Kirsten arrived later, Tia, Lisa and Himmel asked her for her thoughts on Hamburg. Kirsten was busy eating an apple and with her mouth full, she said, 'Uh huh, I'll go. Hamburg is great. We'd get work easily enough and would just need to rent an apartment big enough for the four of us.'

Himmel announced she had to get home, and Kirsten said she'd walk back with her. Himmel said she would write to her friends in Hamburg the next morning. She gave Tia a hug and a kiss and off they went. Kirsten didn't bat an eyelid at the two girls kissing rather more than what friends would normally do. I looked at Kirsten and winked at her. She winked back and smiled as if to say, 'I know you know!' Then the girls disappeared down the road arm in arm, chuckling to themselves like children. I took Tia's hand and said, 'Come on lovebird' and we went inside the lodge, locked up and went up to bed. Before dozing off I recall Tia saying loudly from her room, 'We still need a wireless.' I shouted back, 'Well, we can buy one if we go to Hamburg.' I'd had a good weekend with Erich, and I was blissfully happy. I was a bit concerned for Tia and Himmel, but then I thought, *Fuck the world; if they're in love, let them be in love. Does it change anything? Just fuck the world.* Within minutes I was fast asleep.

We rejoin the girls in Chapter 8 where their story continues from 1950.

Chapter 7

Allied in Love

British Army veteran Mark Arthurs spoke briefly of what he termed a whirlwind romance between himself and a beautiful young German girl he met during his service stationed in West Berlin. Today, although a married grandfather and great-grandfather, that brief romance now so long ago is still as much a haunting as it is a now distant memory:

> Her name was Elise and she lived in an area that I can only best describe as rough. It was a deprived area of the city and the children who played outside the houses resembled something out of the Dickensian abyss. I felt saddened at the scene; the grimmest recesses of London's East End somehow couldn't even compare to this. Elise's family had not been supportive of the Nazis, yet these people had been dragged mercilessly down to the tawdry levels of those who did. It was bitterly sad as Elise's parents were fine people. I looked around; few of the buildings on her street remained fully intact, testimony to the ferocity of our Allied strategic bombing offensive and the heavy street fighting which once took place here. I stood there for a few minutes, deep in contemplation on how these people had managed to survive all that they had been through. Momentarily, I felt a sense of guilt and shame, as if a murderer sneaking in to observe the proceedings of his victim's funeral. Elise was a typical German beauty with flawless skin, blue eyes and shoulder-length golden hair. I wanted to bring her home with me and marry her, but everything was against us back then. It was a dream we knew could never become reality. We saw each other up until the day I left Germany. I gave her some keepsakes with which to remember me by and she gave me a hand-embroidered handkerchief which she had made

herself. When we parted, she gave me the handkerchief which was damp with her tears. I still have that handkerchief today. I hope that she had a good life as today she lives only in my memories.

Aero engine mechanics Keith O'Brien and Dave Sims both joined the British Royal Air Force in August 1944, both at the age of 18. Both had entered Europe as the RAF began to relocate to bases in France following D-Day on 6 June 1944. During that period of their service their tasks were primarily in support of combat operations which meant they were constantly being moved from one location to another as the dynamics of the Allied war plan demanded. When the war ended, both admitted to being a little peeved that they themselves had not entered Germany. Upon their return home at the end of the war, both men were encouraged to remain in RAF service as they possessed specialist skills needed to be taught to those who would be replacing them in future. As luck would have, it both Keith and Dave were posted to western Germany in early 1948. 1948 would certainly prove to be an exciting year for the two young Englishmen who had hoped to throw in some sightseeing alongside their obligations with the RAF. It would be exciting but not for all the right reasons. Dave recalled:

> When we arrived in western Germany, it was a bit of a shock. We expected things to have been a little better than what they were. We were stationed at Bückeburg base, which was to the northeast of the town of Bückeburg in the Lower Saxony region. The huts where we spent free time and slept were cold, draughty and sometimes leaked when it rained heavily. It certainly was no hotel. The NAAFI wasn't much better, but we'd go in there and drink mugs of tea, play cards and smoke. My first thoughts were, *Oh, bloody hell, we've really landed in the shit coming here, haven't we?* Either way, I said to Keith, 'We're here now and we'll have to knuckle down and make the best of it.'
>
> We didn't really go off camp much at first and I admit it got a bit melancholy, but this was due to the cold weather: it was bloody cold there at that time and it seemed to be either snowing or raining or in between. We got to know some of

Allied in Love

the other lads and, as spring approached, they would say, 'Come into town with us. We're going for a few beers and to check out the local talent [girls].' We would go out with them and come back absolutely bladdered or shitfaced, as they say.

There were girls in our NAAFI but most of these were the wives or elder daughters of serving RAF officers. It didn't do to get involved with them at all and we were warned off them by the other lads. When we went into bars in Bückeburg, we used to see German girls, but most of them kept themselves to themselves. There was a problem with the language barrier and neither me nor Keith knew much German. We had this little booklet with German phrases in it but going up to a girl then trying to talk to her while trying to find the right things to say through this book was laughable. They would just look at you and start laughing, saying '*Nein, nein*', basically trying to tell you, 'I don't understand you'. We were lucky in some ways as you couldn't have done that a few years previous, as there were these anti-fraternization laws in place which said you weren't allowed to talk to the German people, take German girls as girlfriends or visit them as guests in their homes, things like that mostly. In the end the ban on fraternization was impossible to enforce so it basically got abandoned. It was a stupid idea really, a product of old-fashioned military thinking by the British commander, Field Marshal Montgomery. Monty didn't like the Germans at all, we were told; his attitude toward Germans didn't endear him to the Americans either who felt his views were out of place in the post-Second World War Europe.

Another factor was that good relations had to be developed due to the situation with the Russians; things weren't going as we had planned, quite the contrary really. Should we have expected anything different from Mr Stalin himself though? Stalin was not the kind of political leader that you could really trust in doing business with. We all sensed trouble ahead and I recall one lad saying, 'You wait and see, we'll be at bloody war with the Russians next.'

Keith O'Brien concurred with his friend Dave on the evolving dynamic of Western Allied–German relations:

> We had all seen the films of the Holocaust victims, but to me that should have never implied that all Germans were guilty of supporting the Holocaust, because they didn't. I think personally we had come a long way since the end of the war in 1945; by the time we were in western Germany, it was 1948, and we had to look to the future of Europe. There was only one problem that most of us could foresee in maintaining peace in Europe and that was keeping Russian leader Joseph Stalin in check geographically. We knew he had ambitions toward the whole of Germany – he wanted all of the cake to himself – and in the end we were there to make sure he didn't get his hands on it.
>
> When we started going out into Bückeburg, we found it a beautiful place and the German people were always polite to us and we had no trouble there at all. I suppose mine and Dave's worlds were turned upside down one Saturday evening in the first week of June. We went into a bar in the city which was often frequented by Allied servicemen off camp or on leave. We saw these two German girls and I said hello to the one of them and was shocked to get a hello back in English. I asked her, 'Blimey, do you speak English?' to which she replied, 'Of course I do, silly' and they then laughed. I asked them if Dave and I could join them and so we introduced ourselves and asked them their names. The one who had said hello to me introduced herself as Deborah Klinsmann and her friend said her name was Heike Friedl. I had to admit I was immediately smitten with Deborah Klinsmann; she was lovely and when I asked her age, she said she was 24 and her friend piped up and said she was 23. I thought to myself, *Great! At least we're not too old for them* and then I asked if they would like a drink each on us, to which they both replied, 'Yes please' and 'Thank you.' I went and bought drinks for the girls and then went back to get mine and Dave's. We then began to talk about all sorts of things. Deborah told me to talk slowly and clearly so as

she could understand me better. We found we had much in common, really, Dave was talking to Heike like he had known her for years, bless him. When the girls had finished their drinks, they told us they had to get home, so we offered to walk them back, but they politely declined. So, we asked them if they would like to meet up again for a drink and a chat, to which they agreed. We were off duty all weekend so I suggested we could meet here on the Sunday, the next day, and the girls agreed a time and we said we would see them tomorrow.

As they walked off out the door, I can remember thinking, *God, help me, I think I'm falling in love*. Dave told me, 'I feel the same, but we have to keep it under control, as we could never take these girls home and marry them.'

'If that girl were to ever agree to marry me, if need be, I would come and live in Germany. I don't care a fuck what anyone else thinks about it either, Dave,' I said forcefully.

I think he was shocked by my remark. 'Fucking hell, you really are in love, aren't you?'

I had never believed in love at first sight and I wasn't really one for speaking aloud about my emotions – not many blokes did back then – but that girl changed something in me. Don't tell me how I knew, but I just knew she was absolutely the girl of my dreams. That night in bed I couldn't think of anything else but Deborah Klinsmann, her blond hair, blue eyes, beautiful lips and smile.

Dave felt exactly the same way about Heike. He admitted the next morning at breakfast in the NAAFI that she had been on his mind 'all bloody night'. The other lads teased us about it, and we said to them, 'Well, we've not long arrived, and we've got German girlfriends … must be our English charm.' They all laughed and slapped our backs and wished us both well with our meeting later.

When we arrived at the pub, because that's what it was, although in German it's a brewhouse, we bought a couple of beers and sat down and waited. Twenty minutes later there was no sign of the girls and my heart began to sink a little. Dave pretended that he wasn't that worried, but I could tell from his body language that he was. We had been gulping down our beers more from nerves than anything and had just finished when in walked Deb – I always called her Deb for short – and Heike. We both jumped up and pulled chairs out for them to sit down. I think this impressed them and showed we had manners and were respectful toward them. They both offered to buy some drinks, but we insisted we pay for them. It felt more relaxed this time and we told them of our homes and what things were like in England and they told us about theirs. The time seemed to go nowhere and as the girls had to work in the morning they soon had to leave.

The best thing of all is that they let us walk them some of the way home. As we walked, I asked Deb if I could hold her hand. She looked at me and smiled and said, 'Yes, of course you can.' I could see Dave and Heike walking a few yards behind us then do the same.

When the girls stopped and said, 'We will be okay from here,' I held Deb's hands and said, 'Can I give you a kiss? I really do like you, if you don't mind, that is.'

At that she wrapped her arms around me and gave me a kiss. After the kiss I asked her, 'Are you my girlfriend properly now?' She laughed at me and reminded me that I hadn't yet asked her, so I asked her, 'Will you please be my girlfriend?'

She looked into my eyes for a minute then said, 'Yes, of course I will. You are very kind, sweet and you are adorable, you know.'

At that we arranged to meet again the following weekend to go and see a film or something and we headed back to our base, both feeling ten foot taller than when we left.

The two young British servicemen's relationship with the two German girls had not gone unnoticed by their superiors. On the Monday afternoon, after the two young men had finished their work for the day, their commanding officer asked if he could see them one at a time in his office. Both were very nervous as they couldn't think of any reason why the CO would want to speak with them, other than about the girls they were seeing. Keith recalled the interview as he was first into the office for what he called 'a chat without the coffee':

> The CO asked me in and told me to be at ease and take a seat. Then he sat there, lit up his pipe and began puffing away. 'Now, about these girls you are seeing … are they German girls?'
>
> I replied, 'Yes, sir, they are German girls from the city whom we both met recently.'
>
> 'Do you think it's a good idea to have German girlfriends? There could be problems should one or both fall pregnant. It would not look good from the point of view of local relations,' he continued.
>
> I assured him that neither Dave nor I had slept or had any sexual relations with the girls as we had only just began seeing them.
>
> He then said, 'Think about it. You could never take these girls back home to England; they hate the Germans back in England – there's still a lot of bad blood from the war, you know. Besides, it's still early days yet.'
>
> 'Yes, sir, I understand what it is your saying and I respect the point you are making, but I am serious about this girl. It's not just a case of looking for sexual comfort, sir,' I replied.
>
> He then said, 'Well, what if I were not happy about two of my men seeing two German girls?'
>
> I swallowed hard before replying, 'I would think that is a bit unreasonable sir, as both myself and Mr Sims perform our duties to the very highest standard; our conduct has been exemplary and we were both invited to remain within the Royal Air Force due to the specialist skills we had acquired.'
>
> The CO sat there, silent, for what seemed an eternity, clouds of smoke temporarily obscuring the expression on his face, a little like a steam train as it disappears into a tunnel. Then he said, 'Well, we will leave it here for the time being. I have made you aware of my thoughts on the issue, and will just ask you to be discreet as you are still in the service, representing our fine country.'

I said, 'Thank you sir and I respect both your authority and that of my country.' At that I was told I could leave the room. Then it was Dave's turn to face the 'Beak'. I waited for him nervously.

When he came out some twenty minutes later, he just said, 'I can't see her anymore. I'm going to have to break it off before it goes any further, Keith.'

I tried to persuade him that he was being a little hasty over this and asked what the CO had said that had changed his mind. He just sat there and said, 'Oh, I don't know mate. If it came to anything, what would we do? I can't take her home with me, can I? My old man and the old dear would go berserk if I came back with a German girl. They wouldn't like it and would probably disown me.' He sighed. 'I like that girl, but the thought of the trouble it would cause me … and it wouldn't be fair on her either.' Dave said he would tell Heike the following weekend that he would not be able to see her anymore.

I was determined that nothing was going to stop me from seeing Deb. I couldn't get her out of my mind, and I couldn't eat at times. All I thought about was seeing her the next weekend. When that weekend came, I was both scared and apprehensive, as I knew Dave had to break things off with Heike and I hoped it would not mess things up for me and Deb as she was Deb's best friend. As it happened the four of us met up and Dave took Heike aside and told her the bad news. She was upset but dried her eyes and then turned to Deb and said, 'You go to the cinema and enjoy yourself; you have a good one there.' She smiled and turned and walked off home.

It put a damper on the night to start with as I could tell Deb was a bit upset for her friend, but as we settled down to watch a film, the mood improved. We held hands throughout the film and stole the odd kiss during it too. It was an enjoyable evening in all and by the time we walked out of the cinema, I had my arm around Deb, and we gazed at one another as two people in love do. As I walked her back home, we passed a group of off-duty British Army guys, and

Allied in Love

one of them made a remark, something like 'kraut shagger', so I turned and asked, 'Do you have a problem? It doesn't look like you're having much luck, does it.' For a minute there was this standoff until Deb said, 'Leave them ... come on, just ignore them.' It made me very angry, but also aware of the kind of issues that I might face if I ever took Deb back to England with me.

Before we parted I couldn't help it: I tried hard not to get upset but I began crying – the thought of not seeing her again just hurt too much. She was very concerned and said, 'My dear, whatever is the matter? What's wrong? You must tell me.' I apologized to her and then told her I was in love with her and couldn't bear the thought of ever being without her.

'You won't ever be without me. I will be yours for as long as you want me, if you want me that is,' she replied.

I told her, 'Yes, yes, yes Deb, of course I want you. I want to spend my life with you if you will have me after all this blubbering.'

She looked at me all puzzled and asked what I meant by 'blubbering', so I had to explain this English expression which she found very amusing. We both started laughing and then she gave me a lingering goodnight kiss and we arranged to go swimming the following weekend as she knew a lake where we could go. So, I wished her a good night and headed back to the base. As I walked back, I made up my mind that I would go into Bückeburg and try and find a suitable ring which I could use to propose to Deb. I hadn't a clue what size her wedding band finger was so had to try potluck. At worst, if the ring didn't fit properly, I could get it adjusted. I wanted it all to be a surprise for her, though the thought of proposing to her this early in the relationship made me nervous. I looked in a few jewellery shops before I found a ring I liked and hoped she would like. My pay at the time was pretty good and just as well as the ring was not cheap. It was a little diamond and eighteen-carat gold, and I was pleased with it.

The next weekend I met Deb in the city, and we took a short tram journey to where the busy metropolis ended and the countryside began. Germany has some of the most breath-taking countryside in the world, and is simply stunning during the warmer months. We held hands and walked to a lake situated in a meadow around a mile and a half from the suburbs. Deb had her swimming costume on beneath her clothes. I hadn't thought about this and realized I would have to take off my underwear to change into my swimming trunks but there were no trees nearby for me to do this.

Sensing my predicament Deb said, 'Look, I can hold the towel up for you while you put on your swimming shorts.' So, she held the towel around my waist while I fumbled with my trousers, not easy when you're standing on one leg. In the event, I was able to complete this difficult manoeuvre with little embarrassment on her or my part. She did laugh at me and told me I was very funny. Then we jumped into the lake. I marvelled at how well she swam – she was a better swimmer than me by far. She told me that in the girls' Hitler Youth, which she had no choice but to join during the war years, swimming was something they had to master. The lake wasn't that deep at around ten feet, but the water was cool as it was still early in the year for swimming, but we had lots of fun splashing around and seeing who could get to the other end of the lake first, I'm afraid she beat me every time. We climbed out of the water and walked back hand in hand to where we had left our clothes and towels.

It was idyllic and felt a thousand miles away from my duties on the base. I had spent many hours in a stuffy room instructing new mechanical recruits on the latest engines then in use with the RAF, so to get out here into the countryside did me some good. We both flopped down on the blanket and it was at that point I felt was the right time to propose. I asked Deb to pass me my trousers and ferreted in the pocket for the small box within. I took it out and held it in front of Deb's face. She looked shocked for a second, as I flipped open the lid, took out the ring and asked, 'Deborah Klinsmann, I love you. Will you marry me?'

She looked at me then at the ring with a broadening smile and said, 'Oh, oh my god, yes of course I will, yes I will marry you.'

At that I slid the ring onto her finger and to my utter amazement it fitted without any need for any adjustment, as if it had been made for her. We spent much time by the lake kissing; it was wonderful, and our swim was followed by a picnic which Deb had packed earlier. When we headed back to the city, neither of us could stop looking at the other. We stopped to share kisses on the way back and I lost count of the times she said, 'I love you Keith'.

We still had some obstacles to overcome: if I wished to marry Deb, I would be subject to a six-month 'cooling off' period as it was termed by the military. This meant I would have to return to England for a period of six months' leave from the date of application, by myself before I would be permitted to marry Deb. I would also need a permit from a senior military commander who had to be satisfied there were no security risks in the event we married. I hadn't even told my mother and father back home that I had got engaged and had yet to meet Deb's parents.

We put in our marriage application and prepared ourselves for the hard times which lay ahead. Before I returned home for the six-month separation, I was invited to meet Deb's mother and father, Heinz and Inge Klinsmann. Their English wasn't that good, but I liked them, and they were very kind and respectful to me. Deb warned me before taking me to meet them not to mention the war or anything to do with Hitler. Deb's father had despised Hitler and would tolerate no talk of him under his roof. I promised her I wouldn't be that insensitive and at the end of our meeting they were happy their daughter had made a good decision and they gave us their blessing. I shook her father's hand and her mother gave me a hug and they both welcomed me into their family. I sent a telegram to my mother and father to tell them the news, followed by a lengthy letter enclosing a photograph of me with Deb. I told them I would be returning home soon and would see them then. Deb and

I made the most of my last days in Bückeburg before I had to leave her behind for six months; it was the hardest thing I have ever had to endure, to leave her at the front door of her house crying her eyes out, and her mother and father trying to comfort her.

The trip home was long and tedious and left me in a very melancholic state. By the time I had reached the front door of my home, I felt emotionally drained and very low in spirit. My mate Dave was still in Germany and had two months left to go before he returned home. I wished I was him and could still be there. My parents had been shocked at the telegram and the news I was now engaged to a German girl. I think they could see how dejected I looked from the experience of having to leave Deb behind. They made me a cup of tea and then we began to discuss the engagement. As I spoke of Deb and her family, my father sat looking at the photograph of Deb and said, 'Hmm, she's a very pretty young lady' before passing it to mother for a look. Dad aired his fears if I brought Deb back here to live, wondering what people might think or at worse say. My reasoning was I wasn't the only one, and what should it matter to anyone else whom I fell in love with and wanted to marry? I knew my mother and father were concerned but before they sent me up to bed, as I was dead on my feet, they said, 'Look son, if at the end of your six months you are still as in love with this young lady as you obviously are now, you can go back to Germany and bring her back home if you wish. Naturally, we want to meet her ourselves and see what she's like.' I felt better at hearing dad say that and went up to bed yet found it difficult to sleep. All I could see when I closed my eyes was Deb weeping at her front door. That night I dreamt of her, waking up feeling even worse, and I lay awake thinking how on earth I would get through these six months – it would be an emotional hell for me. The next day I wrote a letter to Deb enclosing a photograph of my parents and told her they were happy about our engagement and that they were anxious to meet her.

The six months away from Deb were the longest of my life. Dad kept me busy most days, bless him, and found me some work locally – anything he felt to take my mind off things. Both mum and dad were really very good and helped keep me together. I was some four months into my six months' leave period when I had an unexpected call from the RAF. I was asked to return to Bückeburg due to an emergency which had arisen in Germany. The call gave no reasons as to what this emergency was, so I packed my things the next day and left to embark on an RAF flight back to Bückeburg. I asked dad if he could send Deb a telegram telling her I was on my way back to Germany and would be in touch as soon as I found out what was going on.

> *Six months away from your warm embrace,*
> *can't bear to see tears run down your face.*
> *Know that I'll come back my love,*
> *as sure as the moon beams down from above.*
> *No obstacles will block our path,*
> *true love forever built to last.*
> *Six months and I'll be coming home,*
> *a wandering soldier no more to roam.*
>
> *Six Months* AV XI

The emergency Keith referred to at this point was the first international crisis of what would become known as the Cold War. The Russians had blocked the Western Allies access to the sectors of Berlin under Western control. The Russians then offered a deal, stating the blockade of the railway, road and canal that were critical to the Western Allies could be lifted on condition they agreed to withdraw the newly introduced deutsche mark currency from western Berlin. The Western powers refused, and so a plan to carry supplies to the people of western Berlin, now effectively cut off by the Soviet blockade, was quickly implemented. This operation, which ran from 26 June 1948 to 30 September 1949, became known as the Berlin Airlift. It was indeed a bold plan given the area and size of the city of Berlin's population, yet the aircrews of the United States, Britain's Royal Air Force, the French Air Force, Royal Canadian, Australian and New Zealand Air Forces, and the South African Air Force would fly 200,000 sorties in one year, to provide the essentials of food and fuel to the population of Berlin. Even though the

Russians far outnumbered the Western Allies in Germany, especially in Berlin, Russian aggression throughout the airlift did not materialize and Soviet forces made no attempt to disrupt the airlift for fear of provoking a full-blown confrontation.

Keith O'Brien continued:

> When I landed at Bückeburg, I was given a brief on what I was told was a serious escalation in tensions in west Berlin. The Soviets had cut off the Western Sector of Berlin, denying the Western Allied forces access. I was told we would be helping to supply the people of Berlin using our transport aircraft, and our airfield here at Bückeburg would be playing a major role in what was going to be known as Operation Vittles, the Berlin Airlift. The plan was we would use open air corridors over the Soviet occupation zone to deliver supplies, fuel and other goods to the people who lived in the western part of the city. It was all very exciting, but we all had a bit of fear of being shot down by the Russians once we arrived over Berlin. Would the Russians react by sending their fighter aircraft up to shoot our transports down? At that time, we just didn't know what to expect, nobody did, it was a huge unknown.
>
> From all of the frantic activity going on at our base at Bückeburg I doubted I would get much chance to get some time to go and visit Deb; I just hoped my dad had sent her the telegram explaining things, that I was called back due to an emergency. Of course, she would have soon discovered through the newspapers and the local gossip of what was going on, so I felt relaxed and at the first chance I had I would go and see her, even if it meant having to skip sleep and things. I felt relieved to be back, knowing I was closer to my future wife. In fact, I thought to myself, *Thank you so much Joseph Stalin for being such an obstinate old bastard – you have brought me back here earlier than expected; you have done me a favour despite the back-breaking work it is turning out to be.*
>
> The first flights into Berlin went unopposed by the Russians which was good as we were carrying in supplies

to British military personnel. This was ahead of the joint operations to supply the rest of the city and its inhabitants. The Russians made no effort to stop our flights and we would land, unload the cargo, turn around and fly back to Bückeburg, load up another cargo then fly back into Berlin again. I was able to grab a couple of days and the first thing I did was to go and see Deb. It was quite some reunion, a reunion which made me even more determined to bring her back to England with me. I went and spoke with my CO and he went up the chain to a higher authority and I was granted permission to marry Deb.

When the Berlin Airlift came to an end in May 1949, Stalin had to concede defeat. He had failed to strangle the Western Allies into submission; we had taught him that we would not be intimidated or back down to Soviet demands. This, I'm sure, set the stage for the future decline in Western–Russian relations. Communist Russia became the next big threat to world peace, not much of an honour, is it?

The day I left with Deb felt like finally my life had everything that it needed. I left the RAF to begin working for an engineering firm. We decided to marry in England, but Deb's parents didn't have the money to come to England, so I paid and arranged for them to come over. We lived in Hereford for four years then decided to go and live in Germany in 1953. Yes, there were some people who would give us strange looks when they heard Deb's German accent, as there were still some who had very anti-German views in 1950s England, but it never bothered us. Going back to live in Germany was the best decision we made. Germany is a beautiful place and we were far happier there. Yes, it meant I was far away from my mum and dad, but I would visit them twice a year and write to them every two weeks or so. I found work almost straight away in Germany as a manager for an engineering company and worked my way up the ladder. In just a few years I was virtually in charge of the business. Our story was a success, but there were many others that weren't, for various reasons.

When Dave Sims returned home from his service in Germany, he recalled:

> One of the first things my parents said to me as I walked in through the door was, 'It's a good job you didn't stick with that German girl, you know, as you couldn't have brought her back here. People would have talked, you know; it would have been so embarrassing.' My mother put a plate of food down on the table, but I grabbed my coat and walked out. I went down to the local pub and got drunk. Once back in England, I began to miss Germany. When Keith got married to Deb, I felt really envious, and when he went back to Germany a few years later, I used to write to him. He would write, 'You should come here; you could get a much better job than in England and the beer is good too!' By 1956 I was back in Germany working for the same company as Keith and at that time he was my boss. I asked Deb if her friend Heike had settled down and married and she told me that she hadn't and that she was still single and living in Bückeburg. Deb set up a meeting for us and at that meeting I apologized to her, asked her to forgive me then asked for another chance as I was now living in Germany and had no intentions of going back to England. All worked out well and we went on a few dates and a year later we were married. A year after our wedding Heike gave birth to twin girls. We had our ups and downs as all couples do, but we never hurt or cheated on each other and we had a great life together. My parents wouldn't speak to me for nearly two years or recognize their grandchildren, but they came around eventually, especially when they saw photos of my two beautiful little girls. That broke the ice in their hearts [he laughs]. It all ended well, and I don't bear any grudges; they could have disowned me for life, I suppose [he laughs] but it was all okay in the end and my folks proved to be wonderful grandparents and in-laws to Heike.

Roberta Steel and her friend Martina Henderson were two 25-year-olds from London who had served in West Germany. Both women had decided to join the Royal Air Force together, in their own words 'to see a bit of the world'. Martina was a leading aircraftwoman while Roberta worked in telecommunications. Much of Roberta's work was of a confidential nature, meaning throughout her service with the RAF she could talk very little about what she was doing. She recalled:

> We were both posted to western Germany, serving on the same base at Bückeburg. Bückeburg was a delightful little town and very typically German with lots of ancient architecture. It was a fairytale setting in many aspects. When we went off duty, we were free to go into the town, and this was something we always did together as friends. We enjoyed the social aspects of life as did many young people back then and yes, of course, we had boyfriends. When we arrived at Bückeburg, we were both single; we had been seeing boys back home but felt the long period of separation would do none of us any good. Before I left for Germany my father went on about being careful of this and careful of that, not to get going out with any German men etc. Father was a little old school; his worries really had little foundation, but don't all fathers fuss over their daughters? When off duty, we often accompanied some of the boys from the base on their excursions into town. We did all the usual things, took snapshots of the buildings and ourselves, went into bars and drank wine, all the normal things, really. We rarely came back drunk as we were careful to stick to our limits with alcohol. To be honest, there were not many young German men around at that time – there seemed to be more old people and young women than young men. When we were in a bar talking about this, we were told this was because so many had gone off to war never to return. One old man announced, 'If you're looking for boys, you're in the wrong place.' We explained we were just curious as to where most of the young men were, as there didn't seem to be many around. The old man told us of a place in town where most of the young people went, so we thought we would have a look. It was just another bar but there were more young people

here than the one we had just been in. As soon as we sat down, we were approached by two young German boys. They introduced themselves to us in English and gathered we were in the Allied forces. We both agreed to have a drink with them and we both thought they were very good-looking young men. We met up with them regularly on Saturday evenings and they would show us all the sights. On Sundays we often went swimming with them, a huge pastime back then, especially during the summer months. All Germans loved swimming as it was, in their opinion, the best way to stay healthy and fit.

I admit that things turned romantic, yet we were not nuns, we were young people and we had been through a war and we lived our lives differently to the young people today. We certainly didn't jump into bed with those boy's straightaway, but we had fun with them. Martina and I called it our 'Summer of Love'. Neither of us were virgins yet we weren't tarts either, and whenever we had sex with the boys, we insisted they wear condoms. The last thing either of us wanted was to be sent home to our parents with a 'bun in the oven'. They'd have killed us as back then having children out of wedlock was considered shameful and dirty. There was a lot of fuss about VD [venereal disease] too back then. It was becoming a common problem and all bases handed out leaflets about the dangers of catching VD, reminding all Allied services personnel to use condoms when having sex, regardless of who it was with. I remember one girl once caught what they nicknamed 'the clap'. She came to us first as she was too embarrassed to see the base medical officer. We took her into the toilets, and I said to her, 'If it's VD, I've seen it before.' She hitched up her skirt, pulled down her knickers and I could see she was very sore. Her vaginal area was red and inflamed and appeared to be surrounded by what looked like a thick salival crust. I said, 'This is serious. You have to go to the medical officer right away, and if you're still seeing the boy who gave you this little present, tell him he needs to go and see a doctor too.' She explained that the boy was working on the base and was English. I went with her to the MO's room and offered to go in with her, but she said she would be fine. When she came out, she told me she had been prescribed medicine to clear up the affliction and warned to not sleep with anyone or have any sexual contact with anyone until it had cleared up. She was told to report back in a week for an assessment. Things like that made you think. It was great going somewhere new, meeting lots of different men and having fun but you had to be careful too.

    I did get very close to one German boy but had to tell him it was over when I had to go back home to England. I could never have taken him back to England with me – we would have had nowhere to live, and my parents would not have agreed to us living in sin, as they called it. Few places in England would have given a job to a German at that time. It was very tough for us both when the time came for me to leave. We met outside the gates of the base; it was very awkward, as neither of us wanted to show how upset we really were. We both pretended it was all okay. He gave me a silver ring inscribed with his name, and told me to keep it to remember him by. It was like something out of a 1930s romance movie. It began to rain. We said our goodbyes, wished each other well and then I turned and walked away. I never looked back; I didn't want to remember him that way, so I kept walking until he was out of sight. Once I had got round the corner, I burst into floods of tears. The trouble was he had been the perfect gentleman: he was kind and courteous with impeccable table manners. I had never met anyone like him before and doubted I ever would again. I stood staring up at the dark sky, crying my heart out. I never heard from him nor saw him again. I met someone and we were married two years later but we separated after eight years and two children later. I never married again and have been happy that way. I still have the ring from my German love. I often wonder how he got on in life. If we could all have been Allied in love, there would have been no problems. Sadly, life back then was never that simple, not like it is today.

Writing verse was once a way many young women expressed themselves without making their emotional pain blatantly obvious to those closest to them. Roberta wrote a short poem in her autograph book, a small, brown, leatherbound book signed by all those she had served with at Bückeburg. At the back of the book on the last page she wrote the following poem. Her words require little analysis:

Within the ruins of my soul,
from the darkest corners of my heart,
I will send you secret kisses,
and take you to the stars,
in a colosseum of our own dreams.
We swap sweets as we kiss;
will I see you once again, lost love,
wearing a veil of Bückeburg mist?

Chapter 8

Adventures in Sorority

By March 1950, Tia, Himmel, Lisa and Kirsten found themselves in the city of Hamburg. Prior to their move, they had spent several weekends there with a young male friend of Himmel's named Franz Sturge. Franz had been born and raised in Hamburg to what many would term a middle-class family. Franz had experienced tensions with his family, and while not being strictly disowned by them, he had been forced to move out of the family home. Franz explained to the girls:

> My parents had discovered that maybe I was not the model citizen they had thought me to be. I never had normal feelings toward girls. I liked them, but I didn't develop any physical attraction toward them, and this became noticeable in my community. I had always preferred the company of males, and these feelings grew as I reached my teens. I knew I was different in a sense to the other boys. This made me a target for ridicule. Things reached boiling point when I began a secret relationship with another local young male. We became increasingly daring with our secret meetings, taking greater and greater risks. At first, he would come to my house when my parents were not there. It started off as just kissing and feeling one another. Then, as time went by, I would push a chair against the bedroom door, and I would put on one of my sister's bras and put lipstick and eye makeup on too. If that sounds perverted then I am sorry, but to me this felt completely normal. I felt comfortable this way. He used to really like me wearing a bra and makeup. For months he would come around to my house; I would take him up into my room, we would undress and have sex with each other. I say sex … at first, we would just masturbate each other, and this was enough for the both

of us. We would simulate sexual intercourse. He would lie on top of me between my legs and he would rub himself against me until he ejaculated. Sometimes I would kneel down and he would simulate sex with me from behind in the same manner. It was in most senses quite innocent. As I mentioned, we took more and more risks and one afternoon as we were having sex, we were compromised by my father. He tried the door to my room but couldn't get in due to the chair against the door. So, he forced the door open and that was it: he saw us both and he knew exactly what we had been doing. He told my friend to get out then hurled abuse at me. My mother was told about it and my sister found out I had been borrowing her bras. She was not best pleased but begged father not to throw me out of the house. Father began to blame what he termed as the 'filth of Western influences', that we might have fared better under the Soviets if this is what our young men were coming to. I stayed at home for some weeks afterwards, yet things remained tense between me and father in particular. After a couple of months, I decided I had to get out. I had another argument with my father, and he shouted at me, 'The best part of your generation was wiped out in 1945.' My sister then got involved, shouting back him, 'Oh, yes, those boy soldiers, those true Aryan warriors went into battle and they all died with hard-ons, didn't they father? And look where that got us all!' By now I had enough of my father and told him and mother I was going. My sister was understanding of my situation and continued to support me, and still does. I had a reasonable job and I was able to rent an apartment. When I got my apartment, my friend came to visit. We both still had feelings for each other. It was nice to be able to have sex without worrying about being caught by anyone. This is how I ended up here.

> *On the surface it seems like our world has changed,*
> *but smiles can be fake and carefully arranged.*
> *Evil lingers within the shadows,*
> *just one breath away from hurt and sorrow.*

Adventures in Sorority

Many scars can still be seen,
physical, emotional and in between.
A life that's built on pain and loss,
still we search for happiness at any cost.
One Breath Away AV XII

The girls listened intently to Franz as he told them his story before Kirsten piped up, 'Those two are in love, you know,' pointing to Himmel and Tia, who were now sitting awkwardly, blushing bright red.

Franz smiled and replied, 'I have known Himmel for many years; she is a loyal and wonderful friend. Tia, you are a lucky girl, I will say that for you, but you both need to be careful about how you behave in public. Hamburg is changing, society is changing, youth is changing, yet we are a long way from where we should be at this time, if you understand me.'

Tia and Himmel nodded in agreement as they sat holding hands on Franz's settee. It was Franz who had helped the girls organize accommodation in Hamburg and introduce them to potential employers.

Tia, Himmel, Kirsten and Lisa had given up their jobs and lives in Schlactensee and had moved into an apartment building which still stands today in the Barmbek-Süd quarter of the borough of Hamburg-Nord. The apartment was five kilometres from Hamburg city centre. To begin with the girls had few of the comforts which they had enjoyed at Schlactensee. The four of them managed to find work at a busy Hamburg restaurant which had recently re-opened following major rebuilding work. The restaurant became a popular haunt for Allied soldiers on R&R and the girls found it a busy if sometimes challenging environment. Himmel had experience of working in food outlets, but to the others it was a baptism of fire, often where stress, frustration and discomfort went hand in hand. Himmel worked out front as a waitress where her figure and good looks made her popular with the male diners. Lisa, Tia and Kirsten were allotted various tasks in the kitchen, tasks which included washing up, preparing food and assisting the chef. Tia recalled their first day at the restaurant:

> Himmel knew what to do as she had some experience of this type of work, but Lisa, Kirsten and I had to learn it all from scratch. There was another young girl who worked in the kitchen and her name was Imogen Brietzl. Imogen was

a tall, pretty, dark-haired 20-year-old from Hamburg whose parents, sister and brother had all been killed in the Allied bombing in late 1943. She had lived with her grandparents in the city after the death of her parents and siblings. She was really nice and very kind, helping us with all the things we needed to know. Kirsten seemed to really click with Imogen; both appeared to have similar personalities with that esoteric sense of humour which tended to irritate a lot of people. On our first day we learned the basics as the chef grumbled his way through his own tasks as chefs always do. We were given two breaks in our day where we could sit down in a small room situated at the back of the kitchen and have a drink and some food. It was during our first twenty-minute break where we talked about home and where we came from.

We had missed the events back in Berlin such as the blockade and subsequent airlift by a hair's breadth, it seemed. Lisa became a little depressed at the time as she had written letters to Erich which had gone unanswered for around a month. When she finally received a pile of letters back from Erich, he explained that the situation in Berlin was very tense and he could not be sure how long the mail might take to reach her. He explained that the Western powers were supplying the city by air and there was nothing to worry about. We had been issued with passes which would allow us to come and go through the Western sectors so there were no real problems with visiting our parents and things. Lisa began visiting Erich again once the blockade of the city had been lifted. During the emergency Erich had advised Lisa to stay in Hamburg. It was also during the previous year [1949] that the FDR [Federal Deutscher Republik] and GDR [German Democratic Republic] were formed in Germany. The FDR, which we lived under, was established from the zones of Germany occupied by the British, American and French after the war. The GDR, also known as the Deutsche Bundesrepublik or DBR, was occupied by the Soviets who occupied eastern Germany. We were thankful that we and our families were not under the GDR. Also, even better was the fact that rationing was now at an end [rationing ended in Germany in January 1950], we were in a secure city with a growing local economy and we had jobs which were well paid for the time. With the four of us sharing a second-floor apartment and pooling our resources, it meant we could live well and afford to go out and buy ourselves new clothes and shoes, and enjoy a good social life into the bargain.

Imogen told us of the horror and trauma of losing her family and how she had lived with her grandparents ever since. She expressed a wish to move out of her grandparents' home but by herself was unable to afford rent on an apartment at the time. I felt sad for Imogen: you could see she was doing her best to be strong whenever she spoke of her family, yet her eyes betrayed her true emotions. Her eyes were so sad, and she was often tearful. It was Kirsten who suggested she could move in with us, saying, 'She can share my room; there's lots of space and it would be great fun.'

Himmel, Lisa and I didn't mind at all and so we said to Imogen, 'If you would like to come and live with us, you would be welcome.'

Imogen began to cry, saying, 'What, you would do that for me?'

We all said yes at the same time. At that, we linked our little fingers into a symbol of female solidarity, inviting Imogen to add her little finger which she did without hesitation. Kirsten then said, 'Agreed it is then! You can move in with us as soon as you're ready.' At that we went back to work, reminded by the chef that we were a minute and a half late back from our break.

The rest of that first day went by well and as that first week progressed, we learned to help make all kinds of foods and pastries and to help prepare and cook various meals. Life seemed to be looking up for us and when we visited our parents, they remarked on how well we looked and what nice clothes and shoes we wore. Our parents had been very apprehensive about our move to Hamburg; Himmel's parents in particular didn't want her to leave home. They had hoped she might settle down and marry – they knew nothing of the romance that had flourished between us at that time – but we were all too busy having fun to worry over these things that we knew some day we would have to face.

At the end of our first full week at the restaurant, we invited Imogen to the apartment to see what she thought of it. As I had explained to Kirsten before this, how did we tell Imogen that Himmel and me were romantically linked? What if she didn't like it and might it affect our jobs if she didn't? Breaking this to Imogen was my greatest worry – after all, she had not known us very long. Imogen came back to the apartment on the Saturday afternoon after work. We all had a bicycle which was our main mode of transport around Hamburg. As we reached the apartment block, we left our bikes in the entrance hall and made our way up the stairs. As Kirsten opened the door to our home from home, Imogen gasped at how big the rooms were and the fact that we had a balcony which overlooked the street outside. She beamed, 'Oh, this is wonderful! I love it here.' She clasped her hands together like an excited child as she looked around.

Then Kirsten in her typically flippant way announced, 'By the way, those two are in love,' pointing to me and Himmel before exclaiming, 'But I'm fine with it and so is Lisa; we're all the best of friends here. Fuck what anyone else thinks – we don't care!'

Imogen didn't seem worried about it at all and said, 'Oh, god, this is so crazy, but you are all so lovely and you are all so kind. When can I move in? I can move in as soon as you'll let me.'

Before the rest of us could say anything, Kirsten said, 'That's good. You can move in tomorrow if you want.'

Imogen looked at us for reassurance so we said, 'If you want to move in tomorrow, we'll help you with your things.'

Kirsten then announced, 'Then it's all agreed: tomorrow it is then!' She then made coffee for everyone. Gone was the dreadful *ersatz* acorn coffee which had almost stripped our palates of their taste buds – now we had real coffee again. We sat together drinking our coffee, talking about the old days. We had to remind ourselves that Imogen had few good memories of the war years and its immediate aftermath, so we tried not to reminisce too heavily while in her presence, though this was difficult at times.

The next day we met Imogen at her grandparents' home which was quite a walk from where our apartment was. It was pitiful really, as Imogen emerged carrying just two small suitcases containing her things. We all said hello to her grandparents as Imogen introduced us one by one. Imogen's grandparents were a very nice couple. I felt they were sad at seeing her go, that somehow she was the last link to a part of their family they had lost in the war. We promised we would make sure she wouldn't forget to visit them. We watched as she hugged both her grandparents, kissing them lovingly. Then we set off back to the apartment, taking it in turns to carry Imogen's suitcases. It was a long torturous walk back to Barmbek-Süd.

Once home, we helped Imogen unpack and put her clothes and shoes away. Himmel opened up the balcony doors to let some of the early summer air in and then we prepared some food. Kirsten had bought some wine the previous day and after our evening meal, she opened the bottle, pouring us each a glass before proposing a toast to our new friend and flatmate. Imogen downed her wine as if it were water, prompting a bemused Kirsten to refill her glass. The second glass was soon emptied and Kirsten refilled Imogen's glass a third and fourth time. We sat watching, somewhat amazed by this girl and how she could drink. That evening we all ended up a bit pissed, with Imogen telling us repeatedly, as drunk people do, how much she loved us all and how happy she was. She then slumped into the settee, letting out a loud belch before falling asleep on Kirsten's shoulder. We sat up until quite late talking as Imogen snored loudly. At 1 am, we finally decided to go to bed. We carried Imogen into Kirsten's room, put her to bed and said our goodnights to each other. Himmel and I washed up and finally got to bed at 1.45 am. We undressed and slid beneath the blankets, soon falling fast asleep in each other's arms. It had been a tough first week, but we were blissfully happy.

On Sunday morning, as the sounds of the city below began to steadily permeate the apartment, the girls were slowly roused one by one. Himmel woke first, going straight into the kitchen to make coffee for the others. Sunday morning was the day the girls enjoyed the most, as Himmel explained:

> Our apartment on a Sunday morning resembled sorority bliss. We would lounge around in just our bras and knickers, drinking cups of coffee and flicking through the morning newspaper. The newspaper was always left at the bottom of the stairs on the doorstep. Each Sunday morning we would take turns to fetch the newspaper. This Sunday it was Lisa's turn; she threw on her gown and made her way wearily down the stairs to the front door. As she had fetched the paper, she had the privilege of reading it first. She threw the paper down on the table and cursed. I asked her what the matter was, and she held up the front page, emblazoned with the news that war had broken out between North and South Korea and that America and Britain were involved. China and Russia were aiding the North Koreans. It seemed the scourge of Communism was cropping up all over the world. We weren't interested in the war: as long as it stayed away from us, we didn't want to know about it. It seemed people had still not learned valuable lessons.
>
> Kirsten was busy slicing pieces of brown rye bread to make toast for us all. Often the air would steadily become void of oxygen due to the fumes coming from the toaster, which tended to get left unobserved to the point where the toast burned. There would be much cursing and much flapping of arms in a vain attempt at dispersing the smoke. I always opened the balcony doors in anticipation of this Sunday morning pollution. We were usually all up and about before 10 o'clock, but Imogen didn't emerge from her bed until nearly 11 am. She came into the living room wearing nothing but an old brown woolly jumper which was two sizes too big for her. With her arms folded, looking somewhat worse for wear, she flopped onto the settee next to Kirsten, announcing, 'Ohhhh, my head hurts.' Kirsten

got up and fetched her a cup of coffee and tried to coax some of the rye bread toast into Imogen's dry mouth. Watching the two of them was something I adored. They looked so sweet. How they looked after one another. The toast was of course fine until Imogen blurted out that she needed to get to the bathroom right away. Kirsten quickly guided her friend to the toilet where the sound of vomit hitting water could clearly be heard from the living room. We sat there, laughing about it and afterwards Kirsten washed her friend's face, ensuring there were no traces of vomit left around her mouth. Imogen would often be like this, fragile for most of the day. It hadn't occurred to any of us at that point that she was developing a problem with alcohol. When Imogen drank, she drank like a fish. She could drink a man under the table with ease. She drank because alcohol helped nullify her emotional pain. She frequently had nightmares too, something that thankfully the rest of us no longer suffered with to any great extent. It was difficult to discuss Imogen's problem with her around. So, we sent her down to throw out the rubbish later that Sunday afternoon after we had eaten dinner. While she was gone, we all agreed we would have to look out for her, especially if she went out into Hamburg to drink. Kirsten said she would make sure Imogen was okay and that she would go with her if she went out. The two had struck up a close friendship and it seemed the logical decision. Although Kirsten waited eagerly for letters from Joel, the young American private we had struck up a friendship with at Schlactensee, she was always keen to go out into the city and she did have boyfriends, though few lasted very long, which didn't really surprise those of us who knew her. Most Saturday evenings Kirsten and Imogen would go out into Hamburg, visiting the many bars in the city. Sometimes they would be out all night. We never worried as we knew they were together and had probably met some boys and had gone back to their place. They never brought boys back to our apartment. Sometimes they would come back very pissed.

One Saturday evening around 10 o'clock, Tia and I went to bed early as we thought we would take advantage of having the apartment to ourselves. It was wonderful. We had started kissing in the living room and had slowly undressed each other as we got closer to the bedroom. We couldn't get into bed fast enough and had left a trail of clothing in our haste. I had just finished making love to Tia when I told her it was now my turn. She had just positioned herself between my thighs, so there I was, kneeling down with my head resting on my hands as Tia slowly penetrated me with our toy. I was on my way to the stars when we heard Kirsten and Imogen opening the front door. I told Tia to carry on as they wouldn't come in. Just as I uttered those very words, the bedroom door was flung open and Kirsten and Imogen were standing there. It was as much as they could do to stand they were so drunk. Imogen just stood there giggling, while Kirsten shouted, 'Woo-hoo! A chick with a dick!' Then they closed the door and we heard them going into their bedroom and within minutes both were snoring loudly. Tia and I continued our lovemaking to the backdrop of their snoring.

The next morning there was much giggling at breakfast before Tia and I started hitting Kirsten and Imogen with the settee cushions in an attempt to silence them both. Then Kirsten and Imogen busied themselves with painting each other's toenails with red nail varnish. It reminded Tia and Lisa of the time they did the same, only to be rumbled for possessing contraband by their parents. We tidied up the apartment, prepared some dinner and then we all headed off together to the nearby park for a leisurely walk. The five of us walked arm in arm while Kirsten and Imogen discussed the previous night – the things those two got up to were pretty crazy in comparison to me, Tia and Lisa. Saturday night was for letting off steam and Sunday was for resting and family time. In a sense, we were like a family, a dysfunctional one in some respects, but a happy one. We passed some ruined buildings which were still to be demolished and rebuilt. We would also see the occasional burned-out German tank. Imogen pointed one out and said, 'Look, a Panther!' Then she and Kirsten ran over to inspect it. The turret of the tank was still intact with its 7.5cm gun and we watched them climb aboard and squeeze down inside the ruined hulk of this once mighty war machine. Lisa, Tia and I slowly made our way over to the tank as Kirsten and Imogen messed around inside it like excited children. We asked, 'What's inside? What can you see?' We heard them scrabbling around and when they emerged from the turret hatch, Kirsten had black soot all over her hands while Imogen had streaks down her face. Imogen was clutching the remains of a shell and we told her to put it back quickly and carefully as it might still be dangerous. We laughed, telling them they could wash the soot off at the park as there was a spring there. When we got to the park, we used some water from the spring to clean them up. There were many people out walking, old men with their sticks, young couples arm in arm and Allied soldiers out sightseeing and taking photographs.

It is important to note here that a Major Cortez F. Enloe, a surgeon in the USAAF who worked on the United States Strategic Bombing Survey (USSBS), remarked that the fire effects of the atomic bomb dropped on Nagasaki were not nearly as bad as the effects of the RAF raids on Hamburg on 27 July 1943. He estimated that 40,000 people died in Hamburg that night. Himmel continued:

> We enjoyed the stroll around the park but Lisa wanted to get back to the apartment as she had a letter to write to Erich. It was idyllic here despite the scars of the war which will undoubtedly remain here for a very long time. When we arrived back at the apartment, our legs ached as we ran up the stairs. There was a fight for the settee and an argument over who made the coffee. As Lisa sat and penned her love letter to Erich, Tia made the coffee while I made us all sandwiches. The two rogues, Kirsten and Imogen, were sitting on the settee reading a book together, *Der Tod in Venedig*, or *Death in Venice* in English, written by Thomas Mann. They were

taking turns reading to each other. Kirsten was reclining and Imogen was lying beside her with her head on Kirsten's shoulder, listening intently while she read.

Our tea that evening consisted of chorizo, sauerkraut and pumpernickel bread, followed by almond cake, which was made locally in the city. This was a feast compared to what we used to have to live on. As we ate, we recalled the days of those horrible vegetable stews and soups we had to exist on. We discussed making our own bread and cakes, but agreed that by the time we finished work we were all far too worn out to do that.

Lisa was still scribbling away, on the fourth page of her letter to Erich. When she finally finished, she placed a big kiss on the letter, folded it carefully and put it in an envelope ready for posting. As we still had no radio, we played cards or chatted or scribbled in our diaries. It was a cosy atmosphere with the subdued lighting provided by two small electric table lamps.

On Sunday evenings we didn't stay up too late as we needed to be fresh for the week ahead. Kirsten and Imogen went to bed, taking their book with them. Lisa followed a short while after, then Tia and I ensured all the electrics were switched off and the doors to the apartment locked before going to bed. We rarely went straight to sleep and often spent some time quietly talking. I watched Tia as she took off her clothes, carefully placing them on the bedroom chair. As she slipped naked into bed beside me, my thoughts were soon consumed with eroticism. As tired as I was, I embraced her and before long we were kissing passionately. Tia was soon reaching for our toy which we kept in the bedside drawer. Within minutes she was making love to me, and it felt so nice. We swapped round and tried hard not to make any noise which might wake the others. Afterwards we collapsed, exhausted and sweating but fulfilled. As we lay staring up at the ceiling, our only dread was that Sunday evening was always followed by Monday morning. We would all soon be getting up again to start another busy week.

Monday mornings were always the worst. As the girls were roused by their alarm clocks, the city below the apartment was already bustling with commuter traffic. Between them they made breakfast and coffee, and changed into their work attire. Lisa went downstairs to check if there had been any mail and found a letter for Kirsten that had arrived from the USA. She excitedly ran back up the flight of marble stairs and handed it to Kirsten who shrieked with delight while tearing open the envelope. It was a letter from Joel, the young American from their time at Schlactensee. The others gathered round as Kirsten attempted to read the contents of Joel's letter. The only issue was that Kirsten could not read English very well, if at all. So, it was Lisa's job to read out the letter. Joel wrote that he had now left the US armed forces and would soon be visiting as a civilian and that he would arrive in around three weeks' time, in mid-May. He wrote many endearments to all of the girls and signed off, sending them all his love and best wishes and telling them he would see them all soon. There were more excited shrieks then panic as they had to get to the restaurant on time to help set up and prepare everything for the day ahead. They ran down the stairs before grabbing their bikes in the hallway and cycling off toward the city. It was a pleasantly warm morning which made the three-mile journey all the more bearable. The girls were in good spirits thanks to the letter from Joel and, on the way, they discussed what they would do when he arrived in Hamburg.

Kirsten told Imogen all about Joel. 'He's very kind and sweet and good looking too; you will like him.'

When the girls arrived at the restaurant at 9 am, the chef was busy baking off pastries he had prepared earlier that morning. He had two large pots of meat cooking on the stove and more meat was cooking in the ovens. He appeared relieved at the girls' arrival: 'Good morning, my dears, now quickly hurry yourselves as we have lots to do.'

Himmel went out front and began laying tables, ensuring everything was clean and tidy, ready for the first customers. At 9.30 am, she opened the doors, propping them open with a large stone. Generally, in the mornings coffee and pastries were served. From midday it would be meals, beers and wines. In the afternoons it would be coffee, pastries and cakes again until 4 pm when the premises stopped serving food to clean down, ready for closing time. The first customers most Monday mornings were two smartly dressed, well-groomed gentlemen in their late twenties. They always ordered the same thing every Monday morning: coffee and croissants. They would strike up a conversation with the young Himmel Boiten, both obviously captivated by her good looks and pretty smile. Imogen watched the scene from the small hatch as Himmel served the two men and walked back to her counter. The one man was staring intently at Himmel's legs.

Imogen remarked to Tia, 'Look at those two creeps, they make me sick.'

'They seem nice enough to me,' Tia replied.

Imogen then said, 'Those two are not all they appear to be; they would take your dear love away and ravish her without a second thought, you know.' She then began to explain her loathing of the two smartly dressed men who sat sipping their cups of coffee while eating their croissants: 'Tia, those two sitting there are former SS, you know. They will sit there, no doubt reminiscing about the good old days when ovens stank of corpses rather than bread. These are the men who made love to death on a daily basis. I'm surprised they are still able to walk around, but they have friends in high places, even now.'

For a moment Tia stared intently at the two men through the hatch before the chef shouted, 'Come away from there! You're not paid to stand around. Come and peel these potatoes.'

The two men finished their coffee and croissants, then wiped their mouths with the white napkins on the table. As Himmel approached to ask if they had finished and if they would like anything else, the one man remarked, 'Oh, yes, there are a few very charming things in this place I would like to have, Fraulein. Could I possibly ask you to maybe have dinner with me one evening? Of course, it will all be on me … so what do you say, Fraulein?' He sat bolt upright like a dog awaiting a bone from his master, his hands placed on the table, a smug grin etched upon his expertly shaven face. Himmel stood before them like an awkward child, not really knowing how to deal with the situation. He asked her again, 'Well, what do you say?'

Himmel said the first thing that came into her head: 'I am very sorry, but I am engaged to be married and could not take up your most kind offer of taking me out to dinner. I am very sorry.'

The man sat there; you could tell from his facial expression that he was not entirely satisfied with Himmel's reply. For what seemed an eternity his dark anthracite eyes pierced Himmel's crystal blue eyes as she felt momentarily polluted by the intensity of his gaze. He then stood up and held out his hand. Himmel assumed he was wanting to shake hands but instead received a kiss on her knuckles. The two men then wished Himmel a good morning and left the restaurant, disappearing out the door and into the crowd outside.

There was something very unnerving about the whole thing. Himmel told her friends all about it on the way back home after closing. Imogen then told Himmel what she knew about the two men, that they had both been former SS officers. Both were well known locally, and had been questioned by the British authorities after the war, yet neither had been found guilty of any crime other than belonging to what the Allies referred to as a criminal organization. Himmel later admitted that she dreaded every Monday morning and having to deal with these two men. They had done her no wrong yet there was something sinister about them, something that told her these two were no good.

Later, as the girls ate their tea in the apartment, Imogen remarked of the two men, 'They think they can still go around expecting girls to fall at their feet as many probably did during the war. Yes, they would take you out, feed you fine food and drink then they would expect you to let them fuck you for the privilege. Yes, they may wear fine suits and smiles with endless pots of money to throw around, yet their breath reeks of tobacco and their fingers of pussy.'

The other four girls almost choked as Imogen angrily spat out her scorn for the two former SS officers. Kirsten was in fits of laughter over Imogen's remark, saying, 'Breath reeks of tobacco and their fingers smell of pussy. I like that! That's good; I must try to remember that one!'

The day of Joel's much anticipated visit soon arrived. The girls were all up uncharacteristically early on the Saturday morning that Joel was due. Himmel and Tia were able to get time off to meet him while Lisa, Kirsten and Imogen worked their half day at the restaurant. It was an arrangement which kept both the boss and the chef happy. Tia recalled Joel's first visit since leaving Germany and the military:

> Joel arrived in a taxi at around 11.30 that Saturday morning. Himmel and I waited for him to arrive at the entrance to our apartment and we both felt a huge surge of excitement as we watched his taxi pull up. He jumped out and flung his arms around us, telling us how well we both looked. Then he asked, 'Where're the others?' We explained they had had to go to work but would be home later. We then helped him

get his bags out of the taxi and told him to follow us up the stairs. Joel remarked at how beautiful the old building was. When we entered the apartment, he said, 'Wow, this is a beautiful place you have here.' It was quite weird as the last time we saw Joel we had virtually nothing, yet here we were offering him coffee whereas before he was giving us coffee and treats from his ration packs. We gave him a tour, showing him the balcony and he was very impressed by it all. We told him we had a new friend named Imogen living with us and that Imogen and Kirsten were now best of friends and would no doubt be taking him out into the city later that evening. We did warn him though about their antics and he assured us that he had 'seen it all' and that 'nothing could possibly shock me'. Himmel and I smiled at each other then looked at Joel: 'Well, don't say we didn't warn you.' He didn't believe that they could be that much mischief. Himmel brought some coffee and we sat and talked about everything that had happened since the last time we had seen him. It passed an otherwise unremarkable Saturday afternoon.

Joel looked so different in his civilian dress and we asked him about how things were in America. He said, 'You really must come and visit if you can. You would be welcome to come and stay with me. It's a huge place, kinda swallows you up in some ways though, but it's a great place. I think most Europeans get completely the wrong idea of American people. America is far from the perceived vision of negroes picking cotton under a hot sun in the fields; it's really not like that.' Then he asked how Kirsten was and how much he was looking forward to seeing her as it had been a long time. Both Himmel and I could tell that he had the hots for Kirsten, as they say, and we hoped they would get together in some way. The only problem would be when Joel had to go back home: would it leave Kirsten broken-hearted?

As we talked the afternoon away over coffee and sandwiches, we would occasionally look at the clock, wishing for 4 pm as we knew the others would not be long coming home. It was 5.25 pm when we finally heard the clatter of excited footsteps coming up the stairs. Kirsten, Lisa and

Adventures in Sorority

Imogen burst through the door and Lisa and Kirsten both threw themselves on Joel as Imogen stood back watching. Joel, noticing Imogen, said, 'And you must be Imogen. My name is Joel. Pleased to meet you,' holding his hand out to her. The only problem was Imogen's English was not very good and she only understood a few words, so we had to act as interpreter. Imogen said she thought Joel was very sweet, admitting later that she didn't wish to appear too flattering of the young American as she didn't want to risk offending Kirsten who she knew liked him in the romantic sense.

'Right, Joel, we must get ready as we are going to take you out this evening into Hamburg.' Kirsten said.

Joel looked concerned until we assured him that there were plenty of Allied servicemen in the city and that the girls would look after him. The poor boy looked like a rabbit caught in the headlights. Kirsten and Imogen grabbed a few sandwiches then vanished into their room to get ready. When they both emerged thirty minutes later in dresses and wearing makeup, I thought Joel's eyes would pop out of their sockets. They both looked so pretty. Kirsten asked Joel if he liked her painted toenails, placing her foot in his lap. Joel blushed slightly at having Kirsten's slender leg and foot placed so provocatively close to his groin. Imogen just smiled shyly in the background.

By the time the three of them left to go out, it was nearly 8 pm. We told them to behave themselves and not get into any trouble and Kirsten assured us all would be fine. Lisa, Himmel and I waited with bated breath for the three of them to return. We sat reading novels, chatting and shared a couple of bottles of wine between us – it was a pleasant evening. We had the balcony doors wide open as it was warm. In the distance, we could hear the very distinctive voices of Kirsten and Imogen as they made their way up the street. Himmel and I went out onto the balcony where we could see them coming. I recall Himmel saying, 'Oh my god!' The two girls were carrying a very drunk Joel between them. She ran down into the hallway to meet them and helped them get Joel up the stairs. Another resident popped his head out of the door to see what the commotion was all about. He shook his head, muttering under his breath before going back inside. Himmel, Kirsten and Imogen burst in and put Joel down on the settee.

'Look at the state he's in! What have you two done to him?' I asked.

Kirsten explained that they hadn't had that much to drink and maybe Joel was not much of a drinker. We couldn't help but laugh after a while, once Joel began to come round from his stupor. We plied him with strong black coffee which slowly seemed to do the trick. Kirsten and Imogen were laughing, and I heard Imogen whisper to Kirsten, 'Well, he's in no fit state to make love to you now, is he?'

Kirsten replied, 'Who said anything about making love?' They both laughed and were pretty intoxicated themselves.

It was clear that Joel was very tired; it was getting late, so we decided to make him a bed out of the settee and turn in for the night. We could take him out and show him some of the sights the next day. Kirsten said he could always share her bed, before Imogen remarked in her charming manner, 'If you're planning a threesome, darling, you can count me out.' We all laughed.

Our whole lives were full of laughter and that was what made it all so wonderful. The next morning, we were all up pretty early as we were excited at having Joel staying with us. We promised to take him out and show him around Hamburg. As we got up and made coffee and breakfast, Kirsten and Imogen seemed to forget we had, for the first time ever, a male guest in the apartment. Those two just walked out of their bedroom wearing just bras and knickers without a care in the world, forgetting all about Joel. The young man got a right eye full before they both quickly ran back into their bedroom and put on their gowns. Joel apologized for passing out on us and we made fun of him and laughed about it. He complained of having a bit of a thick head but was otherwise fine.

After breakfast we took him out into the city and showed him around. I think he really enjoyed it and was amazed at some of the things he saw. That Sunday evening, he wanted to take Kirsten out for a walk and asked us if we minded if they went out alone. We all whooped and cheered, and Himmel said, 'Well, we might have to send Imogen along with you to make sure you two behave properly.' Joel thought Himmel was being serious for a minute until she grabbed Kirsten by the hand and said to Joel, 'Here, take her out but look after her and please don't get drunk again tonight as we have work in the morning.'

The two of them couldn't get out the door quick enough. As they made their way down the stairs, the four of us ran out onto the balcony where we wolf-whistled at them as they strolled off down the road together. Kirsten later admitted to Imogen that they had gone to the park where they found a quiet, dark corner and snogged each other's faces off. Kirsten also proclaimed she had busted his cherry. We asked her what she meant, and she sighed before replying, 'I was his first, you know. He was a virgin, bless him, and I took his virginity.'

'What? You made love in the park?' Himmel asked.

'Well, yes. Where else could we have done it?' Kirsten answered.

'You could have done it here,' I replied.

Kirsten replied, smiling, 'What! With you four ear-wigging on us? No thanks.'

We had a good laugh about it especially when Kirsten stated triumphantly, 'It's an amazing feeling when you have complete and utter control over a man. That it's you teaching him rather than the other way round.' We asked her if she had enjoyed it, to which she replied, 'Oh, yes, I enjoyed it. It was real emotional, loving.'

'You did use birth control, didn't you?' Himmel asked.

Kirsten reassured her that they had and that she had personally rolled out the 'rubber' as she called it.

Kirsten was anxious that she and Joel should not be viewed as some low-budget Ilona Staller-type porn flick. On the contrary, Kirsten reminded her friends that 'it was the theologians of our world that were often the worst perpetrators of wanton lust'. She then remarked, 'I have written a little poem and it is called, *The Priest Who Made Love to Corpses*. The others gasped at such a title.

Himmel remarked, 'You could get into big trouble saying that, so you better keep that to yourself.' Kirsten shrugged then took the piece of paper with the short verse written on it and read it out. The friends listened intently:

> *The fire was blue and freezing to the touch*
> *the girls that walked through it came out with sore guts*
> *they vomited pink neon, they vomited gold*
> *and their black box secrets were opened for the world to know.*

As Kirsten finished, the others applauded, with Imogen remarking, 'That's so weird, but I really like it.' Joel sat smirking, not knowing what to make of it all. Tia and Lisa had both written poetic pieces in their diaries, and both thought Kirsten's piece was very good, even if the verse itself had nothing in common with its overtly blasphemous title. Himmel inquired as to Kirsten's inspiration for this eloquent verse. Kirsten explained when she was younger, she attended a church choir:

> The priest insisted that each week one of us youngsters remain behind with him for extra teachings on religious laws and practices. This was nothing uncommon back then and neither we nor our parents suspected anything untoward. I will not reveal the religious denomination of this man or where he came from, but his interest in us was not of the healthy type. Apparently, some years later he was accused of being a necrophiliac. Whether that's true or not, I don't know, but I wouldn't be surprised as he was creepy in many ways.
>
> After his death a girl I once knew named Andrea revealed that this same priest had asked her and other youngsters to visit his home once a week for a religious discussion. This began innocently enough until the others slowly dropped out and Andrea was the only one still going. It was always on a Wednesday evening after the BDM sports and fitness when she was obliged to attend. She would go straight from the

Hitler Youth class and into the clutches of another devil who proclaimed to be a servant to god. She was 13 at the time and she told me: 'He abused his power on numerous occasions over the course of many years up until his death in 1955. He loved to get you on your own in some dark, grubby little room where he could paw you. If you resisted him, he would use threats and tell you he had powerful friends who would protect him from any lies I might tell the authorities. Yes, he would remark about the softness of my hands in comparison to his, how it felt so much nicer me masturbating him than him doing it himself. That's how it started then things progressed to him commanding me to kneel before him, where he would then "throat rape" me. I was his secret Lolita, his teenaged plaything, powerless to curb his lusting for me. Afterwards, I would wash his foul-tasting seed from my mouth with the same holy water he used to baptize infants. It was a communion of semen, the activities in which many were complicit. Many of these so-called men of the cloth were doing things like this with young girls or boys – they only wanted the young, pure, untainted ones. The last time I plucked up the courage to shout "no" at the top of my voice. He was afraid his dear wife might hear me and quickly tucked away his ugly manhood back into his robes. I am sure had I not protested he would have raped me vaginally. That creep gave me nightmares. I would dream of being in a dimly lit room with him. An insect would flutter about the room – it was like a moth, earthy brown in colour with black crosses on its wings. It somehow symbolized that I was in Satan's presence.'

Kirsten paused for a minute, knocking back a full shot of schnapps before continuing:

His theories on what he termed 'the modern sin of contraception' were somewhat extreme too. He lectured an older girl that there were other alternatives to contraception. He was basically implying that anal penetration was the best answer to an unwanted pregnancy in a young woman. I for one don't agree: it must bloody hurt, and my question is, is it possible to induce a colonic orgasm? Anyway, something just told you that this was a bad man. The church protects its own, you know, it's like the Mafia. They probably ended up putting bromide in his holy water to nullify his desires, I don't know. Either way, he's dead now and he wasn't acting alone.

Ancient anthropological texts and artefacts clearly indicate the practice of anal penetration having been in existence prior to 100 AD. It was a practice favoured by heterosexual couples, for a variety of reasons, long before its common association with homosexuality.

As Kirsten finished speaking, Himmel stood up and said, 'Right, okay Miss Shelley [referring to the influential English poet Percy Bysshe Shelley, 1792–1822], it's getting late and we best get to bed.'

They cleared up, wished each other goodnight before turning out the lights and retiring for the evening.

It was soon time for Joel to leave. He thanked the girls for allowing him to stay with them for the week. For Kirsten this was a difficult parting. She had no idea when she would see Joel again. As Joel's taxi arrived, her eyes began to fill with tears. Joel embraced her, promising to write as soon as he got back home and would try and see her again as soon as possible. Before he jumped into the taxi to begin the long journey back to America, he turned to Kirsten: 'Thank you so much for everything. You do realize that I am in love with you, my sweetheart. I will come back and see you as soon as I can, I promise you. I just think you are one amazing girl.' He had this silver Saint Christopher medallion which he had worn all through the war. It had been a cherished and highly sentimental gift from his mother. He took off the chain and, placing it around Kirsten's slender neck, he kissed her, again telling her he loved her. He jumped into the back of the taxi, and as it drove off down the street, he waved, blowing kisses to Kirsten who stood watching until the vehicle disappeared.

It was odd, the weather had been sunny and warm all week but now, right at that moment, it started to rain. The rain began to fall heavily; a clap of thunder could be heard in the distance. Kirsten stared up at the darkening sky, the raindrops mixing with her tears. Imogen gently took her by the hand, saying, 'Come on. Let's go inside, cuddle up in bed and read a book and listen to the rain outside.' Tia, Himmel and Lisa followed as they made their way up the stairs.

Chapter 9

Let Them Eat Cherry Pie

The 1950s saw West Germany experience something of an economic miracle, or *Wirtschaftswunder* as it became known. Few in Germany could have imagined that a country virtually reduced to rubble would rise from the ashes to become the world's third-largest economy. It was these early post-war years that would set the foundation for Germany's influential position in Europe today. The first chancellor of West Germany, Konrad Adenauer, was also an instrumental factor in West Germany working toward full alignment within the intergovernmental military alliance of the North Atlantic Treaty Organization (NATO). The treaty, which had been implemented on 4 April 1949, meant that West Germany enjoyed the collective protection and defensive strategy of all NATO members. It was a treaty whereby member states agreed to the mutual defence of any member in response to an attack from an external party. This meant that an ever-increasing number of British and American army, air force and naval personnel would be posted to western Germany on tours of duty. It was these servicemen frequenting the Hamburg restaurant where the girls worked that influenced certain changes. Many of the older sectors of German society were not entirely happy with the western influences now intruding into their cuisine and traditions. Yet much of the older generation had to accept that change was evolving far more rapidly than many had ever imagined. When Tia, Himmel, Lisa, Imogen and Kirsten had first started work at the Hamburg restaurant, it was a very different dynamic to the one where they were now working in 1953. The restaurant, although always busy due to its central city location, went from an establishment conforming to traditional German food and beverages frequented by old bottom-watching peppermint-suckers to that which now catered for both western and German tastes, embracing a much younger clientele in the process. As with many such establishments the restaurant, now designated a restaurant/café, was subject to changes in management on two occasions during the girl's employment there. The first managerial change brought about nothing other than an increase in complaints about slow service and a decline in quality. The employees' opinions were never sought. Subsequently, another manager would bite the dust, quickly followed by the old chef whom the girls had grown to like. The second manager was a younger man with more radical ideas, reflected by the new chef he had brought into the business. The two of them had huge entrepreneurial spirit and while the changes both men implemented were not always easy for the girls and the other employees to adapt to, the business began to prosper. The new chef also began offering new dishes and desserts in order to cater to the requests made by Allied servicemen for such things as liver and onions, traditional English and American breakfasts, English-style roast dinners, and puddings such as apple crumble and custard, and cherry pie and cream. The combination of a new, more versatile menu, the introduction of Coca-Cola plus a range of other soft drinks, including the new phenomenon of the milkshake, made the restaurant/café one of the more popular places to frequent if you were a new-generation German or young foreign serviceman. As Himmel recalled:

> It had inadvertently made the establishment where we had been working for nearly three years into what the Americans called 'one of the coolest places to hang out in the whole city'. It was out with the stuffy, aged, hotel-like formality that the old owner had been happy with and in with this new, brighter décor, and a menu with the kinds of drinks that appealed to teenagers who were not permitted to drink alcohol.
>
> One of the biggest successes, beverage-wise, was this thing the Americans kept asking for called a milkshake. We didn't know what it was as we were only familiar with traditional German beers, wines and soft drinks. One of the Americans gave Tia a recipe for this drink which she then gave to the chef. The new, younger chef was an Italian/American who also spoke fluent German. Before we all went home the one afternoon, he asked us to stay behind to try the new drink. It was made with ice cream and milk with fruits added to flavour it. This was before flavouring syrups really became the niche and so everything we put in fruit-

wise was subject to seasonal availability. The one the chef made up that afternoon was made with imported bananas. He said the Americans liked their milkshakes thick enough to stand a straw up in. So, he made this milkshake and poured us each a glass and handed us a straw, saying, 'Go on, try it.' Apprehensively, we began sucking on our straws until the cold liquid was in our mouths. I have to say we all thought it was the most delicious beverage we had yet tasted and soon our glasses were empty. On the way home Kirsten remarked, 'That milkshake stuff was fucking good. I'm going to make some for us at home.'

The chef also made this dessert called cherry pie. It was a sweet pastry with a sugar-coated crusty top with cherries inside in a kind of coulis or thick cherry juice sauce. It was always served hot with cream poured over it and it too was delicious. The dinners were similar to what we ate at family gatherings: roast pork, roast beef and vegetables with gravy. The breakfasts the Americans and British loved were a little different to our taste. We ate mainly toasted rye bread with black coffee, while they liked bacon, eggs, black pudding, mushrooms, tomatoes and baked beans. It was far too heavy for us to eat of a morning and would take too long to cook anyway. They washed it all down with cups of tea and coffee with milk and spoonfuls of sugar. The new chef was a typical Italian/American, exuberant, loud, yet very easily irritated and with a vile temper. Sadly, it was this that put me, Tia, Lisa, Kirsten and Imogen on a collision course with the man. He seemed to have little patience with Kirsten, as if he didn't like her. Kirsten took an instant dislike to him and she enjoyed irritating him. Kirsten was already a very good cook, while Tia, Lisa and Imogen, and Kirsten too, learned many new skills in the kitchen at the request of this chef, including a more hands-on approach to their work and being more involved in the processes which included the formulation of new recipes. For me it was not too bad as I just took orders and served customers, along with clearing away plates and cutlery after they had finished their meal. I always worked out front and was happy there. The others in the kitchen felt they were being screwed by both the new owner and the chef. They were now doing more work yet were not being paid more money for it. Between them they had to also wash up after the chef, clean all the floors in the kitchen and take out any rubbish. They also had to organize the storage areas and check the food for mould or rot on a daily basis, usually before and after the day's work. If the chef went into the food store and something had been overlooked, he would fly into a rage, cursing and hurling insults at them for it. We would not tolerate this for much longer and that's when the real antics between Kirsten, the restaurant owner and the chef began.

To let off steam on their days off the girls would often head off into the city of an evening. Usually, they would watch a film at one of the Hamburg picture houses, followed by drinks in one of the many bars in the city. The cinemas were just as Tia and Lisa remembered from their employment at Wansee. The one they often visited in Hamburg possessed that typically damp atmosphere with its musky, antiquated scent. The seats in the auditorium were pock-marked with cigarette burns and the resulting fog created by smokers was sometimes so heavy it threatened to obscure the screen itself. One chilly Sunday evening in early spring 1953, the girls walked into the city to watch one of the latest flicks on show. Imogen recalled what happened next:

> We didn't normally go out on a Sunday evening, but we felt like going out to watch a film, so we did. The five of us bought our tickets and went upstairs into the stalls to take our seats ready for the film, which, if I remember correctly, was *From Here to Eternity*, an American picture. It was of course all in English with no subtitles. Luckily for us, Tia and Lisa had spent a lot of time teaching us the English they had learned back in Berlin. We had to learn English for our jobs too, so we had some idea of what was happening in the film. We sat down and began to eat our small bags of sweetmeats, as we called them. These were basically fruit-flavoured boiled sweets wrapped in little clear papers. There was a newsreel which came on before the film. It announced

that Russian leader Joseph Stalin had died from a stroke. As this flashed before the eyes of all those in the auditorium, we jumped up and shouted, 'Hooray!' It was the first we had heard about it, as we had not switched our radio on all day (which we'd finally bought a while back) and had not been out either until this evening. We were far from sympathetic upon hearing the news of Stalin's death. We quickly sat down as people turned round and hissed their discontent at us for interrupting their news. We whispered between us that maybe now political relations between East and West would improve with this man gone.

In the event, I don't know, we got a little bored and distracted, despite the fact we were watching a classic film. There was this bright, shiny, bald head several rows in front of us and it was Kirsten who started it. She took a sweet, unwrapped it and placed it between her index finger and thumb and, closing one eye, she said, 'Target dead ahead, two thousand metres!' She began slewing her hand from left to right as if it were the gun of a tank. As she did this, she blew a bubble with her gum. She lined the target up once again, stopped blowing her bubble gum until the bubble could expand no more – there was a loud pop! – and she launched the sweet. We watched it as it sailed, almost in slow motion, through the air, before bullseye! It hit the bald man's head then ricocheted off into the darkness. We slumped into our seats in a desperate bid to make ourselves invisible as the bald man turned round, angrily looking in our direction and complaining to a woman next to him. They were pointing in our direction as the woman hailed the usher. Himmel, Tia and Lisa were covering their mouths, trying to stifle their laughter. Next thing a voice bellows out while shining a torch in our faces, 'Hey, you lot! Come on, come out of there now.' The usher herded us down the steps and into the ticket office, scolding us for our terrible behaviour. Kirsten offered her apology and told him it was just a joke, but he would have none of it. So, having been kicked out of the picture house, we decided to find a nearby bar for a drink

The mischief did not end there, as Himmel explained:

> We went into the bar, ordered our drinks and sat down. There was this poor German girl in there who was getting flustered at how busy it was, and she was the only waitress in the place that night. Her boss kept shouting for her to hurry up and work faster, shouting, '*Arbeit schneller, arbeit schneller, Hilde!*' She came over with our drinks and placed them on the table with a deep sigh.
>
> Imogen then said to her, 'Tell him he's a wanker. Can you say this word "wanker"?'
>
> Hilde replied, 'This word is an English word. He wouldn't understand what I was saying, so what's the point?'
>
> 'That's exactly the point, Hilde.' Kirsten laughed before telling her again, 'Call him wanker.'
>
> So, we sat back as Hilde continued running around like a headless chicken with her boss barking orders from the bar. As he shouted, we then heard Hilde loudly saying, 'Wanker, wanker, wanker!' We were nearly falling off our chairs with laughter. Being a German girl, the way she said the word sounded more like 'vanka' than 'wanker'. Everyone in the bar besides two young males were Germans. The two men were British soldiers and they must have noticed us talking to Hilde and then her replying 'wanker' to every order her boss issued. They looked over at us, then the one got up and came over.
>
> 'I like that and have to give it to you girls – that was very funny. But do you understand what that word means?'
>
> Imogen chirped. 'Yes, of course we know what it means; it means a man wanking himself, a wanker of course. It's often used in a derogatory sense against a male individual!'
>
> The British guy looked both stunned and bemused: here he was in Germany talking to five German girls who knew English and knew most of the swearwords too. He was so impressed he insisted on buying us all a drink which we gratefully accepted.
>
> Then the conversation turned to the death of Joseph Stalin once again. In fact, most of those in the pub were

discussing it. The majority of Germans bore nothing but contempt for Stalin. Stalin had orchestrated the mass rape and murder that the Red Army had been responsible for, not only in Berlin but many places in the east formerly occupied by the Germans. He was a man who few in Germany would care to commemorate. We drank a toast of schnapps to the death of a tyrant and the British boys joined us in doing so. One of them said, 'I hope the next leader of Russia is more diplomatic than their last one!'

Oh, that was such a great night out and by the time we set off home, we were all a bit pissed, despite the fact we had work the next morning. We all held hands and laughed about the things we had done. Once home it was not that late, and we decided to put the radio on. More death of Stalin news blurted out. We tweaked the channel knob until we found one playing some music. Imogen and Kirsten went into their bedroom to read a book while Lisa handed me and Tia a lollipop. We sat sucking lollipops while listening to the radio. Tia came and lay by my side on the settee and I almost dozed off at one point.

Then Kirsten and Imogen came out of their room and Imogen said, 'What's this then, the inaugural meeting of blowjobs anonymous?' She was referring to how we were sucking our lollipops. Lisa tossed Imogen and Kirsten a lollipop, announcing, 'Hmm, well, if that's what you think this is, you're more than welcome to join.' There was more laughter and chit-chat before we switched off the radio and went to bed.

The death of Stalin on that 5 March 1953 would be headline news around the world over the days following his demise. Stalin had suffered a stroke four days earlier following an all-night dinner with Soviet interior minister Lavrentiy Beria and future premiers Georgi Malenkov, Nikolai Bulganin and Nikita Khrushchev. As the stroke struck the Russian leader down, it paralyzed the right side of his body, rendering him unconscious. The infamous Soviet leader would never regain consciousness. Four days of national mourning followed, and Stalin's corpse was put on display at the Hall of Columns in the House of Unions, remaining there for three days. On 9 March the body was brought to Red Square, prior to internment in Lenin's Mausoleum (where it lay in state until 1961). For the girls, they had greater concerns than the death of a hated tyrant, a man, it has been argued, who was responsible for the deaths of six to nine million people.

Monday evening after work the girls received a visit from their friend Franz and spent the evening drinking coffee and chatting. Most of the chat concerned the restaurant the girls worked at and how unhappy they were with their work. Franz said he might be able to help them get other work as he knew plenty of people in the city. The girls attempted to describe the dread they felt on a Sunday, knowing that Monday was to follow. Kirsten remarked:

> Sundays was a nice day, a lazy day in some ways for us, yet it felt like the day before execution. You knew it was back to work again on Monday and all the same old shit would begin. That chef came into work each day looking like a pair of worn-out bollocks. I didn't like him at all, as he always took his temper out on me. I was the focus of his anger. Another thing was the rats that feasted on the bins out the back of the restaurant. The one morning I was pushing some rubbish down into the bin when this rat literally leaped out over my shoulder. I wasn't afraid of rats, but the creature made me jump. Yes, it leaped clean over my shoulder, landed on the floor and vanished under the gate out onto the street.

Himmel's view was slightly more diplomatic:

> I felt for the others as they had to work alongside the chef in the kitchen. I don't think I've ever met a nice chef – you know, one who wasn't actually an arsehole. Most chefs are arseholes as it goes with the territory of stress and pressure which they self-impose. If the chef is pissed off, then everyone else suffers. I tried to keep the others calm until we had sorted out other jobs, but it wasn't easy.

On the Monday morning the girls set off for work as normal. Kirsten had drunk her coffee but couldn't eat her breakfast as she felt stressed about the day ahead. When they arrived at the restaurant, Himmel opened the door for the morning customers while the other four assisted the chef in preparation for the breakfast service. The first customers in were six young British soldiers who announced this was their first time out in Hamburg since their arrival. All were looking forward to a good English-style breakfast. Himmel took their order and passed it through to the kitchen. Immediately the kitchen became a hive of activity as bacon, eggs, mushrooms, beans and black pudding were tossed into pans. Once the food was ready, it was put on the plates and Himmel took it out to the soldiers. The soldiers thanked Himmel and, looking adoringly at their plates, said 'Wow, this is a slice of home right here. Thank you, miss.' Himmel smiled and told them they were welcome. After they had eaten their breakfast, the one young soldier went to the serving hatch in the wall as he wanted to thank the kitchen staff for the food. Himmel recalled what happened next:

> Kirsten came to the hatch in the wall and this young man said, 'Thank you miss, that breakfast was perfect and really made us all feel at home.'
> Kirsten then replied to him: 'Do you know that the black pudding was made from the chef's wife's menstrual blood?'
> I quickly steered the young man away from the hatch, trying hard not to make it obvious that I'd found Kirsten's remark very funny. When he'd left with his friends, I went back to the serving hatch and said to Kirsten, 'You can't say that kind of thing.' I was trying hard to be serious but it didn't work.
> Kirsten just said. 'Well, it made you laugh, didn't it?'
> I just hoped that that soldier wouldn't complain, but there's every chance he had a good laugh about it too. Then there was this grouchy old German man who used to come in for his daily coffee fix. Despite the upgraded decor which he was not happy with, he would still come in. He was partially deaf, and Kirsten used his hearing impediment to her full advantage. The one time she served him and greeted him by saying, 'Good morning, frog face. How are you today?' He would ask her to repeat what she had said, saying, 'Speak up. Fraulein. I can't hear you.' On another

occasion she said to him, 'I'm feeling hot to fuck today. How about you?' She was terrible but god, she was so funny with it.

Lisa said during their lunchbreak, 'Sometimes I just feel like stripping off all my clothes and shouting at the top of my voice, "Fuck, wank, piss, tits." This place is getting on my nerves.'

We were just getting fed up and bored with it all.

The girls spent the rest of the lunchbreak in relative silence. When they had finished their break, they all wearily made their way back to their workstations. On the way Kirsten stopped and looked at a fire notice on the wall. The notice read, 'In case of fire remain calm.' She asked if she could borrow Himmel's pen, then scribbled a suffix: 'In case of fire remain calm – and carry on fucking.' Himmel said, 'Maybe you should rub that off; it will only cause trouble,' but Kirsten pulled her away by the hand, insisting, 'No, let him [the boss] see it.'

In the afternoons things often quietened down once people had eaten their meals. If there was little to do in the kitchen the chef could either send the staff home or give them cleaning jobs to do, as Imogen recalled:

> He would never let us go early; he was mean like that. Oh, no. He would fill up buckets of soapy water and insist we get down on our hands and knees and scrub the floors and walls. Kirsten used to say, 'I bet he only has us doing this so he can look at our arses and fantasize about fucking us.'

Himmel spoke to the chef later that same afternoon, saying that if it helped, she could always come into the kitchen while Kirsten could go out front and serve, which might help things. The chef talked with the boss, agreeing to give Kirsten a trial as a waitress; if it reduced the tension in the kitchen it might help things. Himmel was at home doing kitchen work as she had done it all before and it was clear she soon became the chef's favourite girl and she often helped alleviate any pressure by preparing things the other girls struggled with. Tia loved having Himmel working with her despite the fact that they couldn't be openly romantic at work. This seemed to improve the mood in the kitchen greatly and Kirsten seemed happier in her new role as waitress. She got on well with the other waitress and all seemed well for a while at least. Himmel explained:

> Kirsten's biggest problem was the fact that she got bored very easily. It was some weeks later on a very quiet morning when Kirsten began drumming on one of the countertops. The boss came through and said to her, 'Can you please stop that noise. What do you think you're doing?'
>
> Kirsten replied, 'I am sending a message out to my tribe.'
>
> The boss shook his head and said, 'Fraulein Albrecht, I don't pay you to stand around drumming on my countertops, so stop it now. It's annoying.' He then turned and walked off but behind his back Kirsten gave a Hitler salute. I saw her from the hatch and was shocked. That was a pretty outrageous thing to do back then. I called her over and begged her to behave and not annoy the boss any further. That said, this is what I liked so much about Kirsten, her wild sense of humour, something all her friends loved about her.

If Himmel had been popular with the young men that made the restaurant their regular haunt, then Kirsten soon eclipsed her. Lisa recalled:

> In a way, the fact that Kirsten became very popular with the boys proved good for business. In turn, this would mean the boss would be reluctant to get rid of her despite her antics. Through Kirsten we received many invites and offers to take us out from German, American and British boys. Some would travel many miles just to see us; it was all really weird. We just viewed ourselves as ordinary girls really; we didn't think we were anything special at all. The biggest problem with us accepting these invites was obvious. I was happily in a relationship and was in no way going to have a one-night stand with anyone. Himmel and Tia were in a relationship and Kirsten was becoming more fixed on Joel, especially after receiving another letter from him. The only real single one among us was Imogen, who we felt was a

little vulnerable and we were thus very protective of her, especially Kirsten.

The funny thing was that Imogen was learning lots of tricks from Kirsten, to the point they would compete with each other to see who could shock people the most. We all accepted an invite out with some German boys one Saturday night. It was alright but we found the British and Americans far more fun to socialize with. We went out the one night with some American boys. The bar we went into was pretty busy, so we had to stand and have our drinks. Kirsten and Imogen got a bit pissed and made a beeline for a table where some women were sitting drinking. We knew exactly what they were going to do next, what they called their 'party trick'. They handed their drinks to us, and the women at the table looked on in horror and disgust as Kirsten and Imogen began snogging each other right in front of them. It was proper, full-on snogging too, with tongues. It had the desired effect: the women got up, calling the two of them disgusting creatures and walked out. Then, as usual, Kirsten and Imogen said, 'Here, we have some seats; let's all sit down.' Our American friends didn't know what to make of it.

Another time we were at a café having coffee and cakes with some British boys when Imogen picked the cherry from off the top of her slice of cake, held it up and said, 'My cherry, does anyone want to come and get my cherry?' Some boys at the next table almost choked on their tea. Imogen just laughed and then popped the cherry into her mouth. We got banned from a couple of places due their antics. Kirsten and Imogen brought out the devil in each another. We couldn't imagine life without them though; it was inconceivable.

Since moving to Hamburg, the girls had been so focused on work and their apartment. They now began to yearn for a break from the normal social scene, to go swimming as they had done back in Schlactensee. Tia recalled:

> We just thought the one Saturday afternoon at how long it'd been since we went swimming together. By now it was

mid-summer 1953 and there would not be too many more hot days for us to go swimming. Our friend Franz and his boyfriend took us to a lovely spot outside the city where you had to walk down a long country track to get to this big lake full of clear, fresh water. When we arrived, a mother and her three children were already swimming there; they greeted us, and we said hello to them. We couldn't wait to get into the water. We had our bathing suits on under our clothes, so we threw off our dresses and ran into the lake. Himmel dived into the water and sped out like a rocket into the middle of the lake, then began to do some fast laps. We all watched, in awe of her; she was simply an amazing swimmer. Franz and his companion both tried to race her, but she was far too fast for them. We then played with the ball, generally splashing about in the water.

It was while we were splashing around that we heard the panicked cries of the young woman with the three young children. We looked over to see that the one child had somehow got out of its depth and was struggling. By the time we could shout, 'Himmel, go and help her', she was swimming out to the child. Within a few seconds, she had the child in her arms and was bringing her back to shore, the child's mother was crying more out of fright than anything. Himmel carried the little girl out of the water in her arms and put her down next to her mother. The child had swallowed a lot of water and was coughing it up, but she was fine. Himmel told the mother the child would be fine but to keep her from going out too far next time. The mother revealed she couldn't swim, so Himmel offered to teach her some time if she liked. The woman thanked Himmel and gave her a contact address to contact her for some swimming lessons. Himmel then jumped into the water and swam back over to us. We all hugged her and told her how great she was and what might have happened had we not been there that day. This was not the first time Himmel had saved someone in trouble in the water. She had saved at least four people from drowning, yet she never expected anything in return and would say, 'Oh, you fuss too much; it's nothing.'

After drying off and putting on our clothes, we went back into Hamburg and went and had some of this cherry pie the Americans raved so much about. We sat outside eating the warm cherry pie with cream, and we loved every single mouthful of it. Franz and his boyfriend had never tasted it before and they both enjoyed this slice of the American dream. The swimming had invigorated our souls and we felt fit and ready for the working week that lay ahead the next morning.

That evening we sat in the living room with the balcony doors wide open and the warm breeze blowing in. We had the radio on and tuned in, listening to this music they called jazz. It was quite good and made for a relaxing atmosphere. Kirsten and Imogen were sitting together on the settee looking through another book. If I hadn't known them, I would have thought they too were lovers by the way they lay with their legs entwined. Himmel was sitting out on the balcony, looking over the rooftops. It looked like something from a fairytale with all the little windows lit up by the subdued lighting. I went out to her. She stood up and we embraced, kissing. Our kissing became more passionate and she flicked her tongue against mine. I whispered, 'Come and make love to me, my sweetheart.' I took her by the hand and led her to the bedroom where we spent the next hour making love. When we had finished, we discovered that Kirsten and Imogen had fallen asleep on the settee. Imogen had her head on Kirsten's stomach, snoring loudly. Rather than disturb them, we covered them with a light blanket. Lisa was lying on her bed, writing a letter to Erich. She said she would be going to Berlin to visit him again the next weekend. We kissed her goodnight. It had been in every respect the perfect day, the kind of day one might look back on when old and think of those perfect summer days of our youth. Himmel and I then went to bed, soon falling fast asleep in each other's arms.

The following weekend Lisa left Hamburg to visit Erich in Berlin. At the last-minute, Kirsten decided to go with her as she wanted to visit her family, particularly her younger sister Petrianna who her parents said was missing her terribly. Kirsten felt guilty at having to leave her friend Imogen behind, but their boss would not give her the time off on the Saturday to go. Franz had very kindly offered to drive them to Berlin, happy to take the girls as he had some friends in Berlin whom he had not seen for some months and, in his own words, kill two birds with one stone. Berlin was approximately a three-hour drive from Hamburg. Franz had to frequently stop along the route when Kirsten announced that she 'needed a piss'. They felt slightly nervous as they approached the checkpoint to the western sector of the city, yet after showing their personal identity cards were soon waved through. Franz ensured both girls arrived safely at their respective houses before arranging to collect them on the Sunday afternoon for the trip back to Hamburg. Kirsten recalled:

> It was lovely to see my family again as it had been a long time since I last saw them, and lots had happened. My little sister, Petrianna, was as excited as a puppy; in fact, she cried when she saw me walking in through the front door. For a few minutes I felt awful – she was my little sister and I know she must have missed me as we always went around together before I moved to Hamburg. I spent the whole time in Berlin with her and I took her out for some lunch and ice cream and in the evening, I took her out to the local picture house.

Lisa's parents and brother were overjoyed to see their daughter and remarked at how well she looked and how finely dressed she was. Her father remarked, 'You must be doing very well indeed in Hamburg.' Lisa recalled:

> It was just as I had remembered it. Very little had changed – all the terraced houses looked just as they did from that day I left back in 1950. I had some lunch with my family and then set off to see Erich. To say Erich was pleased to see me was an understatement. He scooped me up in his arms and spun me round. His mother remarked, 'For goodness sake, Erich, be careful. You'll make her dizzy.' Erich said to his parents, 'Dizzy? I'm dizzy with love; this is marvellous.'

That evening Erich took me out and we had dinner followed by drinks at a nearby pub. When we came out, we were a little merry from the alcohol. We walked back to Erich's and the house was all in darkness as Erich's mother, father and brother had gone out. We stood outside and kissed for a moment. We were both feeling very horny indeed, so we looked at each other, both thinking the same thing. Erich opened the door and we quickly rushed upstairs into Erich's room, slamming the door behind us. We literally tore our clothes off, throwing them onto the floor before collapsing onto the bed. We writhed around kissing and were so overcome with passion that when Erich rolled on top of me, pushed my legs apart and began to make love to me, I didn't stop him to put on any birth control. It was the first time I'd ever made love without using birth control. The sensations were so different; it felt so nice that I couldn't have stopped him had I wanted to. We made love with him on top of me and me on top of him and finished with him making love to me from behind. The sensations tore through my entire body: it was the most powerful orgasm I had ever had. I gripped the ruffled sheets with my fingers and held them to my mouth as I was worried someone might hear me with the noise I was making. When he climaxed in me, I felt the warm jet of semen as if it were going right up inside my belly. For a few minutes he remained inside me, the weakening pulses of his manhood still sending shivers of delight through my body. We collapsed in each other's arms and lay there for a few minutes.

I remarked, 'We didn't use any birth control; I hope that was a blank you just shot inside of me.'

He just smiled and said, 'I don't care; to have a child with you would be a dream for me.'

I reminded him that before you have children you first have to get engaged and then marry. It was then that Erich turned to me and said, 'Look, Lisa, I do not have a ring with which to place upon your finger, but I love you and I am asking you now: will you please marry me? Will you be my wife?'

I looked into his eyes and said, 'Erich, you are one of the most wonderful men any woman could wish to have. I love you very much, and yes, I will marry you.'

Erich was so happy he cried; he'd had visions of me saying no, that I was happy with the way things were.

> *Right here in your arms is where I belong,*
> *your cherry pie kisses linger on my tongue.*
> *In a sea of faces, still feel alone,*
> *but with you my love I've found my home.*
> *With pure abandon I offer my hand,*
> *not just offering a wedding band.*
> *I give you the earth, moon and stars,*
> *the past is behind us, the future is ours.*
>
> Home AV XIII

With hindsight it was lucky for us both that we had reached this decision in our young lives. The next day we announced to our parents that we were engaged, even if I didn't have a ring to show to my friends; rings weren't important to me, love was the most important thing of all – a ring could wait until later as far as I was concerned. Before I returned to Hamburg, Erich and I made love a second time without the rubber barrier that dulled the true sensations of intercourse. This time he made love to me by placing a pillow in the small of my back before drawing my legs back and apart and placing my ankles over his shoulders. It was so erotic. As he slowly moved back and forth inside me, he remarked, 'This is what they call the baby-making position.' Again, I couldn't have cared at that moment: it felt so nice I just lay there as the sensations built up and we both exploded in a shower of cries and moans.

When I left Berlin, I felt a little sad about leaving, but promised Erich I would return in a few weeks' time. Erich promised by then he would have an engagement ring. I met up with Kirsten and Petrianna was with her, so I gave her a quick hug and a kiss. We told her next time we came down she could come back and stay with us for a few days in Hamburg and we'd take her out and spoil her.

When we arrived back in Hamburg Tia, Himmel and Imogen were excited to hear what we'd got up to. I announced that I was now engaged to be married to Erich, and there were loud cheers, hugs and kisses for me. I couldn't stop smiling as Imogen remarked, 'Well, we know what you've been doing all weekend!' That Sunday night I felt so tired that I went to bed early. My leg muscles ached from the weekend's sexual athletics, but I was very happy and felt content with life.

As their alarm clocks summoned the girls from their dreams, another working week began. By now all had reservations as to their future at the restaurant/café. Kirsten revealed that she was no longer happy working there despite being transferred out of the kitchen to out front. The others had also grown tired of the chef's fiery temperament. Himmel remarked that she'd had enough of walking on eggshells all day. They agreed between them that there had to be better employment prospects around. As they began the day's work, rebellion was certainly in the air – they'd all had enough. Kirsten, being the catalyst for dissent, was in a particularly mischievous mood that Monday morning, as she recalled:

> I just thought to myself, *Fuck it; if anyone starts today then they'll get it.* There were lots of other opportunities out there at that time; we felt we were unnecessarily constraining ourselves and that the conflict might be good motivation toward better things. We had plenty of money saved anyway, so we really didn't have to put up with shit from any employer.

As the doors of the restaurant opened for business that morning, it was ironic that the first group of customers would set the mood for that day. Kirsten recalled:

> All they did was fucking moan about everything. The British-style breakfast which they had specifically requested they described as awful. Then they complained about the coffee and asked for tea instead. I took the coffee back and brought them the tea. They finished and then instead of

paying their bill, they began to haggle, saying it was all so bad they shouldn't have to pay for it. I called the boss and naturally he blamed me for the fact that they had issues with the food and drink. I bit my lip to the point where I could taste my own blood in my mouth.

When lunchtime arrived, the girls went and sat outside in the backyard in the sunshine. Some leftover Bratwurst was stacked up on a plate in the kitchen and the chef insisted they take the plate out with them and eat as much as they wanted. The girls sat eating the Bratwurst with buttered bread rolls washed down with coffee. Kirsten then noticed a group of young servicemen walk in through the front door. She made eye contact with one of the young men who smiled at her. She smiled back, the devil within her now straining to get out. As she got up from her chair and grabbed a Bratwurst, the others sat watching in anticipation of what she was going to do next. Himmel described the scene:

> It was useless asking Kirsten what she was going to do as she would never tell you. She kicked off her shoes and walked to the doorway which led into the spacious dining area. Then she took the Bratwurst sausage and started simulating oral sex with it in full view of the young men who were by now sitting down in the restaurant perusing the menu. Lisa almost choked on her food as she watched Kirsten sucking on the Bratwurst, slowly moving it in and out of her mouth. One of the young men tapped his friend busy looking at the menu on the arm, saying 'Well, fuck me. Look at that, look what she's doing over there.' They all looked over and began to laugh then one of them whistled so loudly that the chef came out of his kitchen in the same way a spider alerted by the presence of a fly might dash out onto its web. Kirsten heard the kitchen door open and bolted back to the table where we were all stifling our laughter.
>
> The chef asked, 'What's going on here? What are you up to?'
>
> I looked at him and said, 'Nothing, nothing's going on here. We're just sitting down eating our lunch.'

He knew we'd been up to something but had no proof until he walked back out and tripped over Kirsten's shoes which she'd left by the door to the dining area. He looked down and asked, 'Whose shoes are these?'

'They're mine,' said Kirsten.

'Well, what are they doing down here?' the chef asked.

'My feet were hot, so I took my shoes off to give them some air,' Kirsten replied.

'Well, please put your shoes back on,' he barked. He then threw the shoes across to her.

The group of young men in the dining area called him over and said, 'That girl hasn't done anything wrong. We called her over to ask her for her recommendations on what's good to eat here.'

The chef, unconvinced of their story, glanced across at the girls who were nodding their heads in agreement, then surveyed the young men suspiciously, asking, 'And what recommendation did she make, may I inquire?'

The quick-witted young Brit answered immediately: 'Cherry pie with cream of course, my good man.' They then broke the ice with the chef by asking him about his accent and where he was from, small talk designed to diffuse his frosty demeanour; it was reverse psychology at its best and it worked a treat.

It was then time to get back to work. Before the young Brits left, Kirsten thanked them, to which one said, 'Blimey, that was quite some show you put on. You're certainly not shy, are you.'

Luckily for Kirsten there were no requests to take her out on a date. It was a situation which might easily have resulted in some misconstrued intentions.

The second half of the day appeared to go well until more customers came in and one requested some bacon which they had ran out of earlier. A delivery was not immediately forthcoming and the disgruntled customer felt that this was just not good enough. As the old man moaned and grumbled as to the virtues of bacon, Kirsten stood waiting impatiently with her notepad in hand. She recalled:

He kept on and on and I asked whether he would like to consider something else from the menu. His grumbling continued to the point where I just said, 'Oh, well, would a pig's ear suffice then?' He sat there with his mouth agape, his false teeth clearly slipping from the roof of his mouth and he went very red in the face. He stood up and said, 'Disgusting! Come on, we're leaving.' Like little elves the others with him followed closely behind, walking out the door. The chef didn't hear any of this and as the boss wasn't around, I thought to myself, *Well, Kirsten, that's one up to you.*

The last straw came an hour before the restaurant closed for the day. The boss had decided to come in to check on things. Kirsten thought that maybe the miserable old man whom she had upset earlier had reported her. The boss was his usual overdemanding, unpleasant self. When the girls had a few moments to relax, he demanded they get some buckets and mops and get on with cleaning jobs. Kirsten filled a bucket with water and got down on her hands and knees to clean the pipes that ran along the skirting boards of the establishment. She called across to one of the other girls doing the same over the other side of the room, 'I'm Cinderella, you know; in fact, look at us – we're two Cinderellas. He [the boss] is probably watching us, you know; he likes to get us down on our knees, and is probably fantasizing about fucking us from behind again.' The other girl smiled nervously at Kirsten's scorn as they continued cleaning. Next thing Kirsten slipped, skinning her knuckles on the sharp edges of the pipe brackets; she began cursing, loudly. The boss told her to shut up and get on with her work.

Kirsten's temper finally snapped. She threw the cloth into the bucket, sending water all over the floor. She got up and began singing, 'He's big, bald and fat and he looks like a rat, he looks like a rat and he's big, bald and fat.'

The boss shouted, 'Right, that's enough! Get out of here and don't come back.'

Kirsten asked sarcastically, 'What? Are you trying to tell me I'm being fired?'

'Yes, if that's how you wish me to put it to you. Yes, you are fired, dismissed, whatever,' the boss shouted.

Tia recalled:

> We could clearly hear Kirsten and the boss arguing in the kitchen. We stopped what we were doing to see what was going on. The chef demanded to know where we were going but Imogen told him to shut up. We walked out into the restaurant to see Kirsten standing before the boss with her hands on her hips. We asked her what was going on and she said, 'He's dismissing me, that's what.'
>
> Imogen chirped, 'Well, if she goes, I go too.'
>
> Then Himmel, Lisa and I told him the same. It was like catching a rat in a trap; he didn't know how to deal with the situation or what to say. Himmel attempted some diplomacy and calmly asked him to reconsider his decision, that we had all got angry over something so silly. It was like *Mutiny on the Bounty*. There was this deathly silence as we all eyed one another to see what the next move might be. But the boss was adamant he did not want Kirsten working in the restaurant anymore, so we all took off our work clothing, placed it on a table and walked out the door. The boss followed, shouting, 'Where are you going? Come back now or you can all leave and not come back.' It was the classic bluff most employers used and still do. We carried on walking. Kirsten was last out. When she got to the door, the boss was still shouting, 'Come back here right now. You will not be paid, you know.'
>
> Kirsten shouted at him, 'Oh, yes, you will pay us what we are due, or you will get more trouble than you ever bargained for.'
>
> Then the chef came running out, shouting for us to come back, saying, 'What am I supposed to do now?'
>
> Imogen shouted back, '*Schlupfer!* [Knickers!]'
>
> We caught the tram and made our way back to the apartment. As we ate our meal that afternoon, we decided that over the next few days we would go and find new jobs. The great thing about Hamburg back then was that there were lots of jobs available, especially for smart German girls who could speak English. As for the rest of the world and its people, we just thought, 'Sod it, let them eat cherry pie.'

Chapter 10

Black Dogs and Near Misses

1955 would prove a challenging year for the girls despite them having settled down into new jobs. Himmel and Tia worked together in a newly opened café in the city. It was a place which over the next few years would become the preferred hangout of many Hamburg teenagers. The combination of a jukebox, milkshake, Coca-Cola and fast food proved irresistible to the fifties rock 'n' roll generation of young Germans, now just a year or so away from fruition. In 1955, the café was popular with young people as it embraced modernist décor and had bars lined with stools as opposed to tables and chairs. The flooring comprised black and white lino squares in direct imitation of an American-style café/diner. On the walls hung black and white photographs of American and British movie stars. It could not have been more different from the many traditional German brewhouses, cafés and restaurants in the city. It was considered stylish, chic and modern in concept, thus attractive to the young people of Hamburg. Himmel recalled:

> Yes, it was what some today would call very swanky and bright. The use of very light colours, stainless steel, chrome and the most modern décor made it a place young people preferred to the dingy old bars or restaurants the older people frequented. It provided a very distinct gap in the market between old and new, cool and uncool. I recall the walls being decorated with these silver-framed portraits of British and American movie stars. The most striking of all to me and Tia was this young starlet named Audrey Hepburn. Oh, she was beautiful, so pretty with the most beautiful face. Tia and I had a joke that she was the only girl we'd ever consider a threesome with. It was just a joke of course – we'd never have done that but it was something we used to say every time we looked at her picture. We loved working there as

there was no stress at all. We started at 10 in the morning and finished at 5 pm. We had to work Saturday mornings but only up until midday when it closed, and we had Sundays off and a half day on Mondays. The uniform was based on those worn by American café waitresses. The building belonged to a German man named Peter Erbst, yet the café had been financed by a young American entrepreneur whom we only ever knew as Eddie. That's how he introduced himself: 'My name is Eddie, call me Eddie.' Eddie, who was in his late twenties, was pretty fashionable, wearing what to us at the time were strange-looking clothes. He had a strong vision of the future and possessed excellent marketing and promotional skills. The café at that time was one of the few places you could buy American-style food like hot dogs, fries and cheeseburgers. You could buy Coca-Cola and thick American-style milkshakes which became really popular with the young people. It made a good profit even during the winter months. Tia and I had to learn the art of creating the perfect thick milkshake but this, along with popping the bottle tops off Coca-Cola, was all we had to do really. We didn't have to do any food preparation or cleaning bogs or anything. Before we went home each day, we would wipe down the tabletops with disinfectant and that was it. The two guys who did the cooking were two young Germans who had been to the USA and were committed to American-style food and culture; they were also really nice friendly guys, so we were very happy with it all. In many respects, Tia and I had landed well and truly on our feet, intending to stick with this job as it was really good, including the pay.

Lisa found herself a job in a small Hamburg cosmetics outlet. The work was straightforward, advising the mainly female clientele on the various new beauty products and perfumes that had just come in. Often, she worked on her own, having full responsibility of the shop, which she thoroughly enjoyed. The owner of the shop was a pretty 31-year-old divorcee named Ilse Hubber who lived above the shop in a small yet adequate flat. Lisa worked Monday to Friday, nine till four. Ilse always gave Lisa Saturdays off and she would run the shop herself. Lisa recalled:

Ilse was a tall, pretty lady, immaculate just like a fashion model. Yes, she was what men today would call eye candy. Yet she appeared scornful of males, and I had guessed that her recent divorce had much to do with her attitude. One quiet afternoon she came down into the shop and said, 'Let's close for the day. It's quiet. We can go upstairs and have a coffee and chat before you go home.' I agreed, the shop was locked and bolted, and I followed Ilse up the narrow stairway to her flat. Was it odd being invited for coffee by a woman? Often this was how boys used to test your receptivity for romance with them. Her living room was small, yet cosy. It had just one sofa and chair and a beautiful coffee table with a vase of flowers in the centre. Ilse made coffee, bringing it in on a tray and placing it on the coffee table before sitting down. She sat in the chair, separated from me only by the coffee table. She drew her long slender legs up beneath her, pushing her shoes off onto the floor. She took a sip of coffee and lit a cigarette, drawing heavily, the tip glowing bright red in the fading light of the afternoon. She exhaled and blew a series of smoke rings which had me momentarily captivated. She quickly apologized before offering me a cigarette, which I declined. She then began talking about her ex-husband who a friend had seen in the city with another woman.

'My friend saw them on a tram, sitting and holding hands and laughing. I don't know why he sought the company of other women as I had always done my best to keep him happy. I am a good cook, a good housewife and the proverbial whore in bed. I don't understand men at all, Lisa.' She continued, 'I had revenge in mind, maybe a fine meal of steak and red wine before bed and love balls. I could have inserted them up his arse and started him up like a chainsaw.'

We both burst out laughing and this frank discussion really broke the ice between us. When we finished the coffee, she showed me around her small yet comfy abode. The kitchen was much like one you'd find on a boat, comprising an oven, sink, refrigerator and a set of four cupboards. It made our

Hamburg apartment feel like a warehouse in comparison. The bathroom was spotlessly clean; I could imagine her reclining in a bath of bubbles with a glass of wine in her hand at the end of the day. The last room she showed me was her bedroom which was, as I expected, cosy, warm and clean. The double bed had these huge cushions on top of the pillows; it looked warm and inviting. Ilse then sat on her bed, gesturing for me to join her. I sat down beside her, feeling both a little excited and nervous at the same time. She asked me, 'Now, I can imagine a pretty girl such as you would have a boyfriend?' I explained that I had a boyfriend in Berlin and I visited him every few weeks, to which she added, 'He's a very lucky young man, I'd say.'

I knew where all of this was heading and as she put her hand on mine, my heart began to pound in my chest as she gently grasped my hand. She smiled, leaning closer to my face until our lips were almost touching. At that point I tried to stop her from kissing me, telling her I had a boyfriend and we had planned to be married soon, that I couldn't do what she wanted me to do. She just whispered, 'I will not stop you from marrying him, sweetheart. I promise. I just want to kiss you.' I don't know why I allowed this to happen, but our lips brushed and before I knew what was happening, we were kissing passionately. I tried hard to resist, to just keep talking, but I was powerless. Before long, we were removing each other's clothes. She did things to me I could never have imagined. I had never had sex with a woman before in my life as I had never felt that aroused by a woman until that moment, yet here I was having sex with the woman I worked for, my boss. It was crazy. I knew Himmel and Tia had what they called their toy, a rubber penis that a girl could strap on to herself in order to pleasure her partner like a man would. Ilse pulled this thing out of her bedside drawer and I gasped at its size. I was so excited and turned on by what was happening I couldn't stop; it was as if I were under the devil's spell. She laid me down, then lay between my thighs, kissing me. I felt the tip of the toy nudging at my orifice. I lifted my hips inviting her to penetrate me but each time I did this she withdrew it, teasing. This went on for some minutes as she kissed and bit at my neck sending shivers of ecstasy through my body. I lifted my thighs again, begging her to penetrate me. Again, I felt the bulbous end of the rubber penis brushing against my moistened orifice. I bucked my hips up again, and she slid it into me all the way and began to make love to me as if she were a man. The way she fucked me made me feel that I was not her first conquest. She made me orgasm and then insisted I turn over so she could take me from behind, 'like a dog' in her own words. She made me climax a second time before stopping and removing the toy. We lay on her bed for a moment.

I felt guilty beyond words for what I'd just done and told her I had to go immediately. I quickly got dressed as Ilse watched me, saying, 'See you tomorrow' and then I was off down the stairs and out the side door of the shop. I ran to catch my tram and when I sat down, all the events of the past two hours raced through my mind. A little voice in my head kept saying, 'You stupid girl. What have you just done?'

When I arrived home, Himmel, Tia, Kirsten and Imogen were all there and asked me how my day had been. I told them, 'Very, very weird.' It was Tia who suspected that something had happened; she could always tell when there was something bothering me, so she followed me into my room, closing the door behind her and asked, 'Lisa, what's wrong? Are you alright?' Himmel came in and I told her to shut the door behind her as I had something to tell them. When I explained to them that I'd had sex with my female boss who was also much older than me, they were shocked and stuck for words. They didn't know what to say for a few moments and looked at each other with bemused expressions.

Then Tia held my hand and said, 'What about Erich, Lisa? You are to be married at some point. What's going on?'

I explained I loved Erich more than anything else but could not resist the advances of this woman. Both Tia and Himmel said that I couldn't let this happen ever again, that I was probably just being used and things like that. They told me that in future I should not go upstairs with Frau Hubber and just come straight home, to tell her Erich was visiting or something, anything to prevent the same thing from happening again. I felt guilty as hell. If Erich ever found out about this, he would go mad and probably end our relationship altogether. I couldn't risk that ever happening and I decided I would have to just keep it a secret and put it to the back of my mind, pretend it never happened.

Lisa felt the best way to try and get the events of that afternoon out of her mind was to arrange a visit to Berlin to be with Erich. She was not due to visit him for another two weeks but decided under the circumstances she would go to Berlin that coming weekend.

Kirsten and Imogen appeared untouched by any of the dramas that might have surrounded their lives. They had found work together at a factory which manufactured plastics. Kirsten nicknamed it the Brat Shop. It was a steady eight-to-five job and the work was easy and their co-workers mostly young people like themselves. As long as they did their work, they had no grief from their bosses. It was not long after starting their new jobs that Kirsten in particular developed concerns for Imogen. She had begun going out during the week, to drink schnapps, often to the same pub. Kirsten recalled:

> We would get home from work; Imogen would have her tea then say, 'I'm just going out. Do you want to come with me? I won't be long.' To be honest, I didn't really want to go out as I was tired and wanted to stay in. But I felt I'd better, to make sure she was alright – had I let her go out alone, I would have only worried about her. So, this began to form a pattern. We would get home, grab a meal, wash up and go down to the pub, where, more often than not, I would sit watching Imogen getting hammered on schnapps. We'd get back at the apartment around 9 pm where I'd just want to go to bed and sleep. Imogen would be lying in bed and the next thing she'd jump up, throwing off the covers and run to the toilet to be sick. She would make a hell of a racket and I'd sit with her to comfort her as she began to cry. Things got to the point where in the morning I'd try and rouse her for work,

but I couldn't get her up. I'd leave her there in bed and tell the boss that she was ill. When I got home shortly before the others, Imogen would still be in bed. I'd go into our room and she'd be lying in bed, staring at the ceiling. She hadn't eaten all day and I couldn't believe at how rapidly she was going downhill. I could tell she'd been crying but why, I just didn't know, and she wouldn't tell me.

I got into bed and hugged her. 'What's making you so miserable? You can tell me what it is. You're like my sister, so please tell me what's wrong.'

Imogen sobbed her heart out in my arms, saying, 'I miss my family so much it hurts. I just want them back, Kirsten, but I know that's never going to be possible; they are gone, dead.'

I heard Himmel and Tia come in and they came into the room. I gestured for them to give me a few minutes alone with Imogen. It was heart wrenching when she looked into my eyes and said, 'Kirsten, I don't know what's wrong with me. I feel as if I'm standing at the edge of a black hole, just waiting for that one thing to push me over the edge into the darkness.' I knew Imogen had coped over the loss of her family during the war but was concerned that it was coming back to haunt her, just as we thought everything was going so well for us all. When she fell asleep, I discussed with Himmel, Tia and Lisa what we could do to help her.

When our friend Franz called in on us, he noticed we all looked down in the mouth. When we explained, he told us about herbal remedies which might help. We all knew doctors would just send her away to the nut house, or worse, diagnose her as suffering from Communism. Yes, that's true, some people like Imogen were diagnosed as suffering from Communism and sent to the nut house where they used electric-shock treatment or performed lobotomies. There was no way that we were ever going to risk that happening to Imogen. If she was locked in a battle with herself, then we would fight that battle with her, right at her side, all the way until it was won. Franz recommended an elderly Chinese herbalist who ran a small shop in the suburbs. He said he'd go and see him right away to see if he had anything that could help Imogen's melancholy. The Chinese man was named Chi and he prepared this strange infusion made up from the dry roots and leaves of trees and plants from some of the world's most exotic locations. The old man also requested a meeting with Imogen so as he could examine her and try and heal her with other methods. So, Franz drove me and Imogen to Chi's little shop, which was a cultural wonderland of exotic dried flowers, leaves, incenses and teas. A monkey's paw hung above the entrance to the shop and, as Imogen walked in, she was immediately spooked by it. Chi assured her it was an ancient relic and not a recently killed specimen and was there to ward off evil entities. He then asked Imogen to sit down, closed his eyes and placed his hands either side of her head and appeared to be meditating. After some twenty minutes, he opened his eyes and said, 'The war has much to answer for; man has much to answer for.' On the way out he told me, 'Your friend will be fine.' He gave me a small book on yoga and meditation for the wellbeing of body and mind, and told me to make sure she used all the infusion he'd prescribed. I don't know, some might have called him a 'quack physician' but what he did with Imogen that day worked. She drank the tea that Mr Chi had prepared for her and began doing the various yoga routines as explained in the book. To give Imogen confidence we joined her in the yoga and meditation routines. Her recovery was nothing short of miraculous, considering depression was not an affliction best understood back in those days. She improved rapidly and was soon back to her old self, much to my own personal relief.

I don't know how that elderly Chinese man helped Imogen; it was truly amazing. I went to see him to thank him one Saturday afternoon. He invited me to take some green tea with him and we sat and talked. Mr Chi told me that when he had placed his hands around Imogen's head, he felt a torturous sorrow emanating from within her, residues that the war had left behind, and that if not removed would have blighted her life forever. At the time I didn't really think much about it, but I became a huge believer in the ancient arts of spiritual healing and alternative treatments to the curse of the modern world.

> *Waiting for something to numb the pain,*
> *sweet male attraction my novocaine.*
> *Just one more glass of tepid wine,*
> *take any chance to cross that line.*
> *Need a thrill to fill this void,*
> *war has taken and destroyed.*
> *Everything that I held dear,*
> *one more glass to disappear*
>
> *Novocaine* AV XIV

Thankfully, Imogen appeared cured of the episodes that had almost destroyed her. With the continued support of her friends, she returned to both work and active social life as a happy-go-lucky young girl. She went to visit Mr Chi's shop some months later to thank him herself but found the shop empty. She peered through the milky glass windows and all she could see was darkness. She walked along the street inquiring as to Mr Chi's whereabouts only to discover that the old man had died a month earlier. His relatives had had his body transported back to China. She was saddened by the news but felt that somehow the old man's spirit was very much alive and accompanying her through her life. She would never forget the old man or what he did for her and would often talk about him and tell others about how he had helped her with her 'black dog'.

The dynamic of Hamburg's fledgling social scene was rarely afflicted by violence, but one Saturday evening in the late summer of 1955 would change that perception for the girls, as Kirsten explained:

> Imogen and I arranged to go out with Franz and his partner Johann for a drink. We loved Franz and Johann; they were beautiful young men with huge hearts, and they were so gentle with it. We had dressed up and put on our makeup and were looking forward to enjoying a lovely evening. The evening itself was wonderful and we had great fun, and no, we didn't get drunk on this occasion, which I know was rare

for us two. We decided to pop into one of the old Hamburg bars and have a last drink before going home. We sat with Franz and Johann for most of the time, but then got talking to two German boys at the bar. Franz came over and said he and Johann had to go and they'd see us again soon. We hugged them both and watched as they walked out of the bar. I then noticed a group of five men get up from a table and hastily follow them out the door. I don't know, I just had a bad feeling about it, so I said to Imogen, 'You wait here; I won't be a minute.' I pushed my way through the crowded bar and out onto the street to see the five men assaulting Franz and Johann.

I shouted at them, 'What the fucking hell do you think you are doing! Leave them alone!' They were throwing heavy punches and kicking them, and I knew I couldn't just stand there and do nothing. I just ran into them and managed to kick one of them in the balls. I kicked him so hard that he had to be carried off by his mates as they legged it away from the bar. I shouted after them, 'You're fucking cowards!'

By this time Imogen had come out to see where I was. She guessed from Franz's and Johann's bloody noses and split lips what had just taken place. They were quite shaken up but despite the cuts and bruises, they were okay. We insisted on walking them back to their apartment. We went inside and helped clean the blood off their faces and made sure they were okay. We were both so angry and when we got back to our apartment, we told the others all about it. They were very upset by the news; in fact, Himmel cried when she heard. We all decided to go and visit Franz and Johann on the Sunday morning as we were so worried about them. When I got out of bed that morning, I noticed a huge black bruise on the top of my right foot. When Imogen saw it, she made me laugh, saying, 'I wouldn't want to be that man's bollocks this morning judging by that bruise on your foot!' The others agreed with her too, and yes, it was the first time I'd ever been in a fight. I'd kicked him as hard as I could as I was desperate to stop him and I guess I succeeded.

Black Dogs and Near Misses

From out of the city shadows,
a cold wind swirling about him,
comes a man dressed in black,
a man with a knuckleduster smile.

To be young and gay in 1950s West Germany meant discretion was imperative. Virulent hatred against homosexual men was prevalent in many societies around the world at that time, not just Germany. Homosexuality was classed as a 'sexual deviance' and illegal in both West and East Germany up until 1968 when it was decriminalized. Even when the laws changed, there was still much antipathy against gay men in West Germany. Himmel recalled:

> Gay male couples could not go out in public and indulge in obvious displays of affection. Such open displays of affection between two men would in many cases be met with a violent response. I don't think it was as tough for gay women. The reason being those who attacked gay men were more often than not testosterone-fuelled Neanderthals, strictly women-only fuckers. Yet, if two girls started snogging in front of them, they would whoop and cheer and whistle, thinking it was great. Tia and I were always wary in public and didn't kiss in front of people. Kirsten and Imogen did it frequently just to shock people. The women would curse them and call them things but there was never any physical violence, unlike the men. Either way, I never understood it. Who has the right to tell someone they can't love another of the same sex? It just seemed very unfair that two people, whether they were two males or two females, couldn't love each other as heterosexual couples could. Of course, religion inadvertently created the hate thing, as Christian, especially Catholic, religions viewed gay people as being dirty, ungodly, impure, even sub-human. In their eyes we were creatures to be despised, ridiculed and beaten up. There were times Tia and I held hands in public, but it was not often, and when you did you'd always hear some idiot shouting '*Lesben*'. Our families were still unaware of our relationship. We knew we'd have to tell them at some

point, but finding the right time was always going to be very difficult: would there ever be a right time and what would happen afterwards?

To round off what was a challenging year for the girls, another unexpected blow to their otherwise happy existence in Hamburg occurred. It was an event which caused them both great sadness and joy at the same time, reinforcing the theory that life was ever changing, evolving, and at times reminding them that even their lives were representative of a less than perfect world. Tia recalled:

> One morning I shall always remember. I heard someone in the bathroom being sick. When I got up to investigate, I found Lisa hugging the toilet bowl and looking like death itself. She just said, 'God, I feel awful.' There was no way she could go to work that day so I told her to go back to bed and rest and maybe she'd feel better tomorrow. I made sure her boss, Ilse, knew she wasn't well, and she seemed fine about it. We all went off to work and when we got home later, Lisa seemed better. We thought maybe she'd eaten something that hadn't agreed with her. Yet the next morning the same thing happened and again she felt really ill. We made her go and see a doctor to find out what was wrong as we were quite worried. The doctor could do little else other than carry out a few tests to determine what was wrong. It was only after Lisa had gone to bed early one evening and the rest of us were discussing things, that one possibility came to light.
>
> Himmel remarked, 'Lisa could be pregnant; she's suffering all the symptoms of a mother to be.'
>
> We laughed and said, 'No, surely that can't be right?'
>
> Himmel continued, 'If she had sex with Erich without birth control, there's every chance she could be pregnant, you know. It only takes one time to get caught out.'
>
> We all hoped that Himmel was mistaken, but Himmel was not often wrong. We sat in silence for a while before Imogen said, 'Well, what if she is expecting a baby? What will happen then? Will she stay with us or go back home?'

None of us had considered this and again we hoped Himmel was wrong, yet I had that feeling in my stomach that she was probably right. The next morning, I sat on Lisa's bed and talked to her about her sickness. It only occurred during the morning and tended to wear off but left her feeling tired. I asked her if she had used birth control with Erich and it was then she admitted there had been three or four times when she hadn't.

I asked, 'What happens if you're pregnant Lisa? What will you do?'

'I hope you're wrong but if I am, then I'll have to go back to Berlin and we'll have to marry before the child is born,' she replied.

Lisa's results came back a week later and the doctor stated, 'Congratulations. There's nothing wrong with you other than the fact that you are with child – you are expecting a baby, that's all.' The words hit Lisa like a hammer blow. She left the surgery in silence, deep in thought all the way back to the apartment. When the other girls arrived home after work that day, she had to break the news to them. Kirsten recalled:

She sat there and started crying and for a minute we thought there was something seriously wrong with her. Then came the news: 'I'm having a baby – that's what's wrong with me.' We didn't know whether to laugh or cry; it was one of those awkward moments where you had to choose your emotional reaction with care. Then Lisa announced, 'There's nothing left for me to do other than go back to Berlin and marry Erich. I couldn't continue living here with a baby; it wouldn't be fair on Erich or any of you. There's no way on god's earth I will get rid of this baby, so I'll have to make plans to leave you all.' By the time she finished, we were all crying and hugging her. We didn't want to let her go but knew we would have to.

The next morning Lisa went to see Ilse to explain she had to leave her job and return to Berlin. Ilse was very supportive and gave Lisa the money she was owed in wages before wishing her well. Ilse told her, 'Be sure to come and visit me when you find the time and bring your little baby with you when you do. I'm sorry about what happened between us that afternoon, although I did enjoy it very much. Whoever your Erich is, he's a lucky man.'

Lisa smiled and said her farewell. The next thing she would have to do was to tell Erich that he was going to be a father and then the parents would have to be told, then there was a wedding to arrange. So many things were flying around inside her mind as she made the trip back to the apartment that she would soon have to leave for good.

Lisa left Hamburg three weeks after discovering she was pregnant. Erich had been overjoyed at the news and both the Krauss and Sauerstond families came together to arrange the wedding as quickly as possible. Back in Hamburg a letter arrived addressed to the four remaining girls. Himmel opened it first and read it out to the others. The wedding date had been fixed and Lisa was asking them if they would all be bridesmaids. There was much celebration over the good news in Lisa's letter and Himmel quickly composed a reply. However, Tia was apprehensive and when Himmel asked her why, she explained, 'Ernst will be there, won't he? He's Erich's brother, the boy I broke up with before we left for Schlactensee.' Himmel reassured her it would all be okay and that she couldn't say no to such a wonderful offer from her best friend. Over the weeks that followed the girls travelled back to Berlin to see Lisa and their families and to have their bridesmaid dresses fitted. Lisa recalled:

> I moved in with Erich's family into a spare room. Ernst was rarely home as he had a girlfriend and he often stayed with her at her parents' home on weekends. I knew Tia would be nervous about seeing him again but was sure things would be okay between them now after all this time. My four friends looked stunning in their bridesmaids' dresses and we all complimented each other as to how beautiful we all looked.
>
> The wedding day itself was one I can remember for all time as a very happy day. Ernst wasn't unpleasant to Tia and even went up to her and said, 'Hello Tia. You look so well. How are you?' They talked for a few minutes as Himmel looked on smiling. Ernst kissed her on the hand like a true

gentleman and that was that. We had a small celebration in the evening, and I was thrilled to see some of the Berlin Gang there and young Petrianna Albrecht whom I had not seen for a long time. Kirsten had brought Petra along and I couldn't believe how grown up she looked. I asked her how her schooling was coming along, and she told me she didn't like school but was now in her last year. I asked her what she wanted to do, and she told me she wasn't sure. It was then I said to her that if her parents were happy with it, she could take my place at the Hamburg apartment. She would easily get a job in the city, but not with Frau Hubber!

Petra asked, 'Who is Frau Hubber?'

'Never mind about Frau Hubber, it's just a joke,' I told her.

It was a lovely evening, yet it was over so quickly before Erich and I had to say goodbye to our friends to leave for a short honeymoon. Himmel, Tia, Kirsten, Imogen and Petra all wept as we left. They promised to come and visit as soon as Erich and I returned. It was a sad parting and the end of an era really. We had been through so much together that it was a sisterly bond which nothing would ever break.

The last thing Tia said was actually to Erich. She held both his hands in hers, looked him in the eyes and said, 'Just love her, Erich. Don't ever hurt her. She's so special to me, so promise me you will always look after her.'

He smiled, placed a kiss on Tia's cheek before replying, 'I love this girl more than words can ever say. I would never hurt her and promise you I will always cherish her. You don't have to worry about her, really.'

At that we had to leave. It was very sad but at the same time exciting; a new chapter was beginning for me and for my four friends who would be going back to Hamburg without me. I hoped they would be okay and not be too sad.

1955 was a strange year indeed, one which had brought forth black dogs and near misses. As the four girls made the trip back to Hamburg, they did so deep in their own thoughts – happy but sad, hopeful yet pensive of the future. Himmel held Tia's hand on the train; Tia placed her head on Himmel's shoulder and was soon asleep. As Berlin's metropolis slowly gave way to open pasture and countryside, Himmel looked out the window where memories began flooding back. She recalled the days at Schlactensee, how she and Tia became lovers, the move to Hamburg, meeting Imogen and all the things that had happened over the years. She thought to herself, *Will we all be here in another ten years' time or will progression tear us all apart like the yellowed parchment of the manuscript to some doomed theatrical act?* As the train pulled into Hamburg station, Himmel roused Tia and the others and they made their way wearily back to their apartment. It seemed strange with Lisa gone and her room empty. This was to be only the briefest episode of unhappiness for the girls, as the apartment soon returned to its normal, sometimes crazy routine as they settled down again, looking to the future with a newly fuelled optimism. They owed it to Lisa to carry on and keep going forward. They found solace in the fact that they could still visit Lisa in Berlin and, even better, be surrogate aunts to her as yet unborn little angel.

Chapter 11

The Perfume of Purgatory

Lisa's departure left an emotional crevasse in the lives of the girls. It was now just the four of them, yet they understood that life went on as it had to. Christmas 1955 saw all four of the girls return home to their respective families for the festivities. Despite enjoying their time with parents, grandparents and siblings, they yearned to be together again and were relieved to be back in Hamburg two days before New Year's Eve. They had invited Franz and Johann to join them at their apartment to see in 1956. They were sad that their friend Lisa could not be there with them, so Kirsten decided to light a candle to offer Lisa some spiritual good fortune in her life and marriage with Erich. As Tia and Himmel blew up some balloons, Kirsten and Imogen went into their bedroom to change into what they called their posh dresses. They didn't get very far with putting on their fancy attire, as Himmel recalled:

> I heard all this commotion coming from their room and wondered what those two were up to. Tia carried on blowing up balloons while I went to see what they were doing. As I opened the door, there they were engaged in a full-on pillow fight. Kirsten's pillow then exploded, sending white feathers everywhere. Disarmed, Kirsten then launched herself at Imogen. Both wrestled for advantage on Imogen's bed and I watched amazed as the petite Imogen was able to overpower her stronger opponent, sitting astride Kirsten and desperately trying to pin her down by her wrists to force a surrender. The two were momentarily locked in a battle of wills. Imogen said, 'You are beaten as I have the higher ground.' They were both laughing as the struggle continued, with Kirsten's arms slowly weakening as Imogen maintained the pressure. Imogen squealed with delight as Kirsten gave in. At this point I interrupted them, 'Okay,

you two, time to tidy this mess up and get dressed.' Imogen released her hold on Kirsten's wrists, and they both got up. They were both panting like greyhounds after a race but began gathering up the feathers. However, Kirsten was not one to take defeat so easily and when Imogen turned her back, she struck. She dived on Imogen and both fell back heavily onto Imogen's bed again. This time Kirsten had the advantage, holding Imogen's wrists and teasing her: 'Now I can stop you any time I choose.' Imogen protested loudly: 'Hey, that's not fair! You cheated.' No amount of struggling was of use and Kirsten won the battle. Then there was this loud crack and Imogen's bed collapsed in the middle, the wooden frame broken. All I could see were their bare legs flailing among the laughter. They lifted the mattress to investigate and concluded it could not be repaired.

Kirsten said to Imogen, 'No problem, you can share my bed tonight and we'll sort something out later.'

I told them again that Franz and Johann would be here soon: 'Now please tidy up and get yourselves dressed.' I sensed that this was going to be a wild New Year's Eve with these two lunatics on such form.

When Franz and Johann arrived clutching bottles of schnapps, the New Year celebration began. They spent the evening dancing to music on the radio, playing cards, chatting and of course drinking. Kirsten and Imogen drank more than anyone else and by midnight had burned themselves out. Tia recalled:

Those two drank a lot of schnapps and danced with each other for most of the night. When it came to a game of cards, it was as much as they could do to stay awake. They both fell asleep on the living room floor while we continued to enjoy the party. Himmel said, 'Come on, let's get these two into bed,' so we carried them into their room and squeezed them both into Kirsten's bed. We left the door open so as we could keep an eye on them, but they were out cold. As midnight approached, those of us who had paced ourselves with the alcohol were ready with full glasses to toast in

1956. Himmel opened the balcony doors so we could hear the distant chimes of the Hamburg bell towers. Himmel, Franz, Johann and I stood waiting for the midnight bells to strike to signify the dawn of the year 1956. When they began to chime, I felt a rush of emotion run through me. I took Himmel in my arms and kissed her, and I told her I loved her. Franz and Johann too were deep in embrace, kissing and professing the same undying love for each other. We then clinked our glasses for a toast to the arrival of 1956. Some fireworks began shooting up into the sky from nearby rooftops, exploding in showers of coloured sparks and we marvelled at the spectacle. It was a chilly night, so we went back inside, and just talked for the next hour. Himmel and I went in to check on Kirsten and Imogen. As usual they were lying in an embrace, their arms around each other. We gently kissed them on the cheek and whispered, 'Happy New Year, you two drunks.' We felt it best that Franz and Johann stay with us for the night and told them they could sleep in Lisa's old room. We were worried about them walking home so late. Himmel and I went to bed around 1.30 in the morning. Himmel read a book for twenty minutes while I lay reflecting on the evening.

Next morning, around 8 o'clock, I heard Kirsten coming out of her room complaining of a bad headache. She was dressed only in bra and knickers, moaning that it was cold and she urgently needed coffee. Franz and Johann were both up, sitting on the settee staring wide eyed at the half-naked girl who asked them if they'd like more coffee. She made coffee for us all and then went back into her room where Imogen was now stirring. Himmel and I drank our coffee cuddled up in bed. It was a Sunday, which was even better as we could lounge around for as long as we wanted. We kissed, yet the kiss lingered. We put down our coffee and embraced. Within a few minutes Himmel has positioned herself between my legs. She placed one of my ankles on her right shoulder and gently aroused me. When we had finished, we fell into each other's arms and were soon asleep again. We didn't wake again until 11 o'clock. By this time

Franz and Johann had left, having been plied with coffee and toast prepared by Imogen. Kirsten and Imogen flopped themselves down on the settee, vowing not to move all day as they felt like shit. Imogen had her legs resting on Kirsten, and Kirsten was playing with Imogen's feet. That afternoon Himmel and I went out for a walk to get some fresh air. We left the other two in their room, both still fragile from the previous evening. As we walked around the quiet streets of Hamburg, we wondered what 1956 would bring us all.

Something had been steadily stirring in the calm backwaters of American and British youth culture since the arrival of the 1950s. When it erupted in all its fury in West Germany around 1956, it was considered delinquent, dark, lustful and unpredictable. This was no disease or nationwide medical emergency: it was a form of music known as rock 'n' roll. When rock 'n' roll began to gain popularity in West Germany, it was perceived as a threat to the very fabric of German family values, traditions and principles that parents expected their children to abide by. It was greeted with all the warmth of the bubonic plague. Nothing previously had ever threatened to undermine parental control, influence and authority in quite the same way that rock 'n' roll would.

With this new breed of high-energy music came the fashion. The boys either wore suits or leather jackets and jeans with their hair set into a quiff or greased back to their personal style. The girls often wore blouses, poodle skirts with white socks rolled down three times. These socks were known as bobby socks and were often worn with penny loafers or saddle shoes, imitating those of American high school girls. Rock 'n' roll fashion evolved almost as rapidly as the music itself and soon girls too wore jeans and leather jackets, which were considered the epitome of rebellion. Some girls would alter the length of their tight-fitting jeans, cut off to just below the knees. They began to discard the white socks to show more leg and exert greater sex appeal. It was as much about aesthetics as it was the music and most teenagers, boys and girls, fell under the spell of what many older Germans referred to as 'The Western Devil'. Himmel recalled:

> Due to the Allied forces in Hamburg, we had already been introduced to music such as country and western and jazz,

which to be honest didn't really appeal to us. It was Franz and Johann who first played us a rock 'n' roll record when they brought what we thought was a suitcase round with them one Saturday evening in 1956. They were very excited, telling us, 'You've got to hear this.' We wondered what the hell they were doing plugging this thing which looked like a suitcase into the electrical socket in our living room. Franz then explained, 'This is a record player. It's the same as a gramophone and you play these same music discs, or records as they're known, on them, yet they're a bit louder as this thing contains an internal speaker.' He lifted the lid of the suitcase to reveal a turntable with this arm thing attached which contained a needle which worked in the same way as a gramophone. Johann passed Franz this black disc and placed it on the turntable, then he dropped the needle on the now-rotating disc. For a moment crackles of static filled the air before the intro to the song. We all listened intently. The song was by an American band, Bill Hayley and the Comets, called 'Rock Around the Clock'. When it finished, Imogen told Franz to put it on again. In fact, we all loved it so the song was played several more times until, conscious of the neighbours, we turned it off.

It was there and then that we decided that we needed to buy (a) a record player and (b) some new clothes of the kind being worn by the youth in America and Britain, young people who liked this rock 'n' roll. Yes, that music was like the best thing we'd ever heard. After that introduction we sought out other musicians of the genre, including Elvis Presley and Buddy Holly. Elvis Presley had been around a couple years, but we had never really heard any of his music as it was not played on any of the local radio stations. It made us realize we had been hermits to a degree, confining ourselves to the traditional concepts of working, shopping, going out to pubs, seeing the occasional movie and just socializing at home. It suddenly occurred to us that perhaps we weren't as cool as we thought we were. We had all undergone a form of spiritual awakening through this rock 'n' roll and Bill Hayley and the Comets. Yes, we embraced it willingly. We all knew our parents would go mad if they saw us dressed up the way we intended to. So, when we visited them, we'd wear our old clothes, or 'granny clothes' as Kirsten called them. We all knew that it wasn't something which would become acceptable overnight. For the times it was considered extreme, rebellious, even highly sexualized and parents loathed it with a passion.

Kirsten recalled:

Young people from their teens to their late twenties were adopting the rock 'n' roll fashion, even if they weren't all that keen on the actual music. The clothes, particularly jeans, were expensive at first. Some clothing outlets in Hamburg refused to stock the clothes, saying they were pornographic. Yet soon they were everywhere; it was great. I know some of my younger friends living at home with their parents were banned from wearing clothes associated with the new Western youth culture of rock 'n' roll. We were lucky in that respect; we could wear what we wanted. It was a great time to be young. Himmel was the oldest of the four of us, yet she looked stunning in a skirt, blouse, white socks and shoes. She was 27 at the time, yet she looked years younger. Imogen and I preferred wearing our jeans just below the knees, without socks, and we both bought black leather jackets. At first, we were both too scared to wear the leather jackets out on the streets. I remember the looks we got from people when we finally plucked up the courage to wear them out. Leather jackets were associated with bad people; that was the common perception back then. What makes a leather jacket signify anything? It's just a piece of clothing; it's those prejudiced people who invent hatred who have a problem. Imogen and I just thought, *To hell with those who don't like it*. We went out and lots of people stared at us. Two women mumbled 'Ruffians' as we walked past them arm in arm, chewing gum. Another woman standing with her husband in a tram queue said, 'Look at them. They look like prostitutes.' My reply was, 'Knickers, you old goat!'

> After that we tended to go out all together with Franz and Johann and some of the girls and young men they knew. It was safety in numbers, us against the world, but then hadn't that always been the way with me, Himmel, Tia and Imogen? We didn't want to be like everyone else, to get screwed, get to 24, get married, have a couple of crying brats, spend the day slaving over the stove for a husband who sat on his fat arse doing nothing after his day at work. No, to me that domestic lifestyle was a nightmare vision. My parents used to constantly ask me, 'When are you going to settle down, find a nice boy and get married?' I told them one day in the summer of 1956, 'Never!'

Imogen reflects fondly on what she called 'that rock 'n' roll summer' of 1956:

> It was great as soon a lot of young people got involved in the movement. There were no German rock 'n' roll bands; most were from America or Britain. Under the Nazis art and music had been severely supressed and controlled by the state and I think that's why many young Germans found it difficult to get involved in anything other than traditional German concepts on art and music. We went out and bought a record player one Saturday afternoon and the first record we all owned was 'Rock Around the Clock' by Bill Hayley and the Comets. We had just the one copy of it and we played it to death. We soon discovered others like Elvis Presley who had been around a while at that point. My favourite Elvis Presley record was called 'That's All Right'. On Sunday mornings it became a fight to get to the record player first. We were spending more of our money on clothes and records than anything else at that time.

It is certainly true that young women in West Germany were the primary consumers of this Western music culture. This facet of West German female consumerism did cause grave concerns in West Germany. Many West Germans felt that rock 'n' roll fans, particularly young girls, were being dangerously sexualized by the music. The way the girls danced led one West German to remark. 'They danced like wild barbarians in ecstasy.' Rock 'n' roll was also blamed for encouraging promiscuity. Many feared that this new youth culture would destroy that generation. In East Germany, under the control of the Soviet Union, rock 'n' roll was viewed as a form of music which could only ever appeal to 'primitive humans', and, along with all other Western influences, was banned.

With the advent of rock 'n' roll, the café where Tia and Himmel worked underwent a transformation. The owner soon capitalized on the new youth craze and even had a brand-new Seeburg Select-O-Matic jukebox specially imported from the USA. This in turn, with the chic décor, soft drinks, shakes and fast food proved a magnet to the youth of Hamburg. The café soon became a hangout for groups of teenagers and young people. Here they could come and meet friends or likeminded individuals, listen to their favourite rock 'n' roll records and consume greasy food without fear of being ridiculed or told to be quiet. The café itself became a subcultural element of the music and fashion of rock 'n' roll. In time, it would evolve with the youth cultures that were yet to come, but it would always be associated as a rockers' hangout. Tia recalled:

> Himmel and I loved working at the café. We were fans of rock 'n' roll and felt a part of its establishment by providing common ground where fans of the music and fashion could meet in a social context. Some of the girls were very young, like 15 or 16. They weren't allowed in bars as they were not allowed to drink alcohol at that age. Previously, they'd met up in parks or at dances but here they could come and feel they had their own place to hang out. They would sit down and drink their milkshakes, while the boys put music on the jukebox. They were never any trouble – we were the same as them: we wore the same clothes and liked the same music. We got to know many of them, and the younger girls would ask our advice on lots of things. They thought we were cool because we had our own apartment and could do as we wanted. I'd remind them that it was only through hard work that we had the things we wanted in life. The boys used to chat us up and asked us if we'd go on dates with them. We'd tell them we had boyfriends already.

Thanks to the music, Hamburg was rapidly becoming the epicentre of West German youth culture; it was also highly profitable for those who understood the value of this so-called decadence. It led one young West German woman to remark:

> This new era of decadence inducted us to rock 'n' roll icons such as Elvis Presley and Bill Hayley. Men and women alike were soon dancing in the streets. We were often referred to as the *Halbstarke*, the post-war youth who were out to cause trouble, somehow intent on derailing the traditions of society. This of course was not true; we just wanted a taste of freedom and yearned to devour every last piece of it. Our elders wanted us to work in the factories and the fields, rebuilding our infrastructure to make Germany great again. The problem was Elvis Presley showed young men that they could look very sexy for the girls. Girls found a man with a guitar slung over his shoulder far sexier than one with a shovel full of cow shit in his hand. Young men had begun to distance themselves from the military and no longer had to conform. Yet those who embraced the rock 'n' roll religion were often accused of being effeminate or homosexual. The music was blamed for effeminizing German males who had always previously been the masculine foundation of German society. The girls on the other hand couldn't get enough of the leather jackets and jeans. For us girls, gone were the ladylike skirts and blouses – we were equals now and had more control over our individual destinies.
>
> Both the FDR and GDR couldn't stand what they viewed as an uprising and non-conformity among the young. The young began to make a stand and protest, and even riots threatened to break out. While the FDR was more lenient, the GDR tried everything to stop any form of social change, from promoting ballroom dancing to subsidized lessons instructing us how to conduct ourselves with members of the opposite sex. It was bullshit. Our dancing wasn't to their liking, you see, as we had control over our own movements, and we didn't need a man to lead us around a dancefloor. That freedom was intoxicating, to be flung around with

wild abandon which set the hearts racing in our breasts. They tried to tame us with weak imitations like Connie Froboess's and Peter Krause's style of rock 'n' roll and gender-specific fashion, but it was much too late to put the lion back in its cage. Elvis was my idol. They used to say he was channelling black influences as no white man should be able to shake their hips like he did. We didn't care; we thought he was gorgeous and made us young women feel like sex goddesses.

In September 1956, the first rock 'n' roll-specific movie stormed West Germany in the form of Bill Hayley's *Rock Around the Clock* (Hayley's army of adoring West German fans would have to wait until 1958 to see him and Comets play a live show). When it was screened in Berlin, it had teenagers and young people dancing in the aisles, so excited that they started throwing chairs around the cinema. It was little more than youthful exuberance, but the authorities interpreted it differently. Young people began frequenting venues such as the Hot House and Boogie Club, but the GDR in particular was persistent in trying to act as a counter influence with state-funded films like *Why Are They Against Us?* This was nothing more than government propaganda which was shown in schools and youth clubs, anywhere where young people gathered to socialize.

As much as rock 'n' roll might have threatened and unnerved both the FDR and GDR establishments, West Germany soon relaxed to the primal rhythms of rock 'n' roll music while the Communist East German regime continued to construe it as a dangerous disease from the West. Rock 'n' roll was a beast that would sprout many heads; it would become more colourful, aggressive and challenging, the preferred method that the modern youth chose to express their dissent with society and government. Rock 'n' roll was more than just music; it was a weapon which anyone could pick up, as Himmel recalled:

> In late 1956, Franz bought a guitar and began to learn some basic chords. He explained most rock 'n' roll riffs originated from early negro blues music. It was the sound of dissent and protest, it was the sound of the slaves expressing their dejection. All rock 'n' roll did was to play it slightly

differently and through an electric amplifier as opposed to acoustically. Franz had this thing he said was the amplifier. It was a box-shaped thing with a fabric-covered front with these knobs on the top of it. He plugged the amplifier in and said it would take a minute to warm up before he could use it. It had these glass tubes [valves] in the back that glowed like light bulbs when switched on. After a couple of minutes, he plugged a cord into his guitar at one end and into the amplifier at the other. When he began playing, the others came running out of their rooms to listen. The more volume he added the more aggressive the sound became. We thought it was great and we all wanted to have a go. Kirsten had a go first and she just made a noise by striking all the strings at once. Franz tried showing her how to do a barre chord, but she couldn't get her fingers positioned correctly on the frets and she soon lost interest. Tia was better but even she struggled and said it was impossible. Imogen was content with just watching us, shyly declining the offer of a go. When it was my turn, I really tried hard, but the strings hurt my fingers. It was not as easy as it looked, yet Franz said I was a natural and if I practised, I would improve. So, Franz agreed to give me lessons every Sunday afternoon. He particularly loved Chuck Berry, and the song 'Johnny B Goode' was his favourite of all. I later learned how to play that one too, among others.

 As the music scene in Hamburg flourished, we'd often go to these private basement shows where there would be just one man with an electric guitar who would play and sing. Many of these young musicians came from cities in England like Liverpool and London and even from Scotland.

 We went to see poets too. We all liked poetry and back then poets could draw large audiences. Some of them spoke about romance, others about war and social subjects. We showed the one young man some of the poetry we'd written, poems we'd kept in our diaries. He encouraged us to get up and read them out to the crowd. We all wanted to, but our nerves got the better of us each time. It was only after a few shots of schnapps one evening that Kirsten got up and agreed to read one of her poems. When she finished, there was rapturous applause from the crowd. It was great as anyone could do it; it was free, and anyone could be a star. The English pop group The Beatles played in Hamburg in 1960. We didn't really get into The Beatles despite the furore their arrival created in the city. For the time being we preferred these small underground gatherings where there weren't hordes of screaming girls drowning everything out.

It was through these subterranean gatherings that the girls met 25-year-old Christa Hubst. Christa was another young girl who'd had to navigate her destiny through the post-apocalyptic ruins of Germany. She was a tall, pretty blonde from the suburbs of Hamburg who worked in the housekeeping department of one of the city's prestigious hotels. It was a hotel where many western rock stars stayed during their visits to West Germany. As a result, Christa had built up quite a collection of autographs from the various stars who stayed at the hotel. She had a deep passion for poetry, admitting to spending much of her spare time writing and reading poetry. Most of her work was directed at the growing political tensions between East and West. She envisioned a future which once again would be defined by the struggle between nations of differing ideologies. Much of her work proved to be strangely prophetic. Christa's quirky personality endeared her to the girls and she was soon invited to the apartment. Tia recalled her first impressions of Christa:

> She was such a pretty girl, very intelligent with beautiful eyes too. Our only concern at the time was what'd happen when Himmel and I revealed that we were in a relationship. Would she still feel the same way about us all? When we finally told her several months after meeting her, she seemed surprised but said she was okay with it and that it was no problem. We didn't think we'd see her again, but she called on us one evening the following week and brought some flowers for us to put in our room. When we sat down and talked about life, she explained she had been engaged to marry her German boyfriend. They'd got on very well and she thought they'd spend the rest of their days together; however, it was only when she began to listen to rock 'n'

roll music and take a more active role in her poetry that the dynamic of their relationship changed.

She explained: 'It was love, but only so long as I remained under his total control. If I wanted to go and listen to the musicians and the poets, he protested. I told him he was behaving selfishly and not to be so immature. It was then he stood against the door, stopping me from leaving his house. For the first time in my life, I felt intimidated by him, even scared of him. He locked the door and cemented his authority by forcing me into the bedroom and raping me on the floor. All the time he was doing it, he was shouting that I belonged to him and I would do as he told me, that I was his property. Afterwards, I pretended all was well as he calmed down and said sorry for getting mad. When I went to work two days later, I never returned to the house and went home to my parents. I couldn't tell them what he'd done as they'd never have believed me. He began calling at my parents' house. I refused to see him, but my bloody father let him in. Things got so bad I threatened to call the police if he didn't go away. I went to live with a schoolfriend and her husband, then after that I lived in the hotel staff accommodation which was actually really nice. So, there you are. That's my story so far.'

By the time Christa had finished talking, the other girls were all in tears. Kirsten got up and went and hugged her, followed by Imogen then me and Himmel. Her story had inflicted pain in our hearts. None of us had ever suffered such indignity as this lovely young woman and we all vowed no one would ever hurt her again: she was our friend now and as friends we looked after each other.

Christa continued living in the hotel staff accommodation. It was rent free, very comfortable and she often enjoyed free meals too. It would have made little sense to move out of what was an extremely generous and beneficial arrangement. She carried out mainly housekeeping duties but also served behind the bar of the sumptuous establishment when required. She proved to be very popular with the guests who often gave her generous tips into the bargain. The only downside to the job was the fact she could be called on if needed, even on her days off. Either way, she enjoyed her work and was happy being independent.

The summer of 1956 gave way to autumn and winter. As the colder weather and darker nights began drawing in, the girls spent more time in their apartment reading, playing records and listening to the radio. Franz and Johann visited every Sunday afternoon to teach Himmel guitar and the girls felt enriched by the presence of their new friend Christa.

Christa joined them for Christmas Day 1956. Himmel and Tia had got up at six that morning to prepare a roast goose. They also prepared all the vegetables for the festive banquet. It was the first time they were all together for Christmas, though they had visited their families in the weeks leading up to Christmas so as not to cause any upset. Franz and Johann joined them in the afternoon and they played board games, music and cards and drank beer and schnapps. Kirsten and Imogen got drunk and retired to bed early while the others spent the evening quietly in front of the open fire listening to the radio.

The girls' lives continued in much the same fashion over the years that followed, the only difference being they were no longer girls anymore: they were young women. Sadly, space does not permit me to document the next four years of their lives, thus in the next chapter we will join them in the years 1961–5.

Chapter 12

A Barbed-wire Bodice

During the night and early hours of 12/13 August 1961, East German soldiers began unrolling bails of barbed wire across streets and neighbourhoods in East Berlin. This was the result of the escalation in tensions between East and West Germany, the USSR and the West, that many feared might emanate from the uneasy post-war years. The rolls of barbed wire now separating East and West Berlin were the precursor to what would become the symbol of Communist tyranny: the Berlin Wall. This ugly grey snake of concrete would blight the German landscape for twenty-eight long years, becoming the flashpoint between East and West throughout the years of the Cold War. The Berlin Wall was more than just a geographical divide: it represented the ideological stand-off between the superpowers of East and West.

In Hamburg the young women rose from their beds on what was a balmy Sunday morning. Himmel switched on the television that morning as she usually did, to provide some background distraction while making coffee. The news that greeted her made her shout to the others, 'Come quickly, come and listen to this. Oh, my god, this is terrible news.' The others rushed out of their bedrooms and they all sat together on the settee as Himmel turned up the volume. Kirsten recalled that Sunday morning:

> It had been the perfect morning up until that point. We all sat in silence as the news was broken about this barbed-wire now separating East Berlin from the West. A precursor to a more permanent structure. Imogen remarked, 'Well, it is the thirteenth; what a fucking day for this to happen.' The others sat listening intently to the newsreader. Tia had her head in her hands and began to cry. We comforted her as best we could, but we were all worried about the friends, family and relatives we had back in Berlin. We spent most of that morning writing letters to those friends we thought might be affected by the erection of this barrier.

Himmel recalled:

> It left a sour taste in our mouths. Tia was really upset by the news and wrote a letter to Lisa to see if she was alright and try and find out more of what was happening there. Tia was worried about her old friends, the Berlin Gang, and was looking for reassurances I couldn't give her.

Imogen remembers:

> People began going out on to the streets to protest, yet their protests were in vain. The Soviet Union was behind this; we'd feared something like this was going to happen, which was one of the reasons Himmel, Tia and Kirsten decided to move here to Hamburg. Being in Hamburg didn't put our immediate fears to rest though. It was just something we would all have to learn to live with, and over the weeks and months that followed we in the West and the East had to do just that.

> *The grey snake stretches as far as the eye can see,*
> *writhing through the landscape, a concrete monstrosity.*
> *The Soviet Union's threat to their prey,*
> *if rules are not obeyed then the people will pay.*
> *She bears her fangs of authority,*
> *spits in the face of democracy.*
> *Swallows the heart of her enemy,*
> *in a bid to control in entirety.*
>
> Hunt to Kill AV XV

When the young women visited their family and friends in Berlin some months later, they were now confronted not just by a monstrous concrete barrier but also increased security checkpoints with guard towers and heavily armed soldiers with ferocious dogs at their sides. Himmel recalled their first visit back to Berlin after the events of 13 August:

> It was like entering a prison complex; you had to go through the checkpoints, where guards stood armed to the teeth with

A Barbed-wire Bodice

snarling dogs at their sides. Guard towers stood menacingly over us and it was a relief to pass through these things and leave them behind. We visited our families who were all very well. Then we all went to see Lisa and Erich and their young son Bobbi who was now 5 years old. It was so nice to see them again. We had kept in touch by visiting over the years since Bobbi was born. Lisa brought Bobbi up to know us all as his aunties. We all adored the little boy, particularly Kirsten who nicknamed him Beetle Bum. Where she got that nickname from, I don't know – she called all little children Beetle Bum. The only stain on that visit back to Berlin, apart from the wall, checkpoints and guard towers was the fact that one of Tia's and Lisa's friends from the old 'Berlin Gang' was in East Berlin and they were unable to contact her. We were glad to see our families and Lisa but were all happy to get back to Hamburg.

Perhaps the most terrifying development to emerge in 1961 amid the political tensions was the test of the first Soviet RDS-202 hydrogen bomb, the most powerful nuclear weapon ever created. News of this weapon, known as the Tsar Bomba, sent shivers down the spines of every German as it did the rest of the world. The Tsar Bomba was never really designed to be a deployable weapon but more a technological demonstrator of the theory, calculations and principles of multistage thermonuclear weapon design. It was designed by Yulii Khariton, Andrei Sakharov, Victor Adamsky, Yuri Babayev, Yuri Smirnov, Yuri Trutnev and Yakov Zel'dovich. The bomb was tested at Sukhoy Nos ('Dry Nose') Cape, Severny Island, Novaya Zemlya. It weighed 60,000lb [27,000kg] or 27 metric tonnes, had a length of 26 feet and a diameter of 6 feet 11 inches. If the proportions of this three-stage hydrogen bomb sounded impressive, then it was dwarfed by its terrifying destructive power. It was carried by a Tupolev Tu-95v, which had to have its bomb bay doors and fuselage fuel tanks removed to accommodate it. To retard the bomb's fall on release from the aircraft, it was fitted with an 800kg 1,500m^2 parachute. It was released from an altitude of 34,500 feet. The bomb detonated at 1133 hours Moscow time on 30 October 1961 at approximately 4,000 metres above the target area. When it exploded, the blast yield of the weapon was recorded at 50 megatons of TNT.

To place this in perspective, imagine all the explosives used during the Second World War detonating at the same time. The carrier aircraft was lucky to escape the effects of the explosion; though caught rapidly by the shockwave, it landed safely even though the outer skin of the aircraft had been scorched by the heat from the blast. The explosion produced enough heat to cause third degree burns at a distance of 100 kilometres (64 miles). The flash of light from the bomb was so bright it was visible from a distance of 1,000 kilometres. While the blast literally flattened the island, radioactive fallout was minimal due to the altitude that the bomb was detonated at. The Tsar Bomba test sent a clear message to the Western powers, turning up the heat in the rapidly escalating Cold War. When the news broke of this terrifying new development in weapons of mass destruction, it was greeted with much consternation around the world but particularly in West Germany. West German schoolgirl Andrea Rupprecht who was 13 in 1961 remembers the gathering pace of the Cold War in the wake of the Tsar Bomba test:

> In school we had to practise what to do in the event of a nuclear attack on West Germany. It was all very frightening because if the warning came, we would have just a few minutes to prepare. If the siren sounded while we were at our desks working, we were told that we had to get under our desks immediately and curl up as tightly as possible into a ball. We were only to come out if the all-clear sounded and our teachers told us that it was safe. The teacher would tune into the radio that would give instructions to people. If a nuclear explosion occurred, it was far safer to remain in a building under some form of cover than being outside. You had to keep clear of windows or anything that was not securely fitted down. We were all told about radiation and how it kills people which is why you had to stay inside. To go outside after an attack would invite death by radiation exposure. We were told all these things and all schoolchildren were taught what to do if a nuclear attack was imminent. These drills were carried out throughout the 1960s, 1970s and early 1980s until the threat of nuclear war slowly subsided due to political changes in Russia. It was a frightening time and all the time when I was at school, I worried about what would

happen if an attack came, whether I'd ever see my mum and dad again. It was horrible and I am glad no child has to live with that kind of fear today.

Himmel, Tia, Kirsten and Imogen were horrified at the news of the Tsar Bomba testing as it represented a new age of terror where death could fall from the sky at any moment and nothing could stop it. Himmel recalled:

> As tensions grew between Russia and America, they used to broadcast these short films on what you should do if the warning came. Keep away from your windows, seek safety beneath a table or in a cupboard beneath the stairs if you had one. Do not hesitate, act quickly. People were advised to prepare a cupboard with fresh water in it, along with dry foods and medical supplies. In the event of a nuclear attack, this should be where you seek refuge. You should take a radio in the cupboard with you which will instruct you on what to do after the attack. There were radio bulletins about it too. We used to sit and listen to the bulletins, trying to imagine what we would do if it really happened. We had a cupboard which we put supplies in as instructed but I doubt whether we could all have fitted inside it. We never once tried it out to see; we just thought, well if it happens, it's best it comes down right on top of us. That way we'd know nothing about it.

A few days after the Tsar Bomba test, a letter arrived that lightened the mood for the four young women. The letter was for Kirsten and it was from Joel, informing her that he was coming over to Germany to visit her. When he arrived, he booked himself into a hotel then called in to see Kirsten and the others. Imogen recalled his visit:

> I always felt a strange pang of jealousy every time Joel came to see Kirsten. It was not in the nasty sense, as I liked Joel, but I used to think, *How dare you take my friend away from me*, but in the joking context. I remember Kirsten left the apartment with Joel on the Friday he arrived, and

Transforming Hitler's Germany

she did not come back until the Sunday afternoon. When she got back, Joel was not with her. He'd walked her back home then left straight away, saying he had to prepare for his flight back to the USA. I could tell she'd been crying, so I demanded to know what had happened. She explained that Joel had booked them into the hotel as man and wife. She admitted they had spent most of the weekend making love in the hotel room and both had had a good time until the Sunday morning.

I asked her, 'Well, what's happened? What went wrong?'

It was then she explained that Joel had asked her to marry him and to go and live in the USA where they could spend the rest of their lives together. Selfishly, I felt a sharp pain in my stomach as my heart sank at the news. I tried to pretend I was happy for her but inside I was screaming and trying not to cry. I just said, 'Oh, that's great news.'

Kirsten replied, 'But, I told him no, that I couldn't do that.'

I looked at her, puzzled, admitting that I felt a momentary sense of relief before asking her, 'Why, why are you not going to go with him? You love him, don't you?'

'I'm very fond of him but I don't feel the same way about him now, now that it's come to it, Imogen. I won't be seeing him again, but I hope we can remain friends, if nothing else,' Kirsten added.

Tia and Himmel had been out for a walk and when they came back, I left it to Kirsten to tell them what had happened. They gave her lots of hugs and reassured her that if they lost Joel as a friend over this, then better that than lose her.

Himmel recalled of the end of the long-distance romance between Joel and Kirsten:

With hindsight I don't think it could ever have worked between them. Kirsten only saw Joel twice a year and I had sensed Kirsten had somehow drifted in her emotions. By evening she was fine and back to her usual, happy self, maybe relieved of the emotional burden that had been upon her. Kirsten later confided in me while we were making tea in the kitchen that she couldn't bear the thought of leaving Imogen behind, that this was the reason she'd declined Joel's offer. She explained that she'd even given Joel's neck chain back as she knew how much it meant to him.

It was then I asked her, 'Look, do you feel more for Imogen than what you're letting on? Because if you do, you need to talk to her' I then told her that Imogen had confided in me earlier, that she'd cried and said, 'I know it's wrong but I'm glad Kirsten is not going to marry Joel and move to the USA. I don't think I could deal with that. I couldn't imagine life without her now. I adore her, you know, maybe more than she realizes.' I then told Kirsten, 'Well, you two need to talk and put your feelings on the table, find out what's really important and what you both really want from each other.'

She smiled and promised she'd talk with Kirsten when the time was right. It was then I joked with her and said, 'Jesus, I'm not sure Tia or I could handle having two lesbians living here with us.' We both laughed but I reminded Imogen if there was anything that she needed to say to Kirsten, she should talk to her for both their sakes.

That same evening Franz and Johann called in. Franz always brought his guitar along and he and Himmel would 'jam' as they called it. The guitar playing inadvertently created a party atmosphere and although they all had work the following morning, they broke out a bottle of schnapps. After the music, Tia recalled the conversation:

> Himmel, Imogen, Kirsten and I were all sitting on the settee. Imogen was partially sitting on Kirsten's lap and Kirsten had her arms around Imogen in her normal way. Imogen then chirped up and asked Franz, 'Does it hurt when you and Johann do it?' We all laughed, more at the audacity of the question than anything else.
>
> Franz and Johann sat blushing, so Franz replied, 'Now you ask, yes it does the first few times. The anus lacks the

elasticity of a female vagina, yet it also contains many nerves that if stimulated very gently can be just as pleasurable.'

Himmel then got up. 'Right, I'm going to bed before this biology lesson develops any further.'

At that Franz and Johann wished us all a good night, thanking us for the schnapps and the entertainment before leaving.

I told Imogen and Kirsten I was going to bed too as I was tired. They said that they were staying up a little longer to listen to some music on the radio as the TV that night was shit. I left them there on the settee and when Himmel and I got into bed, we both hoped they'd take this opportunity to discuss what was really going on between them emotionally. They both reminded me so much of me and Himmel in certain ways, only they were far more outgoing than us.

As Tia and Himmel drifted off to sleep, Kirsten and Imogen lay on the settee listening to the radio. Kirsten recalled that evening:

> It was very warm. Himmel had left the balcony doors open as it was stifling in the living room after the evening's earlier session with Franz and Johann. There was a light breeze, but it was not cooling in the slightest. Imogen was lying on me with her back against me and I had my arms around her. We always relaxed this way, so it was nothing out of the normal. As we listened to the music, Imogen picked my hand up in hers, slowly sliding her fingers between mine.
>
> I said, 'This is how lovers hold hands.' It was then I continued: 'Himmel told me that you cried earlier because you thought I was going to go away with Joel. Well, the reason I said no to his offer of moving to the USA and marrying him was because I couldn't leave you behind. I mean, I felt love for him at one time, but the reality of going through with moving and marriage made me realize that perhaps it was not the love that I had thought it was, if you can understand that.'
>
> Imogen replied, 'Yes, I did cry. I felt so much pain at the thought of you going away and was relieved when you said

you weren't going to go through with it, and yes, I know exactly what you mean ... you know, when we do our kissing thing, what do you feel when we do it? Do you enjoy it?'

'What would you say if I told you that yes, I do enjoy it very much, perhaps more than I should?' I replied.

It was then that Imogen wriggled around until she was lying down facing me. 'Then kiss me right now.'

That kiss was different to any of the others we'd shared as our 'party trick'. It was slow, soft, deep and passionate unlike any kiss or snog I'd ever experienced before. We both felt ourselves getting wet and aroused. I for one didn't wish to waste any more time. I said, 'Come on, let's go to bed now.' We both got up. I switched off the radio and lights before closing the balcony doors. We hurried to the bedroom, but in our haste we both tripped over a side table, ending up collapsed on the floor. There was a loud crash. For a minute we lay there on the floor laughing.

Himmel got up out of bed to investigate: 'What on earth are you two doing down there?'

I got up, grabbed Imogen's hand, pulled her up off the floor and told Himmel 'We're going to bed, but I doubt very much if we are going to get much sleep tonight.' Himmel shook her head, grinning at us then went back to bed.

The sex between us was sensational. We did everything we could think of, even sucking each other's toes – they were clean of course. We both lay awake afterwards and Imogen whispered, 'I know for me it will be no problem as I don't have any parents to answer to, but what are yours going to say if they find out?'

'I'll cross that bridge once I come to it,' I said. 'I'm not sure what Petra is going to say about it though. She might be shocked at first.'

The following morning Himmel, Tia, Kirsten and Imogen all got up to prepare for their day at work as lovers as well as friends. Himmel remarked to Kirsten and Imogen before they left, 'I knew you two would become an item someday; it took a long time, but I just knew it. Only a lesbian can detect the inner lesbian in others.' At that they all laughed and headed off to work. Later on that day, Tia and Himmel noticed a new entry in the joint diary, a short cryptic piece which read:

> *I walk barefoot over the shrapnel from your broken heart,*
> *these fragments lacerate the soles of my feet,*
> *leaving bloody imprints the only evidence of the love*
> *I once possessed for you.*
> *A love that has not so inexplicably died.*
> *All things have to die, some sooner than others,*
> *the mortician's embrace is the last we ever feel,*
> *to tread the heavens with beheaded angels.*
> *I feel like a beheaded angel whenever I smile.*
> *I think I smile like a liar, not really a smile at all.*

It was clear from the handwriting that Kirsten was the author of the piece. It was a brief literary statement reminiscent of the works of the German philosopher Friedrich Nietzsche (1844–1900). It was a curious irony as Kirsten had never read Nietzsche.

Two days later it was Himmel's birthday. Tia, Kirsten and Imogen had a special surprise lined up for her. Tia had asked Franz and Johann if she gave them the money would they source a guitar and amplifier for Himmel's birthday present from the girls. Franz told Tia it wouldn't be a problem. They arranged to bring Himmel's present around in the evening. The others didn't tell Himmel that Franz and Johann were visiting so when they turned up, it was a huge surprise, as Tia recalled:

> There was a knock at the door. We told Himmel, 'That's for you. You better go and see what it is.' When Himmel opened the door, there stood Franz and Johann holding this guitar and an amplifier before bursting into 'Happy Birthday'. Himmel stood there with her hands over her mouth in disbelief and said 'What, is that for me?' We told her it was her birthday gift from us all. As she cradled the brand-new 1959 'Blonde' Fender Stratocaster electric guitar [worth £25,000 today] in her arms, she had tears in her eyes, tears of joy. Himmel put the guitar down and hugged us all, thanking us for the best birthday ever. Franz and Johann were invited in for cake and tea where Himmel

showed them the birthday cards she'd received from us, friends and family.

After tea we told her, 'Well, come on then, let's hear you play that thing.'

Himmel plugged the amplifier into the socket, then the guitar into the amplifier before switching it on. She sat there for a minute, carefully tuning each string before announcing, 'Right, here we go!' She stood up, cranked up the volume on the amplifier and the guitar began to growl like an aggressive animal in a cage. The vision of Himmel with that guitar strapped to her body as she tore into the intro and main riff to Chuck Berry's 'Johnny B Goode' was the sexiest thing I've ever seen. She was just fucking amazing. I marvelled at the speed and dexterity of her slender fingers as they played the strings, those same fingers that played me like a fine instrument. Had that occurred before a packed audience, it could have been a defining moment for rock 'n' roll in Germany. Yet, this was no public show, it was a personal moment just for her friends and me. When she'd finished, we all whistled and applauded. Kirsten and Imogen were on the settee busy cementing their love for each other with their tongues down each other's throats. Franz and Johann watched them, clearly stunned, but before they could say anything, Himmel said, 'Yes, they're at it too now, just so you both know.'

Franz just shook his head: 'Well, fuck me. I'm really shocked!'

Imogen recalled:

People close to us who knew us were shocked. Yet ever since Kirsten and I had first met, there'd been no sexual attraction; there really wasn't to start with. I can't explain it; it was something that just developed between us. Sometimes the fear of losing someone you care about deeply is a very sobering experience. Yes, I tried everything in my power to not love Kirsten in any emotional sense, to just be friends. We had both dated boys and we enjoyed dating boys. Maybe the business with Joel opened our eyes. The thought of Kirsten leaving for the USA, getting married and the possibility of not seeing her again made me realize that I could be as happy in a relationship with a girl as I could a man. I couldn't see anything wrong with that; only society at that time deemed it wrong. Yet who was society to judge what made us happy? That day when I discovered that Kirsten had declined Joel's marriage proposal because she didn't want to leave me made us both realize we had to be honest with each other. We only had this one chance in life. It was a serious challenge to have to face back then. But we just had to look at Tia and Himmel: they never argued, rarely disagreed over things and adored each other. Their love developed from their friendship. Our love was the same.

Kirsten recalled:

We weren't kids anymore, yet we weren't old women either. We were still young women enjoying our lives and living it how we wanted to live it. Back then it was society's view that you had to marry and have kids before you were 25 or somehow you weren't normal. I just thought, *Fuck society*. I had friends who had married at just 18 and a few years later they were mothers with two or three kids complaining about it all and wishing they were single again. Imogen became my best friend, a best friend I soon began to love. There is no way I could have ever left her behind. Tia and Himmel were just like sisters to us; we all lived in the same apartment and could never have lived life any other way. It was perfect. We were in every sense an eclectic group of musicians and poets enjoying life to the full and never afraid to tell anyone what we thought.

It was in 1962 that Hamburg was struck by a natural disaster of biblical proportions during the night of 16/17 February, with the onslaught of the *Vincinette* low-pressure system. This hurricane swept in from the southern Polar Sea into the German Bight. With speeds of up to 124 mph, the storm surged into the German Bight, which in turn overwhelmed the dykes. Breaches along the coast, and the rivers Elbe and Weser led to serious flooding of vast areas of the city. The most seriously affected area was Wilhelmsburg, 100 kilometres inland. Himmel recalled the traumatic event:

> The authorities issued warnings of very high winds over the TV and radio stations. I remember the gales lashing our apartment building and the electricity tripping on and off. We all prepared for a power cut by setting up some candles. The storm was far worse than what the authorities predicted. There had been fifty odd breaches before the alarm was raised in Hamburg. It was such a horrible night that we all went to bed early as the wind made the apartment very cold. Thankfully, our part of the city was not too badly affected but the floods destroyed over 60,000 homes and killed 315 people. NATO helicopters flew into the affected areas, flying in and out all day long in the days following the disaster. People called them '*Fliegende Engel*' which means 'Flying Angels'. Some areas of the city had to be cordoned off, trams and railway services were suspended, and Hamburg centre was cut off and had to be supplied by air. We had no power in the apartment and had to cook in the small fireplace in the living room. We'd never really used this open fire before but during the power outages it was our only means of being able to cook some hot food and boil water. It was horrible as we heard stories of dead bodies being discovered in side streets and alleyways weeks after the floods had receded. We all volunteered to help wherever we could, along with thousands of other Hamburg residents. We were a community and in times like these we came together to help one another.

The damage caused by the Hamburg floods was extensive and it was some months before the affected areas were fully functional again. The damage to some businesses was so great that they never reopened. Yet Hamburg was resilient, used to coping with disasters and the spirit of its people could not be dented.

As for Berlin, the Grey Lady might now be wearing a barbed-wire bodice, but defiance was in the hearts of her people, and if the USSR felt that she would submit quietly, they were greatly mistaken.

Her fine dress of barbed wire is torn from her shoulders with such force
that her blood soaks the ground at her feet.
It takes a million of them to pull her down, as she stands protesting,
the cold breath of the east against her neck,
her legs forced apart with such violence the bones snap like willow,
excited hell-lit eyes, orgasm death deep within her,
a bullet between the thighs,
lead, flesh and blood forming a solid slug of hatred at the mouth of
her straining cervix,
her lips now taste of blood, her eyes now blackened from pain,
she walks in slender shoes secured by nails,
to take Andromeda's place within the flames.

Chapter 13

The Ever-changing Sculpture that is Fire

The Cuban Missile Crisis of 1962 was the closest that the USSR and the Western powers came to an actual superpower confrontation. It was only stern diplomacy on the part of US President John F. Kennedy that averted conflict. In the wake of this confrontation, where the world held its breath, on 20 June 1963 Soviet Premier Nikita Khrushchev and President Kennedy agreed to the establishment of a special telephone hotline by which both could contact each other in the event of any future crisis which might emerge throughout the Cold War years. It appeared a step in the right direction that both leaders of the two world superpowers would now be open to direct dialogue should the need arise. However, it did not completely dispel fears of war breaking out between the two countries, but it was viewed as an advancement in relations between East and West.

On Wednesday, 26 June 1963, John F. Kennedy visited West Berlin where he was warmly greeted. Kirsten recalled watching his visit on TV:

> Imogen and I were home before Tia and Himmel. We switched on the TV to see the news of the president's visit. He made a speech in front of the Berlin Wall to rapturous applause. He said, *'Ich bin ein Berliner'* which is 'I am a Berliner'. We sat watching and thought it was great that he was saying how committed he was to West Germany and that America would continue to uphold the freedoms of the people of West Germany.
>
> Imogen remarked, 'He's basically telling Khrushchev to fuck off. I wonder what the Communists are going to think to that?'
>
> We liked President Kennedy as he was not going to take any shit from the Communists. On 5 August, Russia, America and Britain signed this treaty which effectively put

a stop to the testing of nuclear weapons. We read about it in the newspapers and we all felt it a positive step, but that reek of paranoia was still overwhelming.

It was a sad turn of events that on 22 November of that same year, US President John F. Kennedy was assassinated in Dallas, Texas. Himmel recalled the reaction of her friends upon hearing the news:

> When Kirsten and Imogen arrived home from work that day, Tia and I told them the US president has been shot dead in Dallas, Texas. We were all shocked by the news; I think the whole world was. I'm not sure what the Russians really felt about it, but we here in West Germany were very shocked and upset at hearing the news. Kirsten and Imogen were pretty upset by the news; they both thought Kennedy was a great leader. They sat quietly that night in each other's arms. I recall Lyndon B. Johnson taking over as president, and he made it clear he would pursue the same policy of firmness over the scourge of world Communism.

By late 1963, the four young women had witnessed some momentous events in world history. They were still leading active social lives, visiting their favourite pubs and underground clubs, as they called them. The music scene in West Germany, far from petering out, was evolving ever further. A new breed of rock 'n' roll was emerging, possessing an uncompromising sound that would soon define the attitudes of the mid-1960s. While shocking the older generation, the aggressive sound and unkempt appearance of bands like the Rolling Stones was readily embraced by youth all over Europe, particularly in West Germany. Tia recalled:

> I first heard the Rolling Stones when Eddie, the owner of the café where Himmel and I worked, put the single 'I Wanna Be Your Man' on the jukebox. He'd had that copy of the single specially sent over from England as it wasn't yet available in Germany at the time. The music was blues influenced and similar to the rock 'n' roll of the 1950s yet it was faster with a rougher edge to it; it sounded more

urgent, more aggressive. The guys in the band had long hair like girls and wore funny clothes. I used to sing 'I Wanna Be Your Man' to Himmel [she laughs]. The only one of us who didn't like the Stones was Petra who preferred The Beatles. I recall Petra coming into the café during her first stay in Hamburg. She stood over the jukebox perusing all the songs, then she suddenly smiled and put a coin in the slot. Next thing, The Beatles' 'I Wanna Hold Your Hand' was blaring out. What made us laugh most was Petra sitting down stirring her milkshake with her straw and blurting out, 'I wanna hold your cock!' when the chorus came. We had to tell her to keep her voice down; the café was pretty liberal, but it had its limits [she laughs].

When asked about her older sister's relationship with Imogen, Petra replied:

I think Imogen was lovely. Yes, I was shocked when Kirsten first told me all about her and Joel finishing and that she had feelings for someone else. I never guessed it was another girl. I wasn't going to fall out with her over it, but I was worried what mum and dad would say when they finally found out about it. Yes, I was apprehensive at first but once I'd met Imogen and spent time with her and saw how happy they both were, I just thought, *Fuck it, what's the problem? To hell with what the world thinks*. It didn't bother me that my sister was in a relationship with another girl. Himmel and Tia had been lovers for some time now and they were just fine. It didn't change anything; she was still my beautiful big sister whom I loved.

The run-up to Christmas 1963 was one of the most memorable for the four young women. They had saved money and were able not only to buy nice gifts for each other but were also able to treat their families back in Berlin. They had decided to spend this Christmas with their families and they could also visit Lisa, Erich and Bobbi. Kirsten decided Imogen would accompany her as she had no real family to spend Christmas with. It would be a little awkward having to pretend to be friends, but they'd carry it off, as they say. Only Petra knew the truth and she might find it hard to keep a straight face at the dinner table on Christmas Day. They left Hamburg a few days before Christmas Eve, their arms laden with presents and determined to have a good time. Himmel recalled:

> It was the first time we had been apart for some time, but we felt it was right we all visit our families, spend some time over Christmas with them then return to Hamburg after Boxing Day dinner. All my parents wanted to know was if I'd met anyone yet and had any thoughts about settling down and maybe having children. It was very awkward. I couldn't sound enthusiastic about an idea I hated. I told them, 'No, I haven't met anyone yet.' I decided that when I got back to Hamburg, I would write to them and tell them the truth and await their reaction. We all met up before returning to Hamburg so we could visit Lisa, Erich and Bobbi. When we arrived at their home, Lisa went crazy with joy: she said seeing us was the best Christmas present she could have had. It was lovely to see her again, and how I wished she was still with us but, looking at her life, she was happy, and Erich worshipped her and Bobbi. Kirsten played with Bobbi all the time we were there, and calling him 'Beetle Bum' – where she got that from, god knows. We shed a few tears when we left but it was nice seeing her again and seeing how well she looked.

New Year's Eve 1963 was a memorable celebration. Kirsten and Imogen went out early to Franz's and Johann's and came back slightly worse for wear at 10 pm. They had spent the evening playing games and drinking with the boys while Tia and Himmel stayed home to watch TV. Tia recalled:

> Himmel and I cuddled up together to enjoy a few glasses of wine with some chocolates to munch through as we watched TV. We heard Kirsten and Imogen coming back, singing loudly. We thought, *Oh, god, they're pissed again.* They greeted us with kisses then went into their room to change into their pyjamas. They came out in their dressing

gowns. Kirsten sat down in the chair and Imogen squeezed in next to her; it was one of those old chairs big enough for two. Within minutes they were both asleep, Imogen with her head on Kirsten's shoulder. We weren't mean though and woke them up before midnight. We celebrated seeing in 1964 with mugs of tea while watching fireworks from the balcony. We all made a wish then went back inside to listen to the radio for a while. It was as we lay in bed that Himmel revealed her plan to tell her parents that we were romantically involved. I told her that if she was going to tell her parents then it was only fair I told mine too. Neither of us relished the prospect but it was something we had to do.

The next morning Tia and Himmel sat in bed with letter pads resting on their knees, busily drafting the letters that would effectively decide whether or not their families might disown them. Letters were torn up and rewritten multiple times as both young women struggled to find the right words. Eventually Himmel said, 'Right, that's it! It's done.' She sealed the letter in its pink envelope, ready to post the next day. Tia took a little longer but, satisfied she had found the right words, she too sealed her letter in its envelope. Both agreed the emotional fallout from their families might dwarf that of the Tsar Bomba itself, yet in a way they both felt relieved. Neither wanted to live a lie anymore, however difficult it might be.

It was not long before the response from their families landed through the letterbox. First, a letter arrived from Himmel's mother which Kirsten handed to her as she arrived home from work with Tia. Himmel paced around the apartment with the letter in her hand, too scared to open it. Eventually, she sat down and tore open the letter. It was a blunt yet unemotional request for Himmel to call her mother on the telephone. They had no telephone in the apartment, but Franz and Johann had one. Himmel went to see them at their flat to ask if she could use it. Franz recalled overhearing the conversation:

> It was pretty heated at first. Both Johann and I really felt for Himmel as she was a lovely girl. She hadn't told us what she needed to speak to her mother and father about but we guessed by the nature of the conversation. She was on the

telephone for around thirty minutes but things calmed down by the end of the call. When she placed the phone back in the cradle, she burst into tears. We comforted her and when she stopped crying, she explained everything. She told us her parents were furious at first, but the thought of disowning her was equally as unbearable. We reassured her that they would need time to come to terms with it, as it must have been a shock. We walked her back home where a concerned Tia stood waiting for her in the cold outside the apartment. The two embraced then we told them we would see them soon.

Once inside, Himmel told Tia what her parents had said. Tia recalled:

> They were very upset and shocked but could not disown her. They told her how much they loved her and couldn't understand where things had gone wrong, how things had come to this. Himmel said she could hear her father crying in the background as her mother spoke, yet by the end of the call, they had both calmed down. I knew it was my turn next and I dreaded what my parents were going to say.

Tia's letter arrived a few days later, and this time it was her turn to face the wrath of her parents:

> I took Himmel with me into the bedroom and told her to open it and read it first as I couldn't do it. I was too afraid of what it might say. Himmel tore open the envelope, unfolded the letter and began to read. After she had read it, she handed it to me and said, 'Come on, you have to read this yourself.' My father had written it and ranted on about how all that westernized tripe had turned me into a 'queer' and that I should come back home right away and sort myself out. Then he went on to say, 'What would the family think, my aunts, uncles and cousins?' I knew my parents well enough to know this would be their response. I decided to leave things for a few days then write to them again. It was hard but they would have to get used to it as I was totally committed to Himmel and would rather die than be without her.

> I showed the letter to Kirsten and Imogen, warning them that sometime soon they'd have to do the same. Imogen broke the gloom in her typical style by saying, 'Hmm, god, if I go and tell my dear granny that I'm now a lesbian, she'll probably drop down dead with a heart attack.' She then went on to say, 'Granny doesn't need to know about this, not yet anyway.' Imogen did make us laugh but Kirsten said, 'My parents will probably go fucking mad.' Her remark made us laugh even more. Himmel and I were glad they were there with us as they always made a joke out of a crisis and we so adored them for that.

After sitting down to dinner that night, the four young women sat and drank mugs of tea while watching TV. Kirsten soon got bored. She stood up, grabbed Imogen's hand and announced, 'Knickers to this! The TV's shit tonight. Let's go and have sex.' Imogen protested, 'But I was watching that,' as she was unceremoniously dragged into the bedroom. The door closed behind them. Himmel and Tia shook their heads and continued watching TV. Then the bedroom door opened again, and a half-naked Kirsten announced, 'By the way, just so you both know – she's the bitch not me.' She stuck out her tongue and shut the door.

1964 dawned in much the same way as many previous New Year's Days. Those who had partied through the early hours were now lying in bed, nursing hangovers, while others made the most of their day off to visit friends and family or just go out for a walk. Tia, Himmel, Kirsten and Imogen spent their New Year's Day quietly in their apartment, watching TV, reading books and writing poetry and notes in their joint journal.

It was just four days later that they received some shattering news from Lisa in Berlin. One of their dear friends from the old 'Berlin Gang', Katrin, had been found dead by her husband. The saddest thing of all was that Katrin seemed to have taken her own life. It was particularly devastating news as Tia and Lisa had been close friends with Katrin during the war years. This dreadful news hit Tia very hard, as Himmel explained:

> The news was conveyed by a letter from Lisa. We knew it was what they called a 'death letter' as it was edged in

black. From what Lisa had said, Katrin had fallen into a deep depression ever since they built that fucking Berlin Wall. They wouldn't let her cross to visit her parents and siblings in the Western Zone. Her husband, who was a Ukrainian by birth, wrote to Lisa explaining that Katrin had suffered three miscarriages during the marriage and the wall being built added to her misery. He said she had used gas to take her own life: she had put her head in the oven and turned on the gas, and that's how she died. There was no way Tia or Lisa could even get to her funeral. It took all my strength to comfort Tia through this dreadful period. She often cried at night and began to have nightmares again. We all gave her our support and love and thankfully she got through it. It brought home to us the reality of that grey slab of concrete known around the world as the Berlin Wall. It symbolized everything that was evil and wrong in our world. People were separated and unable to cross to see their families. If they were lucky, they could stand and wave at them from a distance. The Berlin Wall represented an evil, oppressive regime every bit as twisted as that of the Nazis. I never met or knew Katrin, but Tia talked of her often. She said she was a lovely, happy-go-lucky kind of girl. The fact her life ended in this terribly miserable way cast a shadow over our otherwise happy existence. We felt for her poor husband, as he sounded really nice, but were unable to reach out to him and offer our comfort because of that concrete barrier.

Christa Hubst lightened the mood during one of her visits which the four friends always looked forward to. She always came bearing news of all the latest bands and poets who were visiting Hamburg to perform or just hang out. Christa herself had not long been freed from what she called 'a troublesome relationship with a man she had been dating for three months'. Himmel made coffee then they all sat down to hear Christa's latest news. Himmel recalled the conversation that evening in March 1964:

> Christa began to fill us in on all the latest gossip. She was still living and working at the hotel. She told us of the

visits to her parents who kept badgering her to settle down and how boring it all was, and she was grateful she didn't live at home anymore. She had met this man, a year older than her, while attending one of the basement shows she still went to. She explained that for a while she thought he was 'Mr Right' but it soon turned out to be a nightmare. We asked her in what way. She told us that she would often sneak him into her room, risking her job if caught, and that he had the habit of leaving his dirty underwear all over the floor. He had also introduced her to the habit of smoking, something which she now admitted to being addicted to. Christa also told us he was a great writer of poetry but a lousy and selfish lover under the sheets. On their third date when she sneaked him into her room, they had barely got through the door when he demanded of her: 'Get that beautiful cherry mouth of yours around my Bratwurst, and paint my body with your tongue.' She explained that she'd never performed oral sex on a man before and wasn't sure if she'd do it right. She went on to explain that it was not the most pleasant of experiences and that he blew a great load of his foul-tasting, salty fluid into her mouth, the juices running down her chin and trickling down the gully between her breasts. Afterwards, he told her he needed to sleep as he was worn out. The following morning, she had to get ready for work yet all he wanted to do was fuck. He refused to leave until she agreed to it. Reluctantly, she did it with him, but it was about as romantic as fucking your own brother. She said he dived in there, telling her to relax, to which she replied, 'Relax, how the bloody hell am I supposed to relax when it feels as if you're trying to insert a cucumber between my legs?' She imagined that only death could have been any colder. We were quite shocked by what she was telling us. She continued, 'To truly understand a bad male [or female] in any relationship, one firstly has to understand the psychology of the predator.' We all laughed but understood what she was saying. It wasn't so much making love but more like, 'Hi honey, are your legs open for business?' When Christa left later that evening after having a meal with us, Kirsten, who had been listening intently to the conversation, wrote in our joint diary the following: 'I am an expedient malicious thing, I don't have the right, to put things right.' I thought it was very clever and seemed appropriate. The good thing was Christa soon tired of this oafish male and told him she didn't want to see him again. A girl should be seduced properly and romantically not treated like a whore. Her juices should be savoured like a fine wine, not merely a mouthful of piss, and fingers should conduct a thorough reconnaissance of a girl's receptivity. Steady romance for some can be difficult to procure, steady romance they say, much like a flow of congealing blood.

It was Christa Hubst who kept her four friends entertained with tales of rock star and celebrity excesses, something she had witnessed frequently in her employment at the Hamburg hotel where she worked. Christa regarded these things as one of the perks of her job, yet by the mid-1960s the Vietnam War, which began in 1955 between the Communist North backed by the Soviet Union and China and the South backed by the USA, had escalated significantly. The Flower Power and Hippie movements flourished. Young people all over the world were expressing their dissent against the war through non-violent peaceful protest, and as a result many young people embraced both the Flower Power and Hippie movements. Those who supported the war argued that it was necessary in preventing the further spread of Communism. Few understood this more than perhaps those living in West Germany. For the younger generation the integration of Flower Power into the Hippie movement was seen as a logical mating of ideologies, which appealed to the youth. Himmel recalled:

> We didn't get into the Flower Power or Hippie thing, but we had friends and associates who did. In my opinion it started out as an ethical movement with good intentions, yet it became very seedy very quickly and seemed to spawn these pseudo-religious cults which didn't interest us at all. These cults formed into these independent harems of young men and women presided over by some self-proclaimed

messiah. They smoked marijuana, talked peace and free love and the messiah figure retained the right to sleep with whomever he chose. Many of the followers were just too naïve to see the dangers.

Kirsten recalled:

> These Hippie people were really funny and dumbed out all the time and they smoked way too much weed for their own well-being. Imogen and I didn't smoke, so weed, as they called it, never appealed to us, neither did it to Tia and Himmel. We felt like casual observers to some form of cultural car crash. We liked our music and socializing, but we had our own identities we were perfectly happy with. I had a friend who joined one of these cults. It was a Sodom and Gomorrah of naked, stoned girls fawning over their leader. They cum-swapped as they French kissed, snorted LSD off album covers, ate 'Pinkies' [foetal mice] from cocktail sticks and there was nothing 'groovy' about their lifestyle. They were like, 'Hey man, we're all sailing on snail mucus here, slow it down baby, slow it right down' – fucking idiots. It made you think, *Jesus why we don't just go out and fuck on the street?*

Imogen remembers how she often got irritated by the Hippie friends she encountered in Hamburg: 'The guys would come up and say, "Hey, baby you look really down man; lighten up." I ended up telling one to fuck off once as he just really annoyed me by not shutting up.'

Kirsten also remembered:

> You couldn't have a rational conversation with them about war and Communism and things; they just didn't get it. Most were just naïve young kids who hadn't experienced war like we had. They spent their time smoking and fucking each other and protesting about the war in Vietnam. What they didn't get was they weren't going to change anything. Governments make war and only they have the power to stop them.

The rock music scene of the mid- to late-1960s couldn't have been more different from that pioneered by Bill Hayley and the Comets of the earlier 1950s, as Christa Hubst explained:

> Bill Hayley was lovely, a real gentleman who was courteous and respectful. The new breed of rock bands was completely different. It wasn't about the music anymore; it was about money, sex and drugs and they were self-destructive people. I recall the one rock band – I won't mention who they were here as I know they're still around, playing occasionally to audiences today. They once performed in Hamburg and stayed at my hotel. By the time the band and their groupies left, the room resembled a murder scene. The once crisp white sheets and pillows were stained red with menstrual blood. One of their groupies had drawn a heart on the inside of the door with her vaginal blood. They were asked to leave early due to their behaviour. I recall the one girl groupie, who looked about 18, came out of the room wrapped in a blanket; her eyes were black around the edges and she looked ill. She trudged barefooted down the corridor. When she reached the entrance, the band had left without her and she began cursing. She sat out on the front steps crying. One of the other girls comforted her and she told her that she didn't know if she had enough money to get back home. She spoke with an American accent. They'd basically used her like a whore and dumped her. Before I began cleaning up their room, I sat in one of the chairs and thought to myself, *If this is what rock 'n' roll has now come to, if this is what it's all about, they can shove it.* They were just dirty cunts. It was disgusting. One of them had left behind a piece of paper with a handwritten lyric scribbled on it. I still have it now and it reads:
>
> > *I'm like a character in a film*
> > *with the least chance of surviving to the end.*
> > *I'm gonna send my baby out to buy my pills,*
> > *jerk off in the face of death.*

As for Flower Power and the Hippie movements, both died along with that beautiful actress Sharon Tate and four others on 9 August 1969 when they were slain by members of the so-called Manson Family. The Sharon Tate murder was particularly brutal, butchered to death with knives, and also killing her unborn child which she was close to giving birth to. I remember Himmel, Tia, Kirsten, Imogen and I discussing this one evening and it made us feel physically sick. Sharon Tate was so beautiful; we could not comprehend what evil could drive people to commit such an act. Then Kirsten reminded us all about Hitler, that it was no different in perspective: hate is hate, prejudice is prejudice and murder is murder. We all felt that we were now living in times that in some ways we could no longer relate to. Things were changing too fast. The things you used to have to work your arse off to buy could now be paid for in instalments; life was becoming cheap and society was following that same doctrine.

Himmel concurs with Christa:

It seemed as if the 'old world' was suddenly dying, like it was being subsumed in technological advances. I remember watching the *Apollo 11* moon landings live on TV. Tia, Kirsten, Imogen and I all watched, fascinated by it all. I recall Kirsten saying, 'Werner von Braun helped to make this happen. He helped America design the *Apollo 11* rocket, yet he was also responsible for the creation of the V-2 missiles which brought death and destruction to mankind. It's all so bloody hypocritical when something becomes packaged in the name of science and discovery.' She was correct though, wasn't she?

Tia added:

With hindsight, the late 1940s and the 1950s were the best years of our lives. And social and economic changes enabled us to jointly buy the apartment in Hamburg we had been renting for many years. It just made sense to us; none of us were going anywhere, and we all enjoyed living together far too much to change that.

Kirsten agreed with Tia:

We shared our lives, so we bought the apartment as together we all earned enough money to be able to do the things we all wanted to do. Buying the apartment gave us all security, a place to call home until we were all gone. It was agreed that when the last one of us died, Tia's niece Hedra would act as executor of our wills, distributing our possessions as she saw fit. The apartment was to be sold and the proceeds spread among our families and relatives where applicable.

Imogen summed it up:

Tia, Himmel and Kirsten were the only people I wanted to live my life with. Meeting them when they came to live and work in Hamburg was a blessing, each one a gift from heaven. I had lost my family during the war and all I had was my grandparents. They became my family and Kirsten my best friend, soulmate and lover. Yes, we became lovers, but that was our choice. We would all grow old together and look out for each other; that's how it would be until the end.

As a caterpillar morphs into a butterfly,
we spread our wings and learn to fly.
Together we could face the day,
each joy and heartbreak that came our way.
Lovers and friends standing side by side,
one family with nothing to hide.
No one could break us, although they tried,
a love like ours cannot be denied.

A Love Like Ours AV XVI

The Ever-changing Sculpture that is Fire

Revolution in the Eastern Bloc countries of Poland and Hungary would set off a political and social chain reaction that would bring down the Berlin Wall which had stood for twenty-eight long years, claiming the lives of eighty people who had attempted to escape from East to West. The collapse of the Wall also signalled the demise of Communist domination in Europe with the breakup of the Soviet Union.

On 9 November 1989, crowds of East Germans climbed onto the wall, joined by West Germans. Soon a slab of the wall was cut out and the crowds flooded through in celebration. Many could see that German reunification was now just a matter of time. In East Germany abandoned warehouses were broken into and flooded with young people, who celebrated the demise of the Wall to the backdrop of Acid House music. The atomic flash of silver strobe lighting made it appear as if they were characters in some black and white movie being played out in slow motion. They partied long into the early hours and the cold grey dawn, yet the warmth of freedom was in their hearts. Tia, Himmel, Kirsten and Imogen watched the news on TV, enthralled. Through her existence the Grey Lady had experienced much pain and humiliation. Maybe now she could tear off that bodice of barbed wire and be beautiful once again.

In many aspects the lives of Tia, Himmel, Kirsten, Lisa and Imogen resembled the ever-changing sculpture that is fire. It had once burned so fiercely when first ignited, yet it steadily slowed in its intensity. Eventually it had to die, leaving behind only the warmth it had once exuded.

Afterword

Tia Schuster's niece, Hedra Klems, informed me of the passing of Himmel Boiten at the age of 83 in Hamburg in October 2010. Ironically, just two weeks after Himmel passed away, Tia died. Kirsten and Imogen gave Tia all the support they could muster in what was a traumatic time for them all. Tia had stopped eating and appeared to have come down with a fever; she went to bed early one evening and died quietly in her sleep. Kirsten and Imogen told Hedra that their dear sister Tia had died from a broken heart, that there could be no other reason. When Hedra visited them after Tia's passing, Kirsten handed her a poem she had found beneath Tia's pillow, a poem that had been written over the days after her beloved Himmel's passing. It read:

I fell asleep,
yet within minutes I found myself walking beside you,
down the familiar streets of Hamburg.
All the familiar faces had somehow re-appeared smiling
and saying hello,
we walked around the harbour, drinking from bottles of Coke.
We stopped to share a kiss, saying 'I love you',
but then the skies turned from blue to grey,
as the early morning traffic stirred me from my dream.
I ran my fingers across to where you used to lie.
All I felt were empty sheets.
Someday I hope to be with you, once more be in your arms.
I can no longer live without you my love.
I am dying from this broken heart.

The following piece was written by Annamarie in memory of Himmel and Tia:

Afterword

No words can express my love for you,
you walked into my life and it began anew.
Your crystal blue eyes sought my broken soul,
expelling the darkness that's taken its toll.
Two rebel hearts set the world alight,
your smile will forever shine on bright.
Let's toast to life with a bottle of wine,
while you play my heart strings one last time.
                                    Rebel Hearts AV XVII

In 2015, Kirsten Albrecht passed away and Imogen Brietzl followed in 2017. After Imogen's passing, Hedra Klems became executor of the wills which then came into effect as requested. Hedra recalled her visit to the apartment after Imogen had died:

> I walked around the apartment; far from being melancholy there was this happy resonance in every room. When the apartment was put up for sale, it was bought by a young couple. They were intrigued to hear some of its history, so we sat down, and I told them all about my aunt Tia, Himmel, Kirsten, Imogen and Lisa. To me they were all my aunts and I loved them all dearly. I told the couple they would be very happy here. The apartment was cleared, and I retained many keepsakes, including their huge joint diary. Before I handed over the keys, I had one more walk around before leaving for the last time. It was like saying goodbye to an old friend. I couldn't help but shed tears as I walked down the stairs for the last time. I walked out of the building into the pouring rain. I didn't look back. I caught my train back to Berlin, back home to my husband and daughter.

When Tia Schuster's niece Hedra presented me with the hefty, black, leather-bound scrapbook containing the collective writings, photographs and poems, I was somewhat unsure of what I might discover. Over the course of time, pages, letters and notes had fallen out, only to be hastily put back in the wrong order. Thankfully the task of reorganizing the material did not involve too much time.

The formulation of this book, far from being a chore, has been an absolute pleasure. The only regret is that we could not include all the material due to the word count limit. With each session spent on this project both Annamarie and I looked forward to working on the next with great anticipation, and as the memoir evolved, it was clear to us as part creators of this endearing work that we both felt an involvement. It was an attachment to those whose words were not only entertaining, but reminding us that we were now looking through the broken window into some dark, dusty, long-abandoned room which signified a time now sadly buried beneath layers of eras, some of which now represent our own collective social history and our own pasts.

Annamarie has embellished this work with her eloquent verse in a way the girls would have been proud of. Poetry figured greatly in their lives as it does in Annamarie's today. Poetry was often the chosen means of expression for the girls, especially during times where conversation on certain aspects of their lives was not deemed permissible, particularly societally. Both Annamarie and I would like to believe that this volume so dear to us should serve as a reminder that those from the past helped determine our futures. The girls, and indeed young men, whose words have shaped this book had to fight for much throughout their lives: the right to live their lives the way they wanted to live them, the right to love whom they chose without fear of prejudice and to enjoy the same equality as enjoyed by their peers within a largely male-dominated society. They lived with the constant threat of nuclear war on their doorstep yet lived they did. The social freedoms we take for granted today were won by them.

Before drawing this afterword and ultimately this account to a close, Annamarie and I would like to allow Hedra the final words:

> Of course, I came to know Himmel, Kirsten, Imogen, Lisa, Petra and Christa well over the years as I grew up. It mattered not to me that my aunt had found love with a woman as opposed to a male. Himmel was a beautiful lady: she was kind, warm and loving and I called her aunty as I did the others. I didn't see much of Lisa but the times I was in her company I found her a delight and quite understood

Afterword

how she had figured so highly in my aunt's life over the years. Their friendship had flourished during difficult times, when Germany had temporarily lost its way in the world. Kirsten and Imogen were such amusing characters and I loved them dearly. I remember the jokes they used to tell and the pranks they used to play. Every time I think of them, I smile. Christa too was a delight to know. A real beauty with her blond hair, blue eyes, slender figure and beautiful face, but she was never aloof around people like pretty girls sometimes are and she had time for everyone. Yet today when I think of them, I get very sad. The youth of today appear governed by social media, consumerism and celebrity culture. My aunt Tia and her friends had none of that. If they wanted equality, they had to fight for it; if they wanted new clothes, shoes and decent food they had to work hard for it. They all looked after each other and there was never any bitching or falling out over things. There was no jealousy or envy. They refused to become part of the youth cattle market, to conform to things they did not believe in or take part in unjust actions.

When I look back on their lives, I am filled with sadness, yet at the same time I am filled with a great sense of pride. I love them, and I always will love them. What would they think of their lives down to their most intimate details being documented in a book? Well, that's an easy question to answer: they will probably be sitting up there somewhere [she points to the heavens] and having a right old laugh about it. They wrote down their memoirs so some day they could be heard, maybe far into the future. They would all be very happy and if they managed to shock a few people along the way then all the better. When I was little, Kirsten nicknamed me Beetle Bum – as she did Lisa's son, Bobbi – because of the nappies I had to wear. It is those precious little memories that make me smile so much; anything or anyone that turns a sad face into a smiling one in my opinion is a little angel. My aunt Tia and her friends are my angels now. God bless them and

I say to them again, I love you and miss you all and hope that one day I will see you all again and share your warmth and laughter once more.

Hedra Klems, Berlin 2011

Her touch as gentle as a butterfly's kiss,
words of love promise eternal bliss.
The world may say we don't belong,
but only together can we be strong.
She lifts me up when I can't stand,
offers me a helping hand.
And when our fingers intertwine,
the world is once again divine..

Butterfly's Kiss AV XVIII

Sources & Acknowledgements

Almost the entirety of this book was formulated by the utilization of the extensive memoirs, photographs, writings and the letters of Tia Schuster, Lisa Kraus, Himmel Boiten, Kirsten and Petra Albrecht and Imogen Brietzl. Below is a list of all additional sources, both literary and archival, which were consulted:

City on Leave: A History of Berlin 1945–1962, Philip Windsor, Chatto & Windus 1963.
German Journey, Ethel Mannin, Jarrolds 1948.
Nuclear Dawn: The Atomic Bomb, from the Manhattan Project to the Cold War, James P. Delgado, Osprey 2009. ISBN 10: 1846033969, ISBN 13: 9781846033964.
The Berlin Document Centre (BDC), Berlin, Germany.
The Berlin State Library, Berlin, Germany.
The German Federal Archives, Aachen, Germany.
The German History Museum (DHM), Berlin Germany.
The Imperial War Museum, London.
The National Archives, Kew, Richmond, Surrey.
The Staatsarchiv Hamburg, Germany.
The Stasi Records agency, Berlin, Germany.

Acknowledgements

I must also offer unreserved thanks and appreciation to my co-author Annamarie who has been an absolute delight to work with. I hope that when she holds this, her first book, in her hands for the first time, she will feel rightly proud of her contribution. I look forward to working with her again. Any translation required during the course of the writing of this book was carried out by Hedra Klems who has our admiration and gratitude.

About the Authors

Tim Heath was born into a military family. His interest in military history began at the tender age of 7. His initial research focused primarily on the aircraft and weaponry of the Luftwaffe in the Second World War. He later wrote extensively for the UK's leading military history magazine, *The Armourer*. In the process he has assisted a number of UK and Europe-based military history authors with their published works. During the course of his research, he worked closely with the German War Graves Commission at Kassel, Germany, meeting with war veterans and their families. For the past thirty-five years he has specialized in German social and military history, with particular emphasis on the roles of German females in the Third Reich and beyond. His first title for Pen and Sword Books, *Hitler's Girls: Doves Amongst Eagles*, was published in 2017, followed by *In Hitler's Shadow: Post-War Germany and the Girls of the BDM*, *Hitler's Germany: The Birth of Extremism*, *Women of the Third Reich: From Camp Guards to Combatants*, *Hitler's Housewives: German Women on the Home Front*, *Hitler's Lost State: The Fall of Prussia and the Willhelm Gustloff Tragedy*, *Anschluss and After: Resistance Heroines in Nazi- and Russian-occupied Austria*. He lives with his partner Paula in the old Worcestershire market town of Evesham,

Annamarie Vickers has been writing poetry since primary school. The majority of her poetry is situational, but she has also written many types of formal poetry and enjoys finding different ways to express herself. She has now written over 400 poems covering many different genres, including real-time issues, fantasy and darker works. She has self-published several of her own books through Lulu, including *Aspirations*, *Through a Child's Eyes*, *Heartfelt Thoughts*, *On the Outside Looking In*, *Under the Spotlight* (The People's Choice), *Literary Tattoo*, *Dream Weaver*, *Illumination* and *Reflections* (see www.lulu.com/spotlight/

myjourney and www.amazon.co.uk). She has a keen interest in history and has worked in battlefield tourism for the past twelve years. Her main passions are singing, writing, reading and socializing. She lives in Chesterfield with her partner.